BRITISH SOCIAL REFORM AND GERMAN PRECEDENTS

A FANCY PORTRAIT.

Mr. Lloyd George on his return from Germany.

(By permission of " Western Mail," Cardiff.)

Lloyd George returns from Germany, August 1908.
A contemporary cartoon by J. M. Staniforth. *The Western Mail.*

British Social Reform and German Precedents

The Case of Social Insurance 1880–1914

E. P. HENNOCK

CLARENDON PRESS · OXFORD

1987

Oxford University Press, Walton Street, Oxford OX2 6DP
Oxford New York Toronto Melbourne Auckland
Delhi Bombay Calcutta Madras Karachi
Petaling Jaya Singapore Hong Kong Tokyo
Nairobi Dar es Salaam Cape Town
Associated companies in Beirut Berlin Ibadan Nicosia

Oxford is a trade mark of Oxford University Press

Published in the United States
by Oxford University Press, New York

British Library Cataloguing in Publication Data
Hennock, E.P.
British social reform and German precedents:
the case of social insurance 1880–1914.
1. Public welfare—Great Britain—History—20th century
2. Public welfare—Great Britain—History—19th century
I. Title
361'.941   HV245
ISBN 0–19–820127–3

Library of Congress Cataloging-in-Publication Data
Hennock, E.P., 1926–
British social reform and German precedents.
Bibliography: p.
Includes index.
1. Social security—Great Britain—History.
2. Social security—Germany—History.   3. Great Britain—
Social policy.   4. Germany—Social policy.   I. Title.
HD7165.H45 1987   368.4'00941   87–11082
ISBN 0–19–820127–3

Set by Hope Services
Printed in Great Britain
at the University Printing House, Oxford
by David Stanford
Printer to the University

PREFACE

THIS book has been produced in bursts of concentrated research and writing interspersed with long periods given over to other work. It has been supported at various times by the Research Support Fund of the University of Liverpool, a Wolfson Travel Grant from the British Academy, a grant from the Centre for Insurance Studies, and a travel grant from what was then the Social Science Research Council. I wish to express my gratitude to each of these organizations for their generosity.

Unpublished material from the Public Record Office appears by permission of the Controller of Her Majesty's Stationery Office. I am also grateful to the Trustees of the British Library, the Librarian of the British Library of Political and Economic Science, the Librarian of the University of Birmingham, and the Librarian of the Bodleian Library, Oxford, for permission to quote from material in their possession, and to the Chartwell Trustees and the Clerk of the Records, House of Lords, for permission to consult the Chartwell Papers and the Lloyd George Papers respectively. I owe a considerable debt to the staff of these institutions for their help and courtesy.

Chapters 11 and 12 are an expanded and amended version of material that appeared originally as my contribution to W. J. Mommsen and W. Mock (eds.), *The Emergence of the Welfare State in Britain and Germany 1850–1950* (Croom Helm, 1981).

Among those who have helped me with their comments or knowledge of material I wish to mention in particular Philip Bell, Valerie Cromwell, David Dutton, Joseph Melling, Anne-Lise Seip, Florian Tennstedt, Pat Thane, and Noel Whiteside. I also owe a debt to members of research seminars in various universities in Britain and abroad, as well as to the participants at a conference organized by the German Historical Institute of London, for the opportunity to present parts of the work while it was still incomplete. Mention should also be made of James Maxwell's help in identifying relevant published work at the initial stage of the project.

To Betty Plummer, Angela MacEwan, and Suzanne Robinson,

secretaries in the Department of History at Liverpool, I want to express my gratitude and admiration for their skill with the typewriter and word processor and their seemingly endless patience.

E.P.H.

University of Liverpool,
December 1986

CONTENTS

ABBREVIATIONS

ASRS	Amalgamated Society of Railway Servants
Birm. Univ. Lib.	Birmingham University Library
BL	British Library
Bodl.	Bodleian Library, Oxford
Churchill Coll. Camb.	Churchill College, Cambridge
DNB	*Dictionary of National Biography*
LPES	Library of Political and Economic Science, London School of Economics
Mins. of Ev.	Minutes of Evidence
NAPSS	National Association for the Promotion of Social Science
NCOL	National Committee of Organized Labour for Promoting Old Age Pensions
PRO	Public Record Office
RC	Royal Commission
SC	Select Committee

INTRODUCTION

Features common to Parts I and II

IN the 1880s Bismarck's Germany established a system of compulsory workers' insurance. The new policy was announced in an Imperial Message in 1881 but the first attempts at legislation succumbed to opposition in the Reichstag. The Sickness Insurance Law was finally passed in 1883, the Accident Insurance Law in 1884 after two earlier versions had had to be withdrawn. The Old Age and Invalidity Insurance Law was passed in 1889. Each of these received amendments and extensions during the following years, but in its general outlines the system persisted until it underwent major amendment in 1911. The precedents for workers' insurance by compulsion, which in some fragmentary form went back in Prussia to the 1850s, the political calculations that moved Bismarck at the time, the tactical shifts that shaped the details of the legislation, all these are specific to German history.[1] But the outcome was of wider historical significance. Compulsory social insurance has become a feature of the modern State. Not least because of the publicity which the German government deliberately provided, the outline of its tripartite system of compulsory insurance soon attracted attention in other countries both in Europe and in America. Austria and the Scandinavian countries were quick to respond with proposals for legislation which were heavily influenced by the German precedent, even though only some of these were to be enacted along the lines suggested.[2]

---

[1] The best introduction in English is G. A. Ritter, *Social Welfare in Germany and Britain* (Leamington Spa, 1986), which also contains a select bibliography of the German literature. This translation and revision of G. A. Ritter, *Sozialversicherung in Deutschland und England: Entstehung und Grundzüge im Vergleich* (Munich, 1983), was published shortly before the present book went to press. All references to the German edition have been altered to conform to the pagination of the translation.

[2] Herbert Hofmeister, 'Austria', in Peter A. Kohler and Hans F. Zacher (eds.), *The Evolution of Social Insurance 1881–1981: Studies of Germany, France, Great Britain, Austria and Switzerland* (1982); Hugh Heclo, *Modern Social Politics in Britain and Sweden* (1974); Anne-Lise Seip, 'Motive Forces behind the New Social Policy after 1870: Norway on the European Scene', *Scandinavian Jour. of Hist.*, 9 (1984), 329–41; Stein Kuhnle, 'The Growth of Social Insurance Programs in

Losses of earnings due to sickness, industrial injury, invalidity, and old age were hazards encountered by workers in all industrial societies. It was not just in Germany that they gave rise to problems which brought them, between 1880 and 1914, to the attention of social reformers. The same was true of Great Britain, where they became prominent issues of social policy. Yet, unlike Austria, Britain was not closely linked to the German Reich by common language and a common political past. Unlike Scandinavia, where the educated classes customarily moved within the field of influence of German culture and its institutions, Britain had its own traditions drawn from very different sources.

Herein lies the subject matter of this book. It is concerned with the interest taken by British social reformers of the generation before the First World War in the German system of compulsory social insurance. Did they regard the German laws in any sense as a precedent that was of relevance to their own situation? If not, why not? If they did, to what extent and in what ways? And if there was a change in their attitude, why did this occur?

In fact, as the book will show, the period 1880–1914 saw a remarkable change in attitude. For more than a quarter of a century compulsory workers' insurance as practised in Germany was considered altogether unsuitable for Britain, and as late as 1908 Parliament passed an Old Age Pensions Act based on a deliberate rejection of that concept. Before 1905 there was hardly anyone who believed that German social insurance could usefully be adapted to the British situation. Yet after 1907 the opposite view began to be put forward by a small but well-informed minority, and after 1909 the government embarked on a policy of compulsory insurance to deal with sickness, invalidity, and even unemployment. This was a remarkable volte-face on the part of the Liberal government of which Asquith was Prime Minister, so remarkable in fact that the politicians felt the need to disguise it as much as possible. It was widely asserted at the time that there was a fundamental difference between the problems created by old age and those created by sickness and invalidity. There was indeed such a difference, but it was a difference of political circumstances and not intrinsic to the social hazards themselves. This is clearly demonstrated by the

Scandinavia: Outside Influences and Internal Forces', in Peter Flora and Arnold J. Heidenheimer, *The Development of Welfare States in Europe and America* (New Bruswick, NJ, 1981).

subsequent introduction in 1925, under different political circumstances, of old age pensions based on compulsory insurance. We shall find, as we examine the actual formulation of policy in the crucial years 1908–11, that the issues raised by old age, invalidity, and sickness were in fact very closely related. There is every justification for identifying a volte-face in policy as occurring in those years.

In Germany the consequences of sickness and of industrial accidents had been treated as closely related issues. The legislation to deal with each of them had been hammered out simultaneously. That was not the case in Britain. Here it was the problems of old age, invalidity, and sickness that appeared to shade one into the other, whereas the consequences of industrial accidents confronted British policy-makers as a separate issue. It arose within a different political context and at a somewhat earlier date. The important decisions were already made in the 1890s, and with the legislation of 1906 the period of innovation was in practice over. It is not a subject to which historians of the central themes of social policy in Britain have paid much attention; it is considered a specialist's field of fairly limited significance. Indeed it was originally included in this project merely because without it a study of British social reform and German social insurance would have been incomplete. There seemed at first sight no reason to think that the two parts of the project would have much in common. Yet this is very far from being the case. There are common features to be discerned both in the circumstances from which they sprang and in the issues which they raise, and these are central to the subject of this book.

For one thing in both instances there occurred a sharp change of course, involving the rejection of measures that had been matured over many years within the British tradition of social reform in favour of new measures consciously influenced by Germany. For although in this period there was no compulsory insurance, whether on German or on any other lines, in connection with compensation for injury from industrial accidents, there is no doubt that the 1890s witnessed a sharp change of policy. In 1893–4 the two Houses of Parliament had been deadlocked in a conflict over attempts to reform the law on employers' liability for injury to their servants caused by negligence, and to reform it on lines that had been advocated since the 1870s. It was this traditional approach to the subject that was rejected four years later. By giving the workman injured in the course of his employment the right to compensation from his employer irrespective of any question of negligence, and by defining the limits of that compensation in advance by means of a schedule applicable to all cases, the Workmen's Compensation Act of 1897 signalized the adoption of the legal principles that underlay the German legislation of 1884 on accident insurance. They were consciously borrowed from Germany and put forward on the basis of the statistics generated by the administration of the German insurance system. Thus the Workmen's Compensation Act of 1897 clearly showed the influence of German social insurance on British legislation. Yet because in 1897 British policy was not prepared to go so far as to adopt compulsory insurance, the influence of the German precedent was more limited than it was to be in the case of the National Insurance Act of 1911.

There were special reasons why policy-makers between 1893 and 1897 confronted with the issue of employers' liability should be receptive to new ideas from abroad. Long-standing demands for reform, emanating from the trade union movement and from middle-class sympathizers and dating back to the 1870s, had become politically irresistible and had been adopted by the Liberal Party. Yet in that particular form these demands were unacceptable to the Conservatives, who in 1893–4 used their majority in the Lords to block the Liberal government's Bill. The policy that had been worked out by the Conservatives during the 1880s was in turn unacceptable to organized labour and to the Liberals. The result was a deadlock, which led to the perpetuation of a state of the law of which neither side approved, and which left organized labour with a grievance for which it blamed the Conservatives. By adopting an alternative approach in 1897 the 'Unionist' government under Lord Salisbury broke the deadlock and removed that grievance from the political agenda.

In 1908 it was a Liberal government that was faced with the demands of a pressure group based on organized labour and widely supported by its own supporters in Parliament and outside. The demand was for universal old age pensions at 65 or even 60 years of age, to be financed out of general taxation. Its advocates had left the government in no doubt of their parliamentary leverage. A reluctant Treasury had made a strictly limited sum available, but this was quite inadequate. The government Bill had to be restricted to those over 70, despite ample evidence that that was too late an age for the Bill's professed purpose of saving many hard-working and deserving citizens from dependence on the Poor Law and from the stigma that was attached to it. For this and a number of other reasons the Bill could be defended only as a first instalment and as a pledge of more adequate provision to come. Lloyd George, the newly appointed Chancellor of the Exchequer, was contemplating with a marked lack of enthusiasm the extension of an expensive, tax-financed policy to the under-70s. It had not been his policy in the first place and it threatened to gobble up revenue that either was not available or, if available, was better spent on other projects. He had every reason to welcome innovative ideas from abroad when presented with them.

The differences between the situation in 1893–4 and that in 1908 will receive attention in due course. What matters here is the similarities. In both cases a government embarked on radical innovation in a successful attempt to escape from parliamentary difficulties which had been the result of pressure-group politics. In both cases it was organized labour that played a crucial role in putting forward the demands that were to prove such an embarrassment to the government. Yet neither in the 1890s nor in the 1900s was organized labour in a position to generate numerically significant pressure on its own. On both occasions it was able to work together with important sections of the Liberal Party, in one case even with the party leadership. What made this common platform possible was the fact that labour, far from drawing its programmes from foreign theories or blueprints, was obviously operating within a long-standing native tradition of social reform that had a wide appeal beyond its own ranks. In such a situation a new policy that stepped right outside those traditional terms of reference and drew its solutions from foreign practices acquired an unusual attraction for hard-pressed ministers. By providing a radical alternative it held out the prospect of escape from pressures which in their existing form could be neither ignored nor satisfactorily accommodated.

Potentially, therefore, foreign models provided a way out of a political impasse. But in practice they did so only if three conditions were met. In the first place those who made the crucial decisions had to have access to information on what was being done abroad. In the late nineteenth and early twentieth centuries this was the least difficult of the conditions to fulfil; many channels of information existed, and knowledge of the details of the German insurance system was available in England. Even so, it could not be taken for granted, as we shall see, that those who really mattered in policy-making would always be adequately informed. Nor was knowledge the only thing that was required. Two personal qualities provide the remaining conditions without which such an initiative could not have been successful. To cut the Gordian knot and propose a bold solution that stepped outside the common terms of reference called for imagination of a high order. What is more, not only was such a solution bold, it was difficult to steer through the shoals of politics. It called for outstanding political talent, very different from the ability to temporize, to moderate, and then to yield to the inevitable that would have been the alternative course of action. It should come as no surprise to find that in such cases the initiative was taken by ministers of the first rank: by Joseph Chamberlain in 1897, by Lloyd George in conjunction with Winston Churchill in 1911. For what was involved in both cases was no less than a rejection of part of the common ground of politics. To side-step an irreconcilable conflict was to side-step the common ground over which that conflict was being fought. Therein lay the attraction of a foreign model; therein lay also the peculiar difficulty of that kind of new departure.

This brings us to the second feature that the two cases have in common. If on the one hand it is possible to identify the political circumstances under which the German model appeared unusually attractive, it is necessary also to consider the problems involved in such a process of borrowing from abroad.

Historians or social scientists who have taken an interest in the transfer of technology from one economy to another have recognized that this involves more than the mere installation of a steam-engine, a textile mill, or a computer. The reception given to new methods of production, and their impact on economic and social relations, are complex matters, on which the success or failure of such ventures ultimately depends. By analogy the copying of social institutions with their related norms and conventions has been described as the transfer of social technology. Compulsory social insurance is a social institution with its related norms of precisely this sort. It was to demand forms of behaviour, such as the regular payment of contributions and the adherence to the regulations governing entitlement, that were quite new to a large proportion of those caught up in it, and it was to involve the State in forms of supervision and control that in Britain it was most reluctant to assume. The impact that such a compulsory institution would have on the existing forms of social organization—on voluntary mutual-help associations, profit-making enterprises, and professional bodies, as well as on the machinery of government—was quite unknown, yet the successful operation of any such insurance system would depend on it. In these and other ways the methods of compulsory social insurance, pioneered in a country that was accustomed to compulsory military service, and that possessed a highly developed and greatly respected State bureaucracy and a labour movement weaker both in its legal rights and in its network of mutual-help institutions, to mention only some of the relevant differences, appeared to run counter to British ways and to the methods of the Liberal State.

To take over German social insurance in its totality would have been out of the question. To turn towards it at all meant to distinguish the acceptable from the unacceptable, to borrow the former and to adapt in such a way as to provide a working alternative to the latter. It is exactly because such a process of borrowing and adapting from abroad necessarily obliged policy-makers to clarify their understanding of the nature of the British political system and to make it explicit that it is so interesting. The form that this process of clarification, sifting, and adaptation took was different in 1897 from what it was to be in 1911. Therein lies its value to the historian as an indicator of changing attitudes to the relation between State and society, particularly since on both occasions the challenge posed by the example of Germany was very similar. On both occasions it was recognized that German social insurance was different from comparable British institutions not because it was *insurance* but because it was *compulsory*.

In the case of German accident insurance it was the employers to whom compulsion was applied. On the one hand they were obliged to combine with all other employers in their trade into a mutual association (*Berufsgenossenschaft*) with powers of discipline in matters of safety and the duty to levy whatever contribution to its indemnity fund it deemed necessary. On the other hand they were prohibited from shopping in the insurance marked for the cheapest and most congenial form of cover. They were in a very different position from that of British employers even after the legislation of 1897 and 1906.

In the case of the other two German insurance laws the question of compulsion impinged not only on employers; it had major implications also for the workers. Mutual aid funds, financed by regular contributions from their members and distributed on such occasions as were specified by regulation, had been for much of the nineteenth century an important feature of the lives of British working men. But membership of these insurance funds was voluntary and limited to those able and willing to keep up their regular contributions. Indeed their voluntary nature was considered to be one of their most valuable characteristics. Only those capable of forgoing present gratification for future security were able to belong, and only those whose way of life was sufficiently regular were able to keep up their membership. The capacity to look ahead, to restrain impulsive desires for the sake of future good, and to associate with like-minded people for a common purpose, in other words foresight, thrift, orderliness, and co-operation, were valued both for themselves and for the contribution that they made to the good of society. The growth of the mutual-aid associations was widely regarded as one of the most important indicators of social progress. They were valued as 'schools of providence', i.e. for reinforcing the values on which they depended, for encouraging, training, and disciplining their members in them. Certainly they were valued also for the financial benefits which were the purpose for which they existed, and for these not only by their members but by those who made laws or formed public opinion. Such payments in times of hardship gave security to their members' way of life, they protected the values on which the future of the institutions of mutual help depended, and they saved men from plunging into an abyss in which neither orderly co-operation nor the subordination of impulse to foresight was possible. To set the financial benefits in time of need against the qualities fostered by voluntary providence would have been to subvert this whole way of thinking.

Nevertheless sole reliance on voluntary action was almost inevitably incompatible with total coverage. It provided security for some by means which others could not, or would not, emulate, at least not yet. As long as the main concern was with social progress the dynamic nature of the movement for mutual help was more important than immediate total coverage. Englishmen within the Liberal tradition irrespective of party prided themselves not on having already attained the society in which they believed but on having discovered the means of progress towards it. If immediate total coverage were ever to become the main concern, then compulsion would become more important. It was by raising these closely connected issues of universal provision and compulsory contribution that German social insurance confronted British policy-makers with a significant challenge. In the 1890s we find them prepared to reject compulsion and to be complacent about the lack of universal provision. In 1906 they were no longer happy to strike the balance in that way but lacked the determination to confront the implications of the alternatives. In 1911 they were prepared to confront those implications. By opting for compulsion and wider coverage and turning to German social insurance as their model for achieving it, the architects of National Insurance were embarking on a reinterpretation of the role of the State in a Liberal society and indeed of the fundamental nature of Liberalism.

In theoretical terms that reinterpreation was then being undertaken by L. T. Hobhouse and J. A. Hobson, the distinguished theorists of the New Liberalism.[3] But what it would mean in practical institutional terms would depend on the give-and-take of legislation and the establishment of administrative arrangements.

It is to that process that attention is directed in Part II of this book. Once the decision had been taken to follow the German example and go for a policy of compulsory insurance, it remains to be discovered in what sense and to what extent the existing German system was capable of serving as a model for legislation, and what else it contributed to the making of National Insurance. These are more significant questions in relation to health insurance, for which there was a German model to be scrutinized, than for unemployment insurance, for which there was not. It is for this reason that the book will pay more detailed attention to the former than to the latter. In the latter case it is the basic decision to include unemployment in the new policy of compulsory insurance that matters. Such a selective approach is the more feasible since the details of the two schemes were the responsibility of different ministers working in separate departments with separate teams of advisers.

[3] L. T. Hobhouse, *Democracy and Reaction* (1904); idem, *Liberalism* (1911); J. A. Hobson, *The Social Problem: Life and Work* (1901); idem, *The Crisis of Liberalism* (1909). See P. F. Clarke, *Liberals and Social Democrats* (1978); Michael Freeden, *The New Liberalism* (1978).

The Example of Germany (i): Friendship's Garland

The conclusions to be drawn from that investigation will be found at the end of the book. At this stage it is more appropriate to return to the first of the two features to which attention has been drawn, namely the political advantage of adopting a foreign, and in these instances more particularly a German, model. Nor indeed were these particular instances the only examples of borrowing from Germany. While there were almost certainly areas of policy where models drawn from foreign countries other than Germany fulfilled a similar role of offering a highly relevant alternative course of action, it would seem to be the case that in the years covered by this study, i.e. the generation before 1914, the example of Germany figured particularly prominently in the minds of reformers. Among those who were prepared to look beyond the native tradition, as found in Britain and its self-governing colonies, no country apart from the USA had its institutions so frequently referred to, inspected, and held up for emulation. In the case of the USA, linked to Britain by a common tongue, the closest mercantile connections, and much else, this is not surprising. It had always been the case. In the case of Germany the phenomenon was far less a matter of course and was indeed of quite recent origin.

Just how recent is suggested by the failure of *Friendship's Garland*, the work in which Matthew Arnold had criticized British amateurisms and the bungling nature, as he saw it, of voluntary institutions through the reactions of a Prussian *Junker*. The cool reception given to it demonstrates the very different attitude towards these matters prevalent in the early 1870s from that to be found a generation later. Appearing originally between 1866 and 1870 as individual essays and published in book form in 1871, the work was not to be reprinted in Arnold's lifetime. Yet, significantly enough, a second edition came out in 1897 and was followed by a popular edition in 1903. By then attitudes had changed and the message of the book differed little from much contemporary comment.[4] Not so in 1871. The *Spectator* had no difficulty in summing up the message of the book and its own attitude towards it:

---

[4] W. H. Dawson, *Matthew Arnold and his Relation to the Thought of our Time: an Appreciation and a Criticism* (1904).

That all our national life, our government, our education, even our business is done without discipline and training, without fitness and special preparation in those who do them, without even the sense that these are good things, that in these days when other nations are organizing their material and intellectual resources, this neglect and defect are becoming constantly more dangerous, that we are actually losing or have lost our *prestige*, that our superiority in some things is gone, and in others endangered, is what Mr. Arnold preaches to his countrymen. There is no danger that such prophets will ever be much listened to.

The *London Graphic* admitted that there was truth in Arnold's strictures but added that 'the strictures pall upon the reader by virtue of their repetition and their foreign origin'. The *Examiner* described it as 'the poorest of all the volumes . . . that Mr. Arnold has written', and Herbert Spencer accused him of overvaluing foreign institutions. *Blackwood's* was scornful of Arnold in the role of public critic, while the *Athenaeum*, which found 'much in the book that is very amusing and much also that is too true', thought Arnold was wasting his talent and advised him to return to poetry and to essays in criticism, i.e. literary criticism.[5]

The Example of Germany (ii): Technical Education

What the writer in the *Athenaeum* may have overlooked was that in addition to being a literary figure Arnold was an Inspector of Schools and an expert on foreign systems of education who had written reports for Royal Commissions.[6] While there is nothing to suggest that these had any effect on shaping policy at the time, he was certainly not alone among experts on education in showing a marked interest in German educational provisions. A study of the interplay between German educational practice and British educational reform would have to take for its starting point a

[5] *Spectator*, 44 (1871), 616; *London Graphic*, 3 (1871), 415; *Examiner*, 4 Mar. 1871, 235; Herbert Spencer, 'The Study of Sociology, ix: The Bias of Patriotism', *Contemporary Review*, 21 (1873), 485–502, reprinted in Herbert Spencer, *The Study of Sociology* (1874); *Blackwood's*, 109 (1871), 458–60; *Athenaeum*, 2262 (1871), 271. The review in the *Athenaeum* was the sole even faintly appreciative comment quoted in the comprehensive survey from which these passages are drawn: C. T. Wilkins, 'The English Reputation of Matthew Arnold 1840–1877', Ph.D. thesis (Illinois, 1959).

[6] Matthew Arnold, *The Popular Education of France* (1861), originally written for the RC on the State of Popular Education; idem, *A French Eton* (1864); idem, *Schools and Universities on the Continent* (1868), originally written for the Taunton Commission.

significantly earlier date than is the case with any other set of institutions.[7] Some of the most important texts for such a study were produced in the 1860s, and the themes enunciated then were with variations to surface repeatedly in subsequent years.[8]

What British educational reformers found in Germany and frequently contrasted with the conditions that existed in Britain may be summed up in a few words: comprehensiveness, compulsion, professionalism, systematic funding, and organization.

No matter whether the object of their investigation was the state of elementary education, of secondary education, of technical, or of higher scientific education, when they looked across the North Sea they found that in contrast to the situation in Britain they were confronted with something that could be properly understood only as part of a larger system and whose strength was due to a significant extent to the quality and the comprehensiveness of the other parts.

At an early stage British observers became aware that the comprehensiveness they admired was dependent on the exercise of compulsion and generally of compulsion willingly borne. They found themselves uncertain what conclusion they should draw. Was it true, as A. J. Mundella, a keen educational reformer with an admiration for the German achievements, proclaimed in 1867 with reference to elementary education, that 'if we are to maintain our position in the industrial competition we must oppose to this national organisation one equally effective and complete. If we continue to fight with our present voluntary system we shall be defeated'? Or was there validity in the sentiments which in 1889 led to the rejection of compulsory continuation schools (evening classes for school leavers) on the Saxon model with the words: 'I do not think we are bound slavishly to imitate continental models when

[7] George Haines IV, *Essays on German Influence upon English Education and Science 1850–1919* (Hamden, Conn., 1969); idem, 'German Influence upon Scientific Instruction in England 1867–1887', *Victorian Studies*, 1. 3 (1958), 215–44; W. H. G. Armytage, *The German Influence on English Education* (1969); J. J. McGlashan, 'German Influence on Aspects of English Educational and Social Reform 1867–1908', Ph.D. thesis (Hull, 1973).

[8] *RC on Popular Education (Newcastle Commission), Report on the State of Elementary Education in Germany*, by Mark Pattison, 1861 [2794–IV] XXI, pt. iv; Mark Pattison, *Suggestions on Academical Organization* (1868); *SC on Technical Education, Report*, 1867–8 (432) XV; *Schools Inquiry RC, Report Relative to Technical Education*, 1867 [3898] XXVI.

we know that our habits and character are so very different from those of other nations'.[9]

There can be no mistaking the fact that in the creation of Britain's elementary, secondary, technical, and higher scientific education the example of Germany was repeatedly investigated and held up for emulation. Just how this actually affected the course of British educational reform, dependent as that was on the nature of the British political process, is another question. To pursue that question over the full range of the politics of educational reform is beyond the scope of an introduction such as this. But something may usefully be said on the significance of the recurrent concern over the state of technical and scientific education, a concern which is important not only for its impact on that particular aspect of educational reform but for the way in which it was ultimately to spill over into a much more general awareness of the differences between the institutions of the two countries.

Ever since the wide-ranging international investigations undertaken in the aftermath of the poor performance of British exhibits at the 1867 International Exhibition in Paris, attention had been drawn to the superior facilities available in Germany and Switzerland. Throughout the 1870s and 1880s what is best described as a technical-education lobby, consisting of a stage army of enthusiasts, many of them educated at German universities or with business connections in Germany, had used every means of publicity at its disposal to inform the public of progress made in Germany, Switzerland, and elsewhere and to drive home the need for comparable initiatives in Britain. These means of publicity were formidable, ranging from speeches on ceremonial occasions, articles, and books to a Royal Commission on Technical Instruction appointed in 1881 by one of their own number, A. J. Mundella, who had just become Vice-President of the Council and in charge of education in the Liberal government. The Commission was to all intents and purposes a packed body of believers in international comparison and in the importance of expanding facilities for technical instruction as well as for advanced education geared to the application of science to industry. On the completion of their task the members of what has been very appropriately described by one of its historians as 'a free-lance inquiry by a small pressure

[9] *Schools Inquiry RC, Report Relative to Technical Education*, p. 10; 3 *Hansard* 333 (15 Mar. 1889) 1866; both qd. in McGlashan, op. cit., pp. 24, 95.

group', proceeded to found the National Association for the Promotion of Technical Education. This was explicitly a pressure group and campaigned successfully for the application of public funds for the establishment and support of technical schools. It very largely succeeded in its object when Parliament passed the Technical Education Act of 1889 and the Local Taxation (Customs and Excise) Act of 1890. The former enabled the newly established County Councils and County Borough Councils to finance technical education out of the rates; the latter put the yield of the excise duty, the so-called whisky money, at their disposal for the same purpose.[10]

Success consisted in persuading policy-makers to emulate, not to imitate, what was being done in Germany. Indeed it would not be inappropriate to speak of a native tradition of technical and scientific education, developing since the 1850s along institutional lines markedly different from what was to be found in Germany and in other similar Continental countries. Within that tradition the role played by international comparisons was to stimulate voluntary and philanthropic efforts in the provision of institutions and to persuade Parliament to allow public funds to be used to subsidize the teaching of technical and scientific subjects, while relying on an examination system to ensure both value for money and public accountability. The legislation of 1889–90, by putting substantial resources at the disposal of the major local authorities to be spent on technical education, enabled them to enter a sphere which had previously been the preserve of voluntary associations and philanthropic donors. It thus did for technical education what the Act of 1870 had done for elementary education, namely to fill the gaps. It led to the establishment of new technical colleges and enabled local authorities to support and frequently to take over responsibility for a number of previously very precariously financed institutions.[11]

In 1884 *The Times* had welcomed the Report of the Royal Commission on Technical Instruction with the reflection that

---

[10] Michael Argles, 'The Royal Commission on Technical Instruction 1881–1884: Its Inception and Composition', *Vocational Aspects*, 11. 23 (1959), 98. For Sir Philip Magnus, perhaps the most important of the intermediaries between Germany and the world of English technical education, see Frank Foden, *Philip Magnus, Victorian Educational Pioneer* (1970).

[11] For a more detailed exposition of this argument and an example of the process of sifting and adapting referred to on p. 7, see my forthcoming article 'The German Technische Hochschule and British education: The Uses of a German Model'.

it must be regarded as satisfactory that the Commissioners have been able to terminate their labours . . . with the conviction that whatever may be the progress of other nations in technical education and in manufactures . . . we already possess considerable opportunities for theoretical instruction in the technical sciences and in art applied to industry; that these opportunities are capable of increase on their present lines.[12]

This was a fair reflection on the content of the Report. For all its bold demands for more resources to be devoted to its cause, in its approach to what Englishmen might learn from abroad it was not a radical document.

It was on their claim to hold the key to the future economic strength of the nation that the propagandists for technical and scientific education had always relied to obtain a hearing for their cause. In this they were finally to be successful. Before the century drew to a close the conviction had struck home to the broad mass of public opinion that Britain was indeed losing its former pre-eminent place in the competition for markets, and that it was losing it to Germany.

How the economic strength of Britain in relation to its competitiors is assessed must of course depend on the indicators that are chosen. By keeping their eye on the number of prizes gained by British products at the regular international exhibitions first instituted in 1851 the proponents of technical and scientific education claimed as early as 1867 to detect a critical decline in the relative performance of British manufactures. The consequence was that for close on two decades they elaborated a cure for a disease which only the most sensitive instrument had been able to identify.

In the 1870s the economic experience of Britain had compared favourably with that of Germany; in the 1880s the opposite was true, and from then onwards the growth rates of the two economies began to diverge.[13] But this is a modern view based on a more sophisticated set of indicators than contemporaries were concerned with. The fact that the German economy was benefiting to a significant extent from a boom in domestic demand is of more significance to modern economic historians than it was to contemporary British commentators. To them it was the growth in the

<hr>

[12] *The Times*, 16 May 1884, qd. in Argles, 'Royal Commission on Technical Instruction', p. 103.

[13] S. B. Saul, *Industrialisation and de-industrialisation? The Interaction of the German and British Economies before the First World War* (1980), pp. 12–13.

respective export trades of the two countries that mattered, and it was not until after 1894 that the published foreign trade statistics began to indicate that fall in the value of British visible exports and significant divergence from the figures for German trade that was to be such a worrying feature of the years between 1894 and 1897.[14]

There was, however, another set of indicators available at the time which had given cause for alarm well before. Consular reports do not normally attract much attention, but in 1885 for the benefit of the Royal Commission on the Depression in Trade and Industry the Foreign Office organized a survey of consular opinion on the impediments to British trade and the loss of trade to foreign competitors. The replies were published in the Commission's Report and attracted much attention in the press for their unfavourable comparisons between the sluggishness of British exporters and the vigour of their German rivals. The alarm which this caused was short-lived, however, and after 1889 with the revival of business the German menace disappeared from view. Yet by 1893 it had reappeared. Once again the evidence was drawn from consular reports which tended to draw attention to those instances in which British exporters were failing to compete.

It was largely by relying on these and on material in certain trade journals with a protectionist leaning that E. E. Williams, the author of *Made in Germany*, succeeded in 1896 in convincing the general public that German manufacturers and traders now posed a serious threat to British prosperity.[15] Here was just the sort of danger against which the advocates of technical and scientific education had warned for decades, and Lord Rosebery, speaking at the opening of a technical institute, helped to give Williams's book maximum publicity. Coinciding as it did with the Transvaal Crisis and the Kaiser's telegram to Kruger, the publication of the book induced in the press 'a kind of mid-summer madness'.[16] Such extreme panics are in the nature of things short-lived. But, writing of the years after 1896, the historian of the Anglo-German trade rivalry has concluded that an examination of the press and parliamentary debates makes it very plain that all through these

[14] R. J. S. Hoffman, *Great Britain and the German Trade Rivalry 1875–1914* (New York, 1933), pp. 230–1, 96.
[15] For E. E. Williams, see 'Biographical Memoir', in the reissue of *Made in Germany* (Brighton, 1973).
[16] Hoffman, *Great Britain and German Trade Rivalry*, p. 255.

years there was a fixed recognition of an acute trade rivalry with Germany. Everybody knew it and everybody took the fact for granted.[17]

The men who had cried 'wolf' for so long seemed now to have been vindicated, and the prescription which they had been offering was finally seen to fit the disease.

Williams's *Made in Germany* contained not merely the recital of 'England's Industrial Shame', it also explained 'Why Germany Beat Us' and 'What We Must Do To Be Saved'.

I wish to bring home to my readers the splendid system of industrial education which obtains in Germany, a system which is an integral part of Germany's success. It compares with that available in England as an electric lamp to a rush-light.[18]

Drawing on a recent report, Williams gave wide publicity to the impressive resources of the recently enlarged *Technische Hochschule* at Charlottenburg, near Berlin, about which so much was to be heard in the years that followed.

At about the same time the members of the 1884 Royal Commission returned to Germany for a second visit. They too referred at length to the work at Charlottenburg, drawing on the same source as Williams, but also described in detail the facilities in Southern Germany which they had visited personally. They stressed the progress that Germany had made since 1884.

Twelve years ago there was nowhere in Germany so well equipped a laboratory for electrical engineers as at Finsbury Technical College. Now there are no laboratories to compare with those we visited in Darmstadt and Stuttgart.[19]

Another collection of consular reports highly critical of British methods was published in 1898. *The Times* had no difficulty in drawing the moral that the German 'exports more mind than his rival . . . and this is the secret of his success'.[20]

It is impossible to know what effect this shock to the economic complacency of the nation would have had after a few years if it

---

[17] Ibid., p. 261.   [18] Williams, *Made in Germany*, p. 156.
[19] *Report on a Visit to Germany with a View to Ascertaining the Recent Progress of Technical Education in that Country: A letter to the Duke of Devonshire*, by Philip Magnus *et al.*, 1897 C. 8301 LXXXVIII. 403. The quotation is from p. 9.
[20] *The Times*, 14 Nov. 1898; cf. Hoffman, *Great Britain and German Trade Rivalry*, pp. 81–2.

had not been reinforced by the shock that military failure in the Boer War administered to its military complacency. The highly publicized failures of training and organization that the war revealed helped to bring about a mood of self-doubt and self-criticism. It expressed itself in a preoccupation with, and often a strident demand for, national efficiency, 'an attempt to discredit the habits, beliefs and institutions that put the British at a handicap in their competition with foreigners and to commend instead a social organization that more closely followed the German model'.[21] German methods had to be taken seriously exactly because the Germans 'have every qualification for taking our place', to quote from the correspondence in 1909 between J. L. Garvin, editor of the *Observer*, and Northcliffe, owner of the *Daily Mail*.[22] This gave a hearing to those who believed that Britain had something important to learn from some aspect or other of the German system of higher education, whether it was the emphasis on research in specialist laboratories or the systematic application of scientific knowledge to problems of industry.[23]

In 1901 yet another consular report drew attention to the German provision for education and research in chemistry and linked this with the progress of the German chemical industry.[24] The early years of the new century saw a marked increase in university facilities in the applied sciences, an interest that dominated the vigorous expansion of university provision in the provinces and looked both to the USA and to Germany for inspiration.[25] The parallel movement in London took the form of

[21] See the excellent description in G. R. Searle, *The Quest for National Efficiency 1899–1914* (Oxford, 1971). The quotation is from p. 55.

[22] Qd. in Paul M. Kennedy, *The Rise of the Anglo-German Antagonism 1860–1914* (1980), p. 394.

[23] For the successful campaign between 1895 and 1898 to persuade the government to establish a National Physical Laboratory on lines similar to, though not on the scale of, the *Physikalisch-Technische Reichsanstalt*, see Russell Mosely, 'The Origins and Early Years of the National Physical Laboratory: A Chapter in the Pre-history of British Science Policy', *Minerva*, 16 (1978), 222–50; Peter Alter, *Wissenschaft, Staat, Mäzene: Anfänge moderner Wissenschaftspolitik in Grossbritannien 1850–1920* (Stuttgart, 1982), pp. 157–69.

[24] *Report on Chemical Instruction in Germany and the Growth and Present Condition of the German Chemical Industries*, by Frederick Rose, 1901 Cd. 430–16; *Supplementary Report*, 1902 Cd. 787–9.

[25] For the expansion of applied science teaching and research in British universities, see Michael Sanderson, *The Universities and British Industry 1850–1970* (1972), who emphasizes the difference between the British and the German

an attempt to found an institution that could rival the *Technische Hochscule* at Charlottenburg. This was initiated by Sidney Webb, the chairman of the LCC Technical Instruction Board, in co-operation with R. B. Haldane, probably the leading university reformer of his day, who was himself the product of Göttingen and possessed a detailed knowledge of German universities. The project, which was launched in 1902, was deliberately labelled the British Charlottenburg. By 1907, when the charter was granted to what had by then come to be called the Imperial College of Science and Technology, the government, the LCC, the City Livery Companies, and a clutch of private benefactors had all been brought into line and persuaded to provide resources.[26]

This emulation in the field of scientific and technical education must be understood as part of the preoccupation with the mobilization of national resources in a climate of international rivalry to which attention has already been drawn. From that perspective much that had been achieved in the past by means of voluntary and therefore fragmentary action now appeared ill-organized. More complete organization became the great desi-deratum. In a lecture, 'Great Britain and Germany: A study in Education', delivered in 1901 at Liverpool, Haldane linked organization with instruction as the two matters that had been carried to a far higher pitch in Germany and Switzerland and warned of the need to repair that failing 'if we are to hold our position'.[27] In 1907 Beveridge was to commend the German insurance system for aiming at covering every kind of incapacity for work and added this moral to his exposition: 'This completeness is a thing which cannot be got by rough and ready methods. It depends upon organisation and the willingness to submit to organisation'.[28] In the following year Churchill compared Germany favourably with England: 'She is organised not only for war but

Approach and the importance of the 1870s and 1880s in shaping the British development.

[26] Eric Ashby and Mary Anderson, *Portrait of Haldane at Work on Education* (1974), p. 385; Alter, *Wissenschaft, Staat, Mäzene*, pp. 169–92. The significance of that episode is reassessed by me in the forthcoming article mentioned in n. 11.

[27] R. B. Haldane, *Education and Empire* (1902), p. 30. A large number of similar statements can be found in Searle, *Quest for National Efficiency*, McGlashan, 'German Influence', and Haines, *Essays on German Influence*. Haines's treatment of the wider implications of the interest in German education for social criticism is particularly perceptive.

[28] *Morning Post*, 20 Apr. 1907.

also for peace'; and he urged the Prime Minister to 'apply to this country the successful experiences of Germany in social organisation'.[29]

Organization had become the task of the policy-maker, and his instrument was to be the coercive power of the State. In 1897 the government had explicitly rejected not merely the actual institutions of German accident insurance but the very idea that, merely because new obligations had been imposed on the employer by a change in the law, it was up to the State to prescribe the means by which he was to meet them. That, it was confidently asserted, could be left to the judgement of employers individually, and, if some of them failed to take adequate measures, that was a hazard to be contemplated with equanimity. The view that it was up to the State to insist on compulsory insurance was precisely what had been rejected as 'regimentation and regulation'. Those were the terms repeatedly used to identify the unacceptable aspect of German institutions. It had been contrasted with the capacity of individuals to recognize their own needs and to know better than any civil servant how to meet them.

Perhaps it was here, in the belief in the superior knowledge of the systematizer, that the long-standing respect for German higher education finally acquired a wider and more political application than had been the case before. For behind the quest for completeness lay a faith in the comprehensive view available to the impartial, trained mind, and a conviction that it was superior to the partial views of those whose knowledge was merely derived from experience. In so far as it is possible to detect a common element in the many appeals, made at this time in a great variety of contexts, to emulate the Germans' way of organizing their national life, it is this conception of knowledge as systematic and applicable to practical affairs. It was behind the call for the establishment of a General Staff to emulate the 'scientific spirit' that Germans had brought to military affairs.[30] It was also behind Haldane's call for *Zentralstellen* (Centres of Applied Research), staffed by scientifically

---

[29] W. S. Churchill to H. H. Asquith, 29 Dec. 1908, qd. in R. S. Churchill, *Winston S. Churchill*, ii. *Companion*, pt. 2 (1967) p. 863.

[30] The relation between the German model of a General Staff and the reform of the British Army provides another example of the process of sifting and adapting. See H. Spenser Wilkinson, *The Brain of an Army* (1890); John Gooch, *The Plans of War: The General Staff and British Military Strategy c. 1900–1916* (1974); Edward M. Spiers, *Haldane: An Army Reformer* (Edinburgh, 1980).

trained experts and impartially serving the needs of all firms in the industry which had combined to set them up.[31] Here was a call for the trained mind both in the Army and in industry, and these were very far from being the only spheres for which the same prescription was on offer. In the context of social reform one need do no more than turn to the arch-exponents of this view, Sidney and Beatrice Webb. As they were never tired of explaining, 'Social reconstruction require[s] as much specialised training and sustained study as the building of bridges and railways, the interpretation of the law, or the technical improvement in machinery and mechanical processes'.[32] It was to be one of the functions of the London School of Economics and Political Science, which they had founded, to provide that kind of training.

Such a claim to superior knowledge implied a belief in the capacity of the trained intelligence both to diagnose the defects in the organization of society and to construct a scheme by which the powers of the State, its powers of regulation and control as much as its powers of taxation and financial provision, could be employed to bring about a more complete mobilization of the resources of the nation. To state the matter in this way is not to contradict the explanation usually offered for the demands for increased State intervention, namely that only the State possessed the financial resources required to meet the new aspirations. It is to supplement it by drawing attention to the claims of those with systematic training and of a theoretical perspective to set out the terms of what was required. Such claims were not only being made; they were being accepted to a degree previously unknown in England.

The Example of Germany (iii): Town Planning

Perhaps the best example of such a claim to superior knowledge made in the name of a comprehensive form of organization is to be found in the early-twentieth-century town planning movement.[33] It

---

[31] Haldane, *Education and Empire*, pp. 18–20; idem, 'The Executive Brain of the British Empire', in W. T. Stead (ed.), *Coming Men on Coming Questions* (1905), pp. 133–4.

[32] S. and B. Webb, *The Prevention of Destitution* (1911), p. 331.

[33] For this subject studied both as a national and as an international movement, see Anthony Sutcliffe, *Towards the Planned City: Germany, Britain, the United States and France 1780–1914* (Oxford, 1981), to which the following section is heavily indebted. See also the individual contributions in Anthony Sutcliffe (ed.), *British Town Planning: The Formative Years* (Leicester, 1981).

can be identified in this quotation from one of its leading exponents, the Birmingham municipal politician J. S. Nettlefold.

If it is necessary (and everyone recognises that it is) to plan a house as a whole before starting to build, then a thousand times more is it necessary in the interests of public health, public convenience, and public economy to plan our towns as a whole before new developments are allowed.[34]

People like Nettlefold had been greatly impressed by the relevance to British urban conditions of the German town-extension plan. Here was another case where a German precedent had something to offer British social reformers.

In its most ambitious form the idea of town planning as a way of organizing the layout of a town from its beginnings, and indeed the idea of deciding its location, had been expounded by Ebenezer Howard, whose proposals for the establishment of new towns were first published in 1898, and republished in 1902 as *Garden Cities of Tomorrow*. In that form it led to the establishment of a new town at Letchworth, financed on the joint stock principle of wealthy shareholders. But had the idea of comprehensive urban planning been limited in its application to the establishment of new towns, it would not have made much impact on social reformers. That was achieved by introducing the idea of town-extension planning from Germany.

Town-extension planning was concerned with the controlled development of suburbs. Those anxious to improve the housing of the working classes had, since at least the 1880s, pinned their hopes on suburbs. As the growing demand for commercial premises in the city centres put pressure on the housing market, it was only by working-class families following their social superiors into the suburbs that an even greater deterioration of working-class housing conditions could be avoided. It was well understood that the labouring poor, especially if dependent on casual work, had necessarily to live near their area of work, but the regularly employed workers could be encouraged to move out. It was hoped that by the process of 'levelling-up' the poor would be able to move into the premises they vacated and slum clearance could take place without leading to even greater overcrowding. That was the theory. It depended on the provision of cheap transport and the enterprise of the speculative builder. In the 1890s the electrification of

[34] J. S. Nettlefold, *Practical Housing* (1908), p. 48.

tramways and the multiplication of cheap workmen's fares both on the trams and on the railways coincided with a building boom. The result was the building of working-class suburbs on the edges of the big cities and a marked enthusiasm among housing reformers for the potential of the suburb as a healthier environment.

The potential of the suburb was, however, in marked contrast to what was actually being created. For many of the speculative builders who provided the new working-class housing, the attraction of a suburban site lay not merely in the lower price of the land but in the laxer building by-laws, sanitary regulations, and enforcement machinery to be found outside the boundaries of the major local authorities. Housing reformers were eager for the extension of such controls into the new areas, and this sometimes implied, as in the case of those in Birmingham, a belief in boundary extension. But even where the new development was taking place within existing boundaries, housing reformers were not content. They had their sights set on something beyond merely multiplying the kind of by-law housing that had been erected since the 1870s. Such workers' settlements as Port Sunlight (1888) and Bourneville (1894) had shown that the more open and varied layout previously associated with middle-class developments could be used for working-class dwellings when overall control was exercized by an enlightened owner and his architect. The benefits were reckoned to be great in terms of both health and happiness, reversing the dehumanizing effects of crowded urban environments and bringing the people closer to nature and its influence over body and mind.

Such an objective, with its implications for a healthy race, made a strong appeal to social reformers in the first decade of the twentieth century, disturbed as they had been by the revelation of the large numbers of men volunteering for the Army during the Boer War who had had to be rejected as unfit. The figures for the big cities had been given wide publicity in the writings of Seebohm Rowntree, of Major-General Sir Frederick Maurice, and of Arnold White.[35] It began to look as if the process of urbanization had reached a point where it was threatening the vigour of the race.

---

[35] B. S. Rowntree, *Poverty: A Study of Town Life* (1901), pp. 216–21; 'Miles' (Sir F. Maurice), 'Where to Get Men', *Contemporary Review*, 81 (1902), 78–86; Arnold White, *Efficiency and Empire* (1901), pp. 101–2. See the discussion of B. B. Gilbert, *The Evolution of National Insurance in Great Britain: The Origins of the Welfare State* (1966), pp. 83 ff.

After the investigations of the Interdepartmental Committee on Physical Deterioration in 1904 had laid to rest some of the wilder fears of hereditary decay and laid the blame for the poor physique of the town-bred population squarely on the conditions under which their children were raised, the reform of housing and the urban environment was one of the causes that benefited from the publicity.[36] As this passage from T. C. Horsfall, the Manchester housing reformer and advocate of town planning, demonstrates, it could be made to chime in easily with the anxieties generated by the competition with Germany.

We must remember that already in 1901 we had 77% of our population in towns of considerable size. We must also remember that while we still had a population to a large extent uninjured by town conditions of life, our trade over many parts of the earth met with little dangerous competiton, but that now when so large a part of our people are enfeebled by the influence of gloomy unwholesome towns, we shall have to struggle everywhere against Germany, whose population has outstripped us in numbers and is far better prepared for the struggle by training both of body and mind than we are. Unless we at once begin at least to protect the health of our people by making the towns in which most of them now live, more wholesome for body and mind, we may as well hand over our trade, our colonies, our whole influence in the world, to Germany, without undergoing all the trouble of a struggle in which we condemn ourselves beforehand to certain failure.[37]

In the bigger cities the local authorities found themselves faced with demands to declare more of the worst areas in the centre as unfit for human habitation. But the high land prices in the centre made the statutory obligation to rehouse those displaced by such clearances extremely difficult to fulfil in the central areas. For them the suburbs also provided a way out. Under Part 3 of the 1890 Housing Act they were in any case empowered to build working-class dwellings irrespective of whether there had been any slum clearance or not. The LCC led the way by building its first suburban council estates in 1898, and after the turn of the century some of the other authorities followed suit. But what was done in that matter is less important than what could have been done. The

[36] *Interdepartmental Committee on Physical Deterioration, Report*, 1904 Cd. 2175 XXXII.
[37] T. C. Horsfall, *The Relation of Town Planning to National Life* (1908), pp. 13–14.

purchase of tracts of suburban land for municipal housing schemes appeared to hold out a strategy, but one that would involve the ratepayers in huge expense if pressed very far. To make it more feasible, those who advocated such a course of action proposed that the Treasury should provide local authorities with loans for working-class housing on far more generous terms than was then the case. Town-extension planning, the body of legal powers enjoyed by German municipalities, held out the prospect of a cheaper and therefore more attractive alternative to municipal land purchase and house building.

The man who saw the significance of what was available in Germany and publicized it in England was T. C. Horsfall, a Manchester businessman but by this date to all intents and purposes a full-time social reformer and philanthropist. He had for some years been a critic of the English system of municipal government, considering it vastly inferior to the German system with its salaried and professionally trained *Bürgermeister* able to co-ordinate the work of all departments and to undertake long-term planning. The English reliance on the unpaid voluntary and part-time service of its committee chairmen he thought just silly. By 1900 he was calling for the planning of the street pattern of large areas round every expanding town, insisting on open spaces at the expense of owners of the land to be developed, co-ordinating this with the creation of a suitable transport system, and arguing that under such conditions private capital could be trusted to supply the houses.[38] In support he quoted the experience of Berlin, perhaps an unfortunate example, for the vast and overcrowded tenement houses that had been built in that city under its building plan were the very antithesis of what the English housing reformers believed in. By 1904 he had become better informed and was commending the German planning powers while at the same time roundly condemning the overcrowded German tenements. He argued that it was not merely possible but essential to have the one without the other. That was the year in which he published the book for which he is remembered, *The Improvement of the Dwellings and Surroundings of the People: The Example of Germany*. It appeared as a supplement to a deeply disturbing survey of Manchester's

[38] Idem, *The Government of Manchester: Paper read to the Manchester Statistical Society* (Manchester, 1895); idem, *The Housing of the Labouring Classes*, (Manchester, 1900).

housing conditions which had been sponsored by the local reforming pressure group of which he was President.[39] Once again he expounded the merits of the planning powers exercized by German towns as part of a plea for the reform of the municipal government system on German lines. To him it was inconceivable that the one could exist without the other.

Horsfall's influence was, however, due to the fact that others took a more eclectic view. It was his demand for German-style town-extension planning that gave him a hearing among the broad spectrum of housing reformers who came together to form the National Housing Reform Council. It was similarly that aspect of his book that had attracted the attention of J. S. Nettlefold, chairman of the Birmingham Corporation Housing Committee. In consequence a delegation from the Housing Committee headed by Nettlefold returned from an extensive inspection of the planning practice of German cities convinced of the relevance of at least some of what they had found not only to the specific problems of their own city but to British cities in general.[40]

The National Housing Reform Council linked the world of organized labour with middle-class housing reformers. It had built up links with back-bench MPs by means of a permanent committee to discuss possible legislation, and by 1907 there existed a housing reform lobby of 130 MPs. When a large delegation saw the Prime Minister and John Burns, president of the Local Government Board, in November 1906, they put forward a wide range of different proposals and received a temporizing response. Then the Association of Municipal Corporations, having under the influence of Manchester and Birmingham appointed a Town Planning Committee chaired by Nettlefold, began to press for new powers for the planning of suburbs. By 1907 pressure was being applied through Parliament in a manner very similar to that in which it was being applied over old age pensions, and it became obvious that

[39] T. R. Marr, *Housing Conditions in Manchester and Salford* (Manchester, 1904). For Horsfall's involvement in the Manchester housing reform movements, see Michael Harrison, 'Housing and Town Planning in Manchester before 1914', in A. Sutcliffe (ed.), *British Town Planning: The Formative Years* (Leicester, 1981).

[40] J. S. Nettlefold, 'Speech made to Birmingham City Council on the Presentation of the Housing Committee's Report', in City of Birmingham, *Report of the Housing Committee, 3 July 1906* (Birmingham, 1906). Also idem, *Practical Housing* (1908); Gordon E. Cherry, *Factors in the Origins of Town Planning in Britain: The Example of Birmingham 1905–1915* (Working Paper No. 36, Centre for Urban and Regional Studies; University of Birmingham, 1975).

legislation would have to be introduced. The intervention of the Association of Municipal Corporations, so Sutcliffe argues, had turned town-extension planning from one of several possible reforms into the one with key priority and given it the backing of the big urban authorities. When in 1907 parliamentary pressure finally prodded Burns into action, it was understandable that the legislation that was promised should emphasize town-extension planning in preference to other, more costly courses of action. It was equally understandable that this choice should be encouraged by the housing reform movement in the following months, which saw the slow gestation of the 1909 Housing and Town Planning Act.[41]

There is much in this development that recalls the conditions under which the German insurance model acquired political salience. A pressure group with effective political leverage played a not dissimilar role in moving the Liberal government towards legislation on old age pensions in the years immediately before the 1908 Act. Yet there is one factor that distinguishes the events described in Part II of this book from the political history of town planning legislation as described by Sutcliffe. In the former case the decision to go for the German precedent was made by a Cabinet Minister in disregard of the preferences of those engaged in putting him under pressure. In the latter case it had been largely made already, and the Cabinet Minister was following suit. On both occasions the underlying reason for the decision was much the same. What the German model offered was a course of action at one and the same time cheaper and more comprehensive. What Lloyd George recognized in 1908, when he embarked on contributory insurance, the Association of Municipal Corporations, following the lead of J. S. Nettlefold, had recognized in 1907, when they opted for town-extension planning.

It is striking how much more closely the case of town planning resembles that of workers' insurance than it does that of education, whether education in general or technical and scientific education in particular. In the two former instances the relevance of the German example was discovered at a late stage, and a particular institutional device with a German precedent was superimposed on a long-standing development along native lines. Indeed these were processes in which Britain had played the pioneering role and had,

---

[41] Sutcliffe, *Towards the Planned City*, pp. 61, 72–82.

if anything, at earlier times been considered as the pattern for others to follow. The case of education is different. Here the inclination to pay close attention to the example of Germany was of much longer standing, being merely intensified, not created, by the change of mental climate that occurred around 1900. But the response to that example took the form of emulation rather than of that imitation at the institutional level to which the term 'transfer of social technology' was applied earlier in this chapter. The characteristic German educational institutions in the technical and scientific sphere were usually rejected as unsuited to English conditions, and the spirit of emulation expressed itself through the more energetic development of British institutions. Research and teaching in the applied sciences was developed within the universities, not as in Germany in separate *Technische Hochschulen* of university standard. Compulsory attendance of young workers at Continuation Schools remained a forlorn cause before 1914 and, when incorporated within the sanguine Education Act of 1918, it immediately fell victim to the economy cuts of the early 1920s. There may be exceptions to this generalization, which is based on no more than a survey, and probably an imperfect survey, of the secondary literature. The National Physical Laboratory would seem to be one exception; perhaps another is the adoption of the open-air school. These are minor institutional innovations compared with social insurance and town planning, more akin to the borrowing of technical devices of even more limited implication such as shower-baths for schools. Such relatively minor matters do not seriously modify the generalization in question. It may perhaps be allowed to stand as an interim judgement, designed to encourage those more familiar with the subject either to confirm or to deny it.[42]

Sources of Information

In his study of town planning as an international movement, Sutcliffe drew attention to the piecemeal growth of international

[42] If there is an exception to this generalization it may well be the scientific research laboratory itself, which it has been suggested is the really fundamental invention which Germany has contributed to the organization of science. That would raise questions, which have not been pursued here, about the establishment and funding of research laboratories by private industry, by universities, and by research councils. In that context the establishment of the National Physical Laboratory might be a more significant matter. See D. S. L. Cardwell, *The Organisation of Science in England: A Retrospect* (1957); Haines, *Essays on German Influence*.

organizations that characterized the century after 1815 and to the way in which this process accelerated particularly from the 1890s onwards. He did so in order to explain the relative ease with which the experiences of different countries in the most diverse fields of action became available elsewhere. This growth and its accelertion was in turn connected with the expansion of the professional classes and the improvements in communications. The creation of an international railway network, the conversion of transatlantic passenger shipping to steam, and the improvement in mail services consequent on both of these developments led to a surge of international meetings, whether in the form of exhibitions or of congresses. Starting as a trickle in the 1840s, by the beginning of the twentieth century it had become a flood. Eight hundred and fifty-three congresses were held between 1886 and the end of the century; no less than 2,271 in the next fourteen years, covering a truly bewildering variety of matters.

Unlike many historians, Sutcliffe plays down the importance of international rivalry and sees the receptivity to foreign examples to be found in many countries during those final years before the First World War as part of a surge in creative internationalism.[43] Such an emphasis comes more easily to a study such as his, which is concerned with the formulation of town planning as an ideal. It fits less happily into the present study, which is concerned rather with the political acceptance and actual realization of practices from abroad.

There is, however, no denying the important role played by international congresses during those years in facilitating the communication of ideas and experiences among professional men responsible for a wide variety of tasks. Thus, for instance, the dissemination of the experiments with open-air schools just mentioned functioned through the establishment of triennial International Congresses for Social Hygiene.[44]

The subject matter of this present study was certainly not unaffected by the forces that brought about the proliferation of international congresses, nor was it ignored at the great international exhibitions. An exposition of the German workers' insurance

[43] Sutcliffe, *Towards the Planned City*, pp. 163–6, 176.
[44] Roy Lowe, 'The Early 20th C. Open Air Movement: Origins and Implications', in N. Parry and D. McNair (eds.), *The Fitness of the Nation: Physical and Health Education in the 19th and 20th Centuries* (History of Education Society, 1983).

system was a feature of international exhibitions in Chicago in 1893, Brussels in 1897, Paris in 1900, and St Louis in 1904.[45]

More effective even than such exhibits were the specialist congresses. Among these, the International Labour Congress sponsored by the German government in Berlin in 1890 was rather a special case. This German initiative was treated with the utmost caution by the British government. It did not want to be put under pressure to amend the laws on the employment of women and children in line with some international convention and it ultimately opposed the establishment of further congresses of this sort. When it became clear that it would be expected to send someone of ministerial rank it chose Sir John Gorst, who as Under-Secretary for India had no official connection with any of the departments dealing with labour questions.[46] Nevertheless the congress proved a most effective means of disseminating information on what the Germans were doing. Its impact on Gorst and his subsequent activities as propagandist will need to be considered.[47]

It was more usual for international congresses to be sponsored not by governments but by international committees of specialists. The series of congresses that dealt with problems of accidents at work had been initiated at a meeting held to coincide with the 1889 International Exhibition in Paris, as was not uncommon in the history of such congresses. The next meeting was held in 1891 at Berne, and thereafter meetings were held at intervals of never more than three years in the various cities of Europe. It might have been expected that this series of congresses would have served as an effective means to educate British specialists in the details of accident insurance policies that were being developed not only in Germany but in many other countries. Yet this was far from being the case. Just because the congresses increasingly came to discuss

---

[45] German Imperial Insurance Office, *The Workmen's Insurance of the German Empire: Guide Expressly Published for the World's Exhibition in Chicago* (Berlin and London, 1893); idem, *Guide to the Workmen's Insurance of the German Empire: Newly Composed for the World's Exhibition in Brussels* (Berlin, 1897); idem, *Guide to the Workmen's Insurance of the German Empire*: Revised Edition Brought up to Date for the International Exhibition at Paris (Berlin, 1900): idem, *Guide to the Workmen's Insurance of the German Empire: Revised Edition Brought up to Date for the Universal Exposition at St. Louis* (Berlin and London, 1904). These were all compiled by Georg Zacher.

[46] *Correspondence Respecting the Proposed Labour Conference at Berlin*, 1890 C. 5914 CXXXI. 529.

[47] See ch. 2 below.

social insurance policies the relevant British government departments kept their distance. When a Superintendent Inspector of
Factories was personally invited to present a paper on factory
accidents to the 1891 congress and asked for help with his
expenses, the Home Secretary refused. As he explained, the
congress was bound to discuss the controversial subject of
employers' liability laws, and the Home Office must on no account
appear to be officially represented.[48] In fact the strong German
delegation was so effective at stating its case that the congress
declared itself in favour of insurance against both accidents and
sickness. Thereafter the congress changed its name to Congrès
International des Accidents de Travail et des Assurances Sociales.
The organizers frequently made a point of inviting at least one
Englishman to present a paper, but it is remarkable how small the
British attendance was. In Milan in 1894, when the Germans
numbered 98 and the French 167, there were seven Englishmen and
two of those were local consuls. After 1897 British participation
dropped practically to vanishing point. In Vienna in 1905 there was
no one from Britain apart from the official from the Board of Trade
who had been asked to present a paper. On that occasion the
congress received reports on the progress of workers' insurance in
sixteen countries, and at a time when the British government was
considering enlarging the scope of its workmen's compensation
laws those reports were far from irrelevant.

These attendance figures suggest that official reticence was not
the only obstacle. Unofficial social reformers were equally slow to
show an interest. Not until 1908, by which time matters had
changed in British reforming circles, did attendance improve. That
year when the congress met in Rome, a very popular location, the
British contingent numbered seven and some of those had brought
their wives and daughters. There were even two official delegates
from the Home Office for the first time ever. 1908 saw the
establishment of a permanent headquarters in Paris for what was
now called the Association Internationale des Assurances Sociales,
with national committees, even a British one, composed of
individuals interested in social work. In 1910 there were once more
seven British representatives compared with forty-nine Germans
and thirty-two Frenchmen. On that occasion one of the main items

[48] Minute by H[enry] M[atthews], 11 July 1891, PRO, HO 45/9841/B11058/1.

on the agenda was the role of the doctor in the insurance system of different countries, a matter which was to be of great interest in Britain within less than a year.[49]

More important as a source of information for British social reformers than these international gatherings were visits paid to Germany by interested individuals and groups. In this connection the visits paid by both Beveridge and Harold Cox in 1907 are of particular importance, as were those by Lloyd George in 1908 and W. J. Braithwaite in 1910. To these should certainly be added the visit by the delegation of the Parliamentary Committee of the TUC in 1908. Such purposeful visits of inquiry have their parallel in the histories of town planning and of technical education. They should not be confused with the ceremonial junketing organized in 1906 and after by the Anglo-German Friendship Committee for such miscellaneous groups as mayors or newspaper editors.[50] Indeed the interest taken by social reformers had no necessary connection with friendship for Germany. It could just as well stem from its opposite, or more usually be attended by very mixed feelings. It was due rather to a recognition that, to echo Beveridge's words, Germany was the country which in its industrial development was most closely comparable to Britain.[51]

In this context some notice, however brief, must be taken of the impact of protectionism. Its advocates did more than any others to stimulate discussion of the relevance of German policies to British conditions. As a country sheltered behind tariff walls and conspicuous for its economic progress, Germany was constantly held up by them as an example to be followed. Indeed the impression that Britain was losing world trade to the more efficient German rival had been largely fostered by protectionists, who had an obvious interest in making the plight of British industries appear as critical as possible so as to justify drastic steps in their defence.[52] They also had an interest in giving maximum publicity to German

[49] Figures of attendance and other information, from Congrès International des Accidents du Travail et des Assurances Sociales, *Rapports et procès-verbaux* (1894–1911), *passim*.

[50] For the Anglo-German Friendship Committee, see Günther Hollenberg, *Englisches Interesse am Kaiserreich* (Wiesbaden, 1974), ch. 3.

[51] W. H. Beveridge, 'Social Reform: How Germany Deals With It', *Morning Post*, Sept. 1907, LPES, Beveridge Papers XII.

[52] For a balanced assessment of the state of various industries and of the overall trade situation, see Kennedy, *Rise of Anglo-German Antagonism*, ch. 15.

economic progress. The free traders' argument that a country which taxed imported food lowered the standard of living of its workers caused much attention to be paid by both sides to the well-being of the German working man. Tariff reform organizations sent delegations of British working men to Germany and their opponents followed suit, while descriptions of the condition of the German workers found a ready readership.[53] German unemployment figures, which were lower than the British ones, were much quoted and their significance disputed. In all these debates the Board of Trade played an active role. Its *British and Foreign Trade Statistics* were an antidote to alarmist views on trade, and it was sceptical about the comparability of British and German unemployment figures. To the interest in the comparative well-being of workers it responded by figures in 1903 and 1905 which were much disputed, and finally by launching a massive survey of the cost of living of the urban working classes in Britain and in four other industrial countries. The volume on Germany was published in 1908 and was the first of the foreign reports to appear. It indicated that an Englishman emigrating to Germany and trying to maintain his standard of living would spend one-fifth more on rent, fuel, and food than in England.[54]

Information on many aspects of German policy found its way into the literature that was produced by the debate over tariff reform. Thus for instance, an appendix to *Life and Labour in Germany*, the report of the Gainsborough working men on their sponsored visit, provided a description of German infirmity and old age pensions.

No one ministered more persistently and successfully to this interest in German social institutions than William Harbutt Dawson. From the publication of *German Socialism and Ferdinand*

[53] Gainsborough Commission, *Life and Labour in Germany*, ed. J. L. Bashford (1907); Tariff Reform League, *Reports on Labour and Social Conditions in Germany* (2 vols.; 1910); Sheffield Daily Telegraph, *Life under Tariffs: What we saw in Germany* (1910); Labour Party, *Life and Labour in Germany* (1910).

[54] *British Foreign Trade and Industrial Conditions*, 1903 Cd. 1761 LXVII; 1905 Cd. 2337 LXXXIX. *Cost of Living of the Working Classes: British Towns*, 1908 Cd. 3864 CVII. 319; *German Towns* 1908 Cd. 4032 CVIII. 1., esp. pp. li–lii; see *App. IX, Comparability of British and German Statistics of Unemployment*. These figures were passionately disputed in J. Ellis Barker, *Economic Problems and Board of Trade Methods: An Exposure* (1908). For the most balanced discussion of the validity of the board's conclusions, see the review by A. L. Bowley in the *Economic Journal*, 18 (1908), 657–62.

Lassalle in 1888 and *Bismarck and State Socialism* in 1890 until the war, and indeed until 1933, Dawson poured out a flood of books and articles. A journalist with Liberal leanings and with an interest in social and economic matters, his connections with Germany dated from 1885, when at the age of 25 he was appointed to a post in Berlin as editor of Kislaw's *German Trade Review and Exporter*. He attended lectures at Berlin University and became a disciple of Professor Adolph Wagner, one of the leading exponents of State socialism. *Bismarck and State Socialism*, a careful and well-informed exposition, was also a statement of his own belief in the significance of what had happened in Germany and its relevance for British social reformers. 'In the system of social assurance established by Prince Bismarck we have the model after which we shall have to work', he wrote in the preface to the 1891 edition.[55] In 1890, the same year as his Bismarck study, he produced a book on *The Unearned Increment*, writing from the English standpoint but drawing on the USA and Germany for his illustrations of the principles advanced. He tried but failed to persuade the publisher Swan Sonnenschein that there was a readership for a new periodical advocating State socialist principles with himself as editor. The years 1890–1906 were spent in running the local paper in Skipton-in-Craven, Yorkshire, which he had inherited from his father, but he remained in close touch with Germany and German experts in administration. A two-volume study *Germany and the Germans* appeared in 1894, and a study of social movements and legislation in Switzerland in 1897.[56] From 1901 onwards his publications on Germany followed one another at a rapid rate, as the market for what he had to offer increased.[57]

He had first approached the Board of Trade in 1905 with offers to make inquiries on its behalf while he was preparing material for his 1906 book on *The German Workman*. In 1906 he sold his Yorkshire paper, moved to London, and was appointed to work for the Board of Trade, where he was responsible for much of the cost

[55] W. H. Dawson, *Bismarck and State Socialism* (2nd edn., 1891), p. x.

[56] Idem, *Social Switzerland: Studies of present-day Social Movements and Legislation in the Swiss Republic* (1897).

[57] See titles listed in Bibliography. Also relevant although not specifically on Germany were *Matthew Arnold and his Relation to the Thought of our Time: An Appreciation and a Criticism* (1904); and *The Vagrancy Problem: The Case for Measures of Restraint for Tramps, Loafers, etc.* (1910). In addition he was a frequent contributor to the periodical press.

of living survey. From December 1908 onwards Lloyd George was using him as a source of information on German insurance and in 1912 he was transferred to the newly created National Health Insurance Commission under Sir Robert Morant.[58]

Of his contribution to the making of the National Insurance Act nothing need be said now. But his wide-ranging published writings on German institutions both before and after his appointment to the Board of Trade deserve some comment within the present discussion of the flow of information on Germany.

In spite of the statements in the prefaces, which were expressions of his own genuine belief in the importance of what he was presenting, it would be a mistake to ascribe to him much, if any, importance as an advocate of policies. In that respect he is not in the same class as Beveridge, nor do any of his publications acquire the importance that Horsfall's writings had in relation to town planning. He relied on the existence of a public prepared to attend to what is on the whole a distinctly prosaic body of information.

Nor was there anything special about his emphasis. He was on the whole prepared to reinforce commonly held views. Thus *The German Workman: A Study in Efficiency* (1906) presented thoroughness and system as characteristic of the German mind and the key to all Germany's progress.[59] Yet the information that he provides repeatedly shows the incomplete and spasmodic nature of the institutions in question, depending on local municipal initiative or varying according to the component states of what was after all a federal structure.

In 1914 the bottom fell out of the market for admiring presentations of German ways. Dawson's ambitious book *Municipal Life and Government in Germany* had the misfortune to be published just before the outbreak of war in 1914 and received a very mixed reception by the reviewers.[60] But this did not mean that Dawson's role as a publicist was now over. Far from it! The following year saw the publication of his next book, *What is Wrong with Germany*, the first book on Germany, so he claimed, which he had written without pleasure. In it he blamed the political

---

[58] Biographical information from Birm. Univ. Lib., W. H. Dawson papers. There is a more detailed sketch in Hollenberg, *Englisches Interesse*, pp. 230–42.

[59] Op. cit., p. viii.

[60] See press cuttings in Birm. Univ. Lib., W. H. Dawson Papers.

absolutism of the German state and the personal role of William II for much that had gone wrong.[61]

Dawson provides the most prominent example of a publicist who contributed to the flow of information on German workers' insurance. Alongside such work must be set the careful descriptions submitted to Royal Commissions, such as that on Labour of 1892–4 or that on the Poor Laws of 1905–9, and to all intents and purposes buried in the numerous folio volumes of evidence produced by these inquiries. Nor should the routine channels of information available to the Foreign Office through its diplomatic representatives be overlooked. Yet it must be confessed that overlooked they often were. They played their part in providing ministers and civil servants with information, when such people chose to ask for it, but such a role was distinctly secondary. Far more important were those accounts that would seem to have had some effect on social reformers, not least those in which information and advocacy were combined in a more or less effective way.[62]

---

[61] W. H. Dawson, *What is Wrong with Germany* (1915), esp. pp. viii–xi.
[62] All three kinds of publication are listed in the bibliography.

PART I

The Partial Rejection of the German Precedent
Compensation for Industrial Accidents

I

Towards an Impasse

THIS section is about the creation of a system of workmen's compensation and the circumstances out of which it arose. There is no mystery about these circumstances. The Workmen's Compensation Act of 1897 was an attempt, and a successful one, to break a political deadlock that had arisen over the efforts to reform the law of employers' liability for injury due to negligence.[1]

In common law masters had been held responsible for the consequences not only of their own negligence but also of that of their servants. A legal judgement in 1837, however, laid down that such liability did not exist if the injured person was also in the employ of the same master.[2] The defence of 'common employment', as it was called, meant that in practice an employee had a claim only if there had been negligence on the part of the master personally. Common employment came to be interpreted in the widest possible terms. In the case of large undertakings in which the owner was remote from the actual running of the concern, such as mines and railways, to quote two forms of employment in which accidents were only too common, this left the workman with no claim that he could in practice pursue. There were other obstacles in the way of actually establishing liability,[3] but the doctrine of common employment was the principal one.

---

[1] W. C. Mallalieu, 'Joseph Chamberlain and Workmen's Compensation', *Jour. of Econ. Hist.*, 10 (1959), 45–57. The best book on the period up to 1897 is P. W. J. Bartrip and S. B. Burman, *The Wounded Soldiers of Industry: Industrial Compensation Policy 1833–1897* (Oxford, 1983). The present study had been written before it appeared and has been revised in the light of it. D. G. Hanes, *The First British Workmen's Compensation Act 1897* (New Haven, Conn., 1968), the first book to be based on the Home Office papers in the PRO, is not well informed on British political history. Sir Arnold Wilson and Hermann Levy, *Workmen's Compensation* (2 vols.; London, 1939, 1941), has been an indispensable guide.

[2] *Priestley v. Fowler* (1837) 3 M & W 1.

[3] e.g. the plea that the plaintiff voluntarily encountered the risk by taking employment in this particular occupation, and the plea of contributory negligence for such things as failure to report known shortcomings in the equipment. Hanes, *First British Workmen's Compensation Act*, pp. 5–14; A. H. Ruegg, *The Laws relating to the Relation of Employer and Workmen in England* (1905).

In such cases it was impossible to use the civil law to bring home to owners their responsibility for safety provisions and procedures. Hence whether the matter was regarded from the point of view of safeguarding lives, or of the moral claims of the victim, or of the men's own benefit funds, the state of the law was bound to be a grievance in an accident-prone industry such as coal mining. This grievance was already being voiced in 1863,[4] but the miners' union had to wait until after the extension of the franchise in 1867 and the creation of the Parliamentary Committee of the TUC in 1871 before it made an impact on Parliament.

Alexander Macdonald, the miners' leader, became the first chairman of the Parliamentary Committee and his demand for a reform of the law found a ready hearing at the TUC Conference in 1872. The miners had prepared a Bill that would have drastically curtailed the defence of common employment, and after some initial difficulty the Parliamentary Committee found a sponsor for it in the House of Commons. It was withdrawn after the government had promised to introduce a Bill of its own early in the 1874 session, but by then the government had lost control of the Commons and was in no position to tackle controversial legislation.[5]

The effect of the miners' Bill would have been to place the injured workman, or his dependants in the case of death, in the same position *vis-à-vis* the law as was already enjoyed by the general public. The fact that the law as it then stood deprived the workman *qua* workman of rights which other citizens enjoyed was only too apparent in the event of railway accidents, when injured passengers could sue the company for the negligence of one of its officials but railwaymen injured on the same occasion could not. Such a grievance was bound to appeal to the TUC, which was at this time conducting a campaign against the legal discrimination against workmen sanctioned by the Masters and Servants Acts. After 1875, when the agitation against the Criminal Law Amendment Act of 1871 and the Masters and Servants Acts had been brought to a successful conclusion, the reform of the law of employers' liability became the Parliamentary Committee's principal endeavour.

By then a second initiative had been taken, this time by the Amalgamated Society of Railway Servants (ASRS) that had been founded in 1871. A series of railway accidents had created a climate

[4] S. and B. Webb, *Industrial Democracy* (1898), p. 268.
[5] TUC, *Proceedings*, 1872, p. 5; ibid., 1873, p. 3; ibid., 1879, p. 18.

in Parliament favourable to action aimed at improving the safety of the railways. From 1872 Parliament insisted on obtaining annual returns of the number of railwaymen killed or injured in connection with the movement of traffic. These were so shocking that in 1874 the government was forced to set up a Royal Commission into Railway Accidents as a way of heading off demand for immediate legislation.[6]

The MP closest to the ASRS was the brewer Michael Bass, Liberal member for Derby. He had done much to encourage the establishment of the railway union in the first place, and it was his draft Bill of 1874, rather than that produced by some other parliamentary critics of the railways, that reflected the aspirations of the union. The ASRS had had no close connection with the TUC in its first few years, but now, faced with the likelihood of delay in introducing Bass's Bill, it made contact with the TUC and threw its weight behind proposals to raise the compensation issue in the House. In 1876 Macdonald, now no longer chairman of the Parliamentary Committee but since 1874 MP for Stafford, introduced his Bill and was headed off by the appointment of a Select Committee on Employers' Liability. On the Committee, which finally reported in 1877, a minority, led by the chairman Robert Lowe, the former Liberal cabinet minister, wanted to make the defence of common employment inapplicable in cases of negligence by anyone exercising authority as long as he was not actually engaged in manual labour. The majority wanted to retain the principle of the doctrine of common employment but to take account of the existence of firms not personally managed by the owner. They were prepared to recommend liability for negligence by the one person to whom the overall supervision had been entrusted by the employer. The Royal Commission on Railway Accidents, which had reported earlier that year, went further than that and recommended that railway companies should be made liable to their employees for the negligence of all those to whom in the various branches of railway employment the master's authority had been delegated.[7]

There were not a few lawyers who watched the drift of reforming

[6] For the details of these initiatives by the Parliamentary Committee and the ASRS, see TUC, *Proceedings*, 1874–1880, *passim*; and P. S. Gupta, 'The History of the Amalgamated Society of Railway Servants 1871–1913', D.Phil thesis (Oxford, 1960).

[7] *SC on Employers' Liability, Final Report*, 1877 (285) X. *RC on Railway Accidents, Report*, 1877 C. 1637, XLVIII.

opinion on the subject of the law of liability with profound misgivings. To hold an employer liable for the negligence of anybody but himself seemed to be utterly unjust. They felt that it ought to be possible to mitigate the hardship suffered by the victims of accidents without such injustice. Sir John Holker, the Attorney-General, would really have liked to abolish the right of the public to sue in such cases, and wished instead to compel railway and shipping companies to insure their passengers against accidents.[8] Others, prepared to leave matters as they were, thought that compulsory insurance might be the way to protect the workmen.

This was the view that Joseph Brown, a highly respected figure in this particular branch of the law, put before an expert audience in 1878 at a meeting of the National Association for the Promotion of Social Science, an accepted forum for law reform.[9] His proposal was that in certain hazardous occupations employers should not be allowed to employ anyone unless he was insured against accidents through some Friendly Society or insurance company. The employer should be obliged to contribute a certain proportion of the expense of insurance and should in consequence be exempt from further liability. So as to limit the cost to both masters and men the amount of compensation would have to be limited. He suggested following the Friendly Societies' practice of half-wages for a year at most or a widow's grant of £10 to £25. On the basis of the much criticized statistics of railway accidents he thought a 10 per cent contribution from the employer was about right.

It is amazing for how small a sum he expected workers to be prepared to relinquish the hope of substantial damages under a reformed law in exchange for the certainty of receiving something. He showed no sign of understanding the bitterness and frustration that made trade unionists look on the threat of really swingeing damages as the most promising way of forcing owners to pay more attention to the maintenance of their equipment. He was to be firmly reminded of this aspect in the subsequent discussion.

---

[8] Sir John Holker to R. A. Cross, 8 June 1878, Cabinet Memo, by J[ohn] H[olker], 27 Nov. 1878, PRO, HO 45/9458/72731A. This was within the context of the discussions within the government referred to below.

[9] Joseph Brown, QC, 'Paper on Employers' Liability for Accidents of their Own Servants through the Fault of Fellow-servants, Read 17 June 1878, and Discussion', in NAPSS, *Sessional Proceedings* (1877–78), pp. 169–208. See also Bartrip and Burman, *Wounded Soldiers of Industry*, pp. 140–4, who were the first to draw attention to this incident.

Turning from the financial to the administrative aspect of the proposal, Brown pointed out that there were precedents. Membership of sick funds subsidized by the employers was a condition of employment in some mining districts and on certain railways, although his own suggestion was to leave each man free to choose his own society. How this was to be combined with the payment of the premium by the master, deducting the amount from the man's wages and adding his 10 per cent, was not made clear, and trade unionists were quick to voice their fear of victimization of those who chose a trade union fund. The alternative of a single policy for all the work-force, although simpler to administer, also had distinct disadvantages for the individual.

Brown's terms of reference were entirely British and so were the precedents he quoted. Yet in a strange way the practice current in Prussian mining districts stood godfather to his proposals. In the chair at the meeting was Lord Shand, a Scottish judge of appeal with recent experience of colliery accident litigation, on whose suggestion Brown had produced his paper. Shand knew about the *Knappschaften* in the Prussian mining districts, which provided a wide range of welfare benefits including medical care and financial support for injured miners. Their funds came partly from contributions by the employers, partly by compulsory deduction from the men's wages. In opening the discussion, which was to extend over two sessions and attract many of those involved in the reform campaign in Parliament and among trade unionists, he referred to them at length in glowing terms and also gave examples of German factory-based funds in other industries with contributions from the employer towards the accident component of the benefit.

'It would be well in future not to confine ourselves to observing what was going on in our own country [he said] but to take the benefit of the experience of others'. He had to admit that none of these arrangements actually protected the German employer from being sued under the German law, which (though this he did not say) knew nothing of the doctrine of common employment. Such an admission made the precedent irrelevant on the most crucial point. Nevertheless Shand did manage to convey to his audience that the proposal for obligatory insurance across a whole industry was not just a pipe-dream. The point was quickly taken up by one speaker and firmly rejected.

Lord Shand had cited the case of Germany and had remarked that what he and Mr Brown recommended with regard to England was, in Germany, in actual existence. On this point he would remark that the Germans are a drilled nation—drilled both politically and militarily; and he might almost add, drilled in education and religion. And this he thanked God was not the case with Englishmen.

To the deadening effect of this drilling the speaker ascribed the passive way in which the Prussians had allowed their constitution to be violated in the 1860s, and he ended by protesting against Germany being held up as a model in this matter. The matter of compulsion stuck in the throats of quite a number of others, and although Brown argued back that 'the compulsion he proposed was a very gentle one', few were prepared to support him on this point.[10]

In any case nothing could change the determination of the TUC Parliamentary Committee to obtain the total abolition of the defence of common employment. Macdonald had reintroduced his Bill in 1878 and obtained a Second Reading, but when it became apparent that even those MPs in favour of reform were not prepared to accept so sweeping a change, a breach opened up between the Parliamentary Committee and the ASRS over tactics. Evans, the energetic secretary of the ASRS, saw the possibility of isolating the railway companies by a more moderate measure that had some chance of being supported by other employers in the House. When the Parliamentary Committee refused to compromise, he arranged for a Bill largely along the lines advocated by Lowe to be introduced into the Lords by a Conservative peer, Lord De La Warr, and into the Commons by a Liberal MP and large employer, Sir Thomas Brassey. He had prepared the ground by organizing petitions on a large scale.

By 1878 no one defended the law as it stood and government ministers were casting around for some acceptable basis on which to introduce a measure of their own. They did not much care for the 1876–7 Select Committee's attempt to distinguish between servants in authority and other servants. One senior Home Office official thought it unsound in theory and unworkable in practice. 'Could anything be done in the nature of compulsory insurance on both sides?' asked Ridley, the Under-Secretary at the Home Office,

[10] NAPSS, *Sessional Proceedings*, pp. 200, 208.

echoing the discussions at the National Association for the Promotion of Social Science (NAPSS), but he doubted the practicality of the idea. To compel insurance by Act of Parliament was just not within the bounds of practicality, and the Cabinet finally swallowed its misgivings and that of its advisers and produced a Bill on the lines of the majority recommendations of 1877.[11]

Now there were three Bills before Parliament and in the session of 1879 none of them made any significant progress. In 1880 the government arranged for its Bill to be sent to a Select Committee of the House of Lords, while Brassey and De La Warr as well as Macdonald reintroduced theirs. With a general election due, the ASRS sent out instructions to their branches, and the railwaymen's vote was skillfully deployed to obtain pledges from candidates in favour of Brassey's Bill. At Chester both parties were wooing the crucial railwaymen's vote, and Dodson, the Liberal victor, was well aware of what he owed to them. On becoming President of the Local Government Board he urged on Gladstone the importance of early legislation. A Cabinet Committee, of whose members four had already pledged themselves on the issue during the election, reported in favour of adopting Brassey's Bill as the government measure. It was introduced very early in the new session, timed to coincide with and so to eclipse Macdonald's rival Bill. One railway director was to speak of MPs coming from the hustings reeking of pledges to working men.[12]

The response of the railway company directors and the mine owners to the threat that the Bill contained was to try to construct a common front with other employers' organizations. On the suggestion of the Mining Association they decided that insurance of some kind was preferable to a Bill that would make them liable to court action. They therefore attempted to persuade Gladstone to withdraw the measure in favour of a Select Committee to consider a system of general insurance against such accidents as were proposed to be dealt with by the Bill. An amendment to this effect was moved on the Second Reading. Mine owners from both sides of the House and from various mining districts united behind this

[11] Sir M. W. Ridley to R. A. Cross, 22 July 1878, Memo by G. Lushington, 30 July 1878, PRO, HO 45/9458/72731A. See also Bartrip and Burman, *Wounded Soldiers of Industry*, pp. 145–6.

[12] Sir Edward Watkin, in 3 *Hansard* 252 (3 June 1880) 1135, qd. in Geoffrey Alderman, *The Railway Interest* (Leicester, 1973), p. 72. The whole of Alderman's ch. 4 is important for the reform of 1880.

move, but the government was not prepared to yield, and they were defeated. They tried once more on 6 July when the Bill was in committee, this time widening the scope of the proposed insurance to cover all injuries suffered in the course of employment. During the debates insurance schemes were strongly commended as a means of cementing good relations between masters and men, and of avoiding litigation, but the real object of the move was to press for a wide-ranging inquiry in order to stop the Bill. Vague references to the blessing of insurance, even universal insurance, had a fairly wide appeal. But what it would mean to compel insurance by legislation had not been considered. When the opponents of the Bill got together to see whether they could actually put forward a suitable scheme, they totally failed to come up with anything. The width of support in the House depended entirely on the vagueness of the proposals.

At this juncture Shand re-entered the scene, drawing attention to the *Knappschaften* as a precedent and claiming that the Select Committee of 1876–7 had failed to do justice to their importance. Knowles, chairman of the Mining Association, was interested in anything that would justify a new inquiry, but all to no avail. It was a blatant move to side-track the Bill and was firmly defeated. German precedents for compulsion were regarded as red herrings and ignored accordingly.[13] It was in this context that the government made inquiries through consular channels about the practice in other countries with regard to insurance in mines and the liability of employers in the case of injury. The report on compulsory insurance of miners in the Prussian Rhineland which was published proved to be most unfavourable.[14]

Voluntary insurance through mutual relief funds with contributions by both employer and employee was, however, quite another matter, and one that evoked much enthusiasm. 'The principle of insurance would be of the greatest possible benefit but it could not be treated as a matter of legislation in substitution of the present measure', said the Attorney-General. However, 'masters and men . . . had the power of contracting themselves out of this Bill

---

[13] Charles Knowles, in 3 *Hansard* 252 (6 July 1880) 1759; *The Times*, 24 Aug. 1880. In 1879 Shand had been attacked at the TUC for being hand in glove with the mine owners, see TUC, *Proceedings* 1879, p. 19.

[14] *Reports on the Laws in Force in France and Germany with Regard to the Insurance of Persons Employed in Mines and the Legal Liability of their Employers,* 1880 C. 2607 LIX. 233.

if they liked to contribute voluntarily to a compensation fund'. That was as far as the government was prepared to go. When at a later stage it was suggested that the Bill should be automatically inapplicable to any employer who had contributed at a satisfactory level to an approved mutual insurance fund, the government refused to co-operate.[15]

The Act of 1880 created a number of specific exceptions to the defence of common employment. It made employers liable for the negligence of their supervisory staff, although not of those ordinarily engaged in manual labour. In the case of railways the negligence of train drivers, signalmen, and those responsible for setting the points was specifically included in the liability. But the Act was obsure and badly drafted, and led to many anomalies. It did not abolish the defence of common employment but tried to take account of the fact that in many firms supervision and its consequent responsibility were inevitably delegated through a chain of command.

From the point of view of mine owners these proposals were distinctly unpalatable. Unlike railway directors they were not often sued for damages caused to the general public by accidents. To be liable for the innumerable accidents ranging from great disasters to the loss of life and limb by individuals that were common in mining filled them with apprehension. Their legal liability extended far beyond any measures they personally could take to avoid negligence. They were to be liable for the negligence of their subordinate supervisors even if these ignored explicit regulations.

Some employers responded to the 1880 Act by insuring themselves against the new risks. Most of them did not. Others took up the Attorney-General's suggestion. In exchange for an employer's contribution to their benefit fund the workers were persuaded to waive their right of legal action under the Act. The decision once taken thereupon became a condition of employment in the particular firm. This contracting out of the Act was not, however, very widespread. It was hardly known outside the mining industry and the railways. In mining it was confined to certain collieries in Lancashire, Cheshire, the Midlands, and North Wales; among railways to the London and North Western Railway Company. In South Wales, where contracting out was not

---

[15]   3 *Hansard* 253 (3 June 1880) 1129–30; 255 (6 Aug. 1880) 574–94.

unknown, it was not a condition of employment, merely a condition of membership of the benefit fund. The same was true of the London, Brighton, and South Coast Railway Company, whose employees had the right to contract back into the Act on giving notice, but in practice did not do so, preferring the benefits of their generously subsidized insurance fund. By the late 1880s roughly 20 per cent of colliery workers had contracted out of the Act in exchange for membership of a subsidized accident fund, and of these roughly half had done so as a condition of their employment. But in those areas where the practice existed, its impact was much greater than these national figures would suggest. As for the employers' contribution, in the mining districts it amounted to between 20 and 25 per cent of the miners' own subscriptions. The railway companies were more generous. The London and North Western Railway almost matched its employees' subscriptions while the London, Brighton, and South Coast Railway more than doubled those of its employees.[16]

This then was what the policy of insurance, which had been advocated since 1878 as an alternative to broadening the law of employers' liability, amounted to in practice. Not a scheme of compulsion by Act of Parliament embracing all firms in dangerous occupations, as Brown had suggested, but an arrangement enforced here and there by individual companies or a regional combination of mine owners.

The objection of the trade union leaders to the practice was immediate and vehement. They looked on the Employers' Liability Act with its penalties for negligence as a measure that could be expected to prevent accidents, and regarded contracting out as a means of avoiding the penalties of carelessness. The view that 'mutual insurance fostered neglect' was passionately held. In 1892 the Home Office analysed the accident statistics and found that they lent no support to this view, and it said so the following year in its evidence to the Royal Commission on Labour. Even then the belief persisted in Labour circles. There were in any case other grounds for the objections of the trade union movement. Unions

[16] *Memorandum on the Liability of Employers for Injury to their Servants,* by Sir Godfrey Lushington, *RC on Labour, App. CLIX to Mins. of Ev. Taken before the RC Sitting as a Whole,* pp. 348–59, 1893–4 C. 7063–IIIA XXXIX, pt. i. 805. See R. C. Challinor, *The Lancashire and Cheshire Miners* (Newcastle, 1972) for the imposition of compulsory contracting out in the Lancashire coalfield.

were able to use their funds both to support victims of accidents, sickness, or unemployment and to support strikes. On the other hand the existence of a fund subsidized by the employer and directed specifically to compensation for injury weakened their appeal and hampered their freedom of action. They saw it as an 'insidious attempt to undermine the foundations of their trade associations'. This was so obvious to all trade unionists that it was only rarely spelt out. Another objection was that the organization of benefit funds on the basis of a firm or even of a district could anchor a man to a job which otherwise he might have preferred to leave, and so gave employers additional leverage.[17]

As early as 1881 both the TUC and the ASRS sponsored Bills to make contracting out illegal, and in the following year they combined their efforts behind a single Bill. They obtained a debate on their proposal in 1883 only to discover that there was little support for it in the House. Matters were different after the general election of 1885 had provided an opportunity to put pressure on MPs, and early in 1886 the Commons set up a Select Committee on the operation of the Employers' Liability Act.

It is some indication of the extent to which organized labour's views had gained a hearing in the Liberal Party that the comittee divided evenly on party lines over a proposal to forbid all contracting out of the Act and only the chairman's casting vote ensured its defeat. The Conservatives, far from disapproving of benefit funds supported by employers as an alternative to the Act of 1880, were keen to defend the practice of contracting out by making it proof against abuse. They proposed that funds should have to give adequate compensation for all accidents. Employers should have to guarantee their financial soundness and make a contribution that was proportionate. A competent authority should determine whether the employer's contribution was proportionate to that of the workers and whether the provision made by each fund was adequate.[18]

There was widespread support, well beyond the vested interests of mine owners and railway directors, for the view that insurance funds were much to be preferred to litigation. They made for co-

---

[17] See Henry Broadhurst, in 3 *Hansard* 331 (7 Dec. 1888) 1430–1; John Burns, in 4 *Hansard* 21 (13 Feb. 1894) 439–40.

[18] *SC on Employers' Liability Act (1880) Amendment Bill, Report* 1886 (192) VIII.

operation and good feelings between masters and men, it was said, whereas litigation cast a trade union official or some solicitor as the workers' champion in a conflict in which the employer was the enemy, and which would be costly both in lawyers' fees and in good relations at the workplace.

The recommendations of the Select Committee became the basis of two abortive Bills introduced by the Conservative government in 1888 and 1890. Since both were bitterly opposed on this matter by the parliamentary spokesmen of organized labour, the Bills, intended as a gesture to meet labour grievances, were withdrawn.

The conflict over contracting out should not be allowed to distract attention entirely from the original grievance, the doctrine of common employment. The cautious concession on this point made by the Act of 1880 did not for long remain acceptable to organized labour. By 1885 the original definition of supervisory staff, which had excluded foremen, was being challenged, and the Select Committee of 1886 recommended that the employers' liability should be extended to cover the negligence . of all supervisory staff of every kind. This was accepted by the government and incorporated into their Bills of 1888 and 1890. By then labour spokesmen in Parliament had become bolder and were demanding the total abolition of the doctrine of common employment. That would have made the employer liable for negligence not only of supervisory staff but of all his employees, and would have removed the differences between the legal rights of employees and those of the general public.

In this matter the government concession might well have been accepted as a step in the right direction, had it not been for labour's determined opposition to any legislation that permitted contracting out. It was this that caused the breakdown of the Conservative government's initiatives in 1888 and 1890. Labour's unyielding opposition owed in turn a great deal to the close links that it had forged with the Liberals in opposition. By 1891 the TUC proposals on employers' liability had become part of the Liberal party's programme and labour looked forward confidently to the time when its demand would be met in full by a Liberal majority in the Commons.

With the general election of 1892 that moment had arrived, and in the following year Asquith, as Liberal Home Secretary, introduced an Employers' Liability Bill that proposed to abolish the doctrine of common employment, to remove the upper limit of compensation in cases of death enacted in 1880, thus leaving the courts free to award what compensation they thought fit, and to prohibit contracting out. On the first two issues opinion had moved rapidly since the Conservative Bill of 1890. *The Times* had declared that once you tampered with the common-law doctrine of common employment there was no reasonable halting-place short of abolishing it altogether, and in a confidential memorandum addressed to the Conservative Home Secretary the chief Home Office adviser had said the same thing. On this matter the compromises of 1890 had little chance of being revived. It was over the legitimacy of contracting out that there was to be conflict, and it was to be on party lines.[19]

Before that happened there occurred a diversion of the utmost importance for the future.

[19] *The Times*, 5 Apr. 1890; *Confidential Memo on the Liability of Employers for Injuries to their Servants*, 25 Mar. 1892, PRO, HO 45/9865/B13816/123. The author of the memo was Sir Godfrey Lushington. The memo also contains a strongly argued case in support of contracting out, accompanied by the analysis of accident statistics referred to on p. 48 above.

2

The Emergence of an Alternative

BY 1893, when the Liberal government produced its Bill, there existed an alternative policy potentially capable of breaking the party deadlock that had developed. It was expressed in an amendment moved by Joseph Chamberlain on the Second Reading of the Bill, which declared that 'No amendment of the law relating to employers' liability will be final or satisfactory which does not provide compensation to workmen for all injuries sustained in the ordinary course of their employment, and not caused by their own acts or default'.[1]

Here was a bold plan to settle the issue by ignoring questions of negligence altogether and concentrating on compensation for accidents irrespective of cause, with the one exception just noted. Its origins went back to the early months of 1891 in the wake of the fiasco over the Conservative government's Bill of 1890. It differed from the older Conservative position, which had also emphasized the importance of compensation irrespective of cause, in that it proposed to do this by law, not by contracting out of the law, and above all to put the obligation for compensation entirely on the employer. It thus broke away from a preoccupation with employers' contributions to workmen's benefit societies.

The originator of this alternative proposal was Sir John Gorst, a Conservative MP of great energy and long experience closely associated throughout most of the 1880s with Lord Randolph Churchill.[2] He had thus been on the wrong side in the struggle between Churchill and Salisbury, was generally distrusted and kept at arm's length by Salisbury, and had little influence among those

---

[1] 4 *Hansard* 8 (20 Feb. 1893) 1961.
[2] Sir John Eldon Gorst (1835–1916), barrister, Conservative MP 1866–8, Principal Party Agent 1870–5, MP 1875–1906. Member of the so-called Fourth Party 1880–5, Solicitor-General 1885, Under-Secretary for India 1886–91, Financial Secretary to the Treasury 1891–2, Vice-President of the Privy Council (responsible for Education) 1895–1902. There is no biography, but see *DNB*, 1912–1921.

who controlled the government. Although Under-Secretary of State for India at the time, he had been chief delegate to the International Labour Conference held in 1890 in Berlin.[3] On his return, besides urging the government to set up a Royal Commission on Labour and another on the Poor Laws, he put forward an eight-point legislative programme dealing specifically with labour matters. All but two of his proposals were buttressed by references to precedents in other European countries, and at the head of the list stood a proposal for a new departure on employers' liability, a matter on which he claimed that English law was behind almost every country on the continent of Europe. Taking the German law of 1884 for compulsory accident insurance as his model, he argued that in services which could only be carried on at the cost of a large number of fatal or serious accidents, such as the railways, the State should insist that compensation was provided by the employers, and that, as in Germany, the insurance premium was wholly paid by them. 'No legislation will be satisfactory or final that does not level up English legislation to the level of the Continent'.[4]

This idea immediately attracted the attention of Joseph Chamberlain. Together with a recent proposal for contributory old age pensions subsidized from government funds, it was given an airing at a national conference of the Liberal Unionists.[5] Chamberlain, once a Liberal Radical member of Gladstone's Cabinet, had broken with the Liberal Party in 1886 over Irish Home Rule and had failed to effect a reunion with the party in 1887. Since that date it had become increasingly clear that there was indeed no prospect of a reunion with the Radical wing of the Liberal Party of which he had once been a leader. Now cut off from his former allies on domestic matters and yoked with other Liberal Unionists who had no sympathy with his Radicalism, he was in a highly uncertain political position. He had decided that to reassert his position as a national political leader he needed a programme capable of appealing to a democratic electorate.

On old age pensions Gorst and Chamberlain were to go different ways, Grost advocating compulsion, Chamberlain opposing it. On

---

[3] See above, p. 30.
[4] 'Politics for the People: An Interview with Sir John Gorst', *Help*, 1. 2 (1891). See also *Review of Reviews* (Mar. 1891), 252, 272, for additional publicity.
[5] Joseph Chamberlain, speech at Portsmouth, 2 Apr. 1891, in *The Times*, 3 Apr. 1891, and in pamphlet published by National Liberal Union.

employers' liability they continued to work together, with Gorst making the running in the winter of 1891, Chamberlain taking up the theme during the general election in the summer of 1892 and developing it more fully in November in a long article on 'the Labour Question', published in the *Nineteenth Century*.[6] In it he challenged the claims of various labour spokesmen to represent the interests of the working-class voter, examined their specific demands, and set out a programme of his own. When dealing with employers' liability he demonstrated by means of the German accident statistics (in the absence of any suitable British ones) how inadequate was the demand of the labour leaders for the complete abolition of the defence of common employment when considered from the perspective of compensation for injuries.

He drew attention to the fact that 43 per cent of all recorded German accidents were attributable neither to fellow workmen nor to masters, so that the abolition of the defence of common employment taken by itself would still leave the victims of nearly half the accidents unprovided for. Referring to the attempt of the English law to deal with compensation for injury by distinguishing between different kinds of responsibility, he contrasted it with the very different principle that underlay the German law. The latter, as he put it, granted compensation in every case as a public right arising from the natural obligation of the employer to compensate every workman injured in his service. The recognition of the universality of the right to compensation he considered to be 'the only merciful and the only logical principle' and went on to calculate that the cost would be trifling and could in all cases be passed on to the consumer.

Invited to comment on Chamberlain's proposals in the following number of the journal, neither Thomas Burt on behalf of the trade unions nor Keir Hardie on behalf of the Independent Labour Party showed any sympathy with the new approach to the accidents problem.[7] The trade union leaders had their eyes on the Bill that the recently elected Liberal government had promised for the next session. It seemed to them as if the TUC was about to reap the fruits

[6] Speeches by Gorst in *The Times*, 11 Nov. 1891, 10 Dec. 1891. Speeches by Chamberlain, 25 June 1892, 2 July 1892, Birm. Univ. Lib., Joseph Chamberlain Papers, JC 4/3; J. Chamberlain, 'The Labour Question', *Nineteenth Century*, 32 (Nov. 1892), 677–710.

[7] 'Labour Leaders on the Labour Question', *Nineteenth Century*, 32 (Dec. 1892), 869–73, 886.

of its close relations with the Liberal Party. Indeed, as we have seen, the Bill that Asquith introduced in February 1893 gave them all they had asked for.

By moving his amendment Chamberlain put his own rival proposal to the test of a full-dress parliamentary debate with all its attendant publicity. Once again he used the German accident statistics to demonstrate the limited relevance of the proposals to the suffering caused by injury from accidents at work. Once more he contrasted this with the principle of the German law in words hardly different from those he had used in his article the previous November.

The best speech in his support came from Gorst, who showed an easy familiarity with the German statistics, drawn, as he explained, from a publication in English which the German Imperial Insurance Office had produced for the 1893 Chicago Exhibition. He stated the principle of Chamberlain's proposal in words quoted from a German authority, that 'compensation for injury must be reckoned as part of the cost of production', a phrase which thereafter became part of Chamberlain's vocabulary. Gorst pointed out the similarity between the government's proposals and the German law of 1871, which had been abandoned because it did not work satisfactorily to be replaced by that comprehensive liability which afterwards gave rise to the Accident Insurance law.[8]

Chamberlain had been careful to identify himself only with the principle of the German law, and Gorst made the distinction between principle and machinery very clear. 'There is not a word about insurance in the proposal. The question of insurance is an entirely separate question. It is one that the House may take up on some future day, but the question before the House at present is not a question of insurance but a question of liability'. The distinction was not, however, taken very seriously by the House, particularly since a further amendment had been put down by A. D. Provand, a Liberal MP, in favour of compulsory insurance on the part of all employers. Chamberlain said that he expected that all employers would insure if his proposals were accepted, and added that he would not object to legislative compulsion.

---

[8] The similarity was not as great as he claimed except in the special case of railway accidents. For other occupations the employer's liability was extended no further than the negligence of supervisory staff. Ernst Wickenhagen, *Geschichte der gewerblichen Unfallversicherung* (Munich, 1980), i. 26.

On behalf of the government Haldane declared that it had no objection to the insurance proposal but wanted a great deal more information on the subject, not least on how the law worked in Germany. The trade union spokesmen in the House decided to oppose the amendment and in view of this, Asquith, although not opposed to general compensation in principle, insisted that the Bill to widen liability was needed in any case and nothing should be allowed to get in its way. There was clearly no more to be gained by pressing the issue to a vote and Chamberlain withdrew his amendment. It had given wide publicity to the fact that there was an alternative policy and had embarrassed the government.[9]

Thereafter Asquith's Bill made its slow progress through the Commons, although inevitably overshadowed by the principal measure of the session, Gladstone's Home Rule Bill for Ireland. There was now no longer any disagreement over the abolition of the defence of common employment, and conflict centred on the workman's right to contract out of the Act. Here the government was on weaker ground. Whereas the abolition of the defence of common employment would create formal equality of rights between workmen and the general public, the proposal to prohibit contracting out did the opposite. It prohibited workmen from doing what the law in general permitted, i.e. to enter into contracts of their own choosing.

Whether the contracts in question could, however, reasonably be regarded as of their own choosing was the crux of the matter. Much effort was expended on establishing, or else denying, the legitimacy of the petitions that now flowed in from workers in defence of the established benefit funds, in particular that of the London and North Western Railway Company. However, the government's resolve did not weaken nor its majority fail, and the Bill went up to the House of Lords with the clause prohibiting contracting out still intact. The Lords had no compunction in removing it and the two Houses clashed so sharply over this issue that in the end the government withdrew the Bill altogether.

There was in fact no prospect of a compromise to be discerned. The furthest that the government was prepared to go was to permit existing contracting-out arrangements to remain in force for another three years. But under Salisbury's leadership the Lords

---

[9] 4 *Hansard* 8 (29 Feb. 1893) 1961–9; ibid. 10 (24 Mar. 1893) 1072; ibid. 11 (25 Apr. 1893) 1206–10.

were determined that contracting out in exchange for comprehensive arrangements agreed between workers and employers should continue to be legal. By abolishing the defence of common employment altogether and removing any upper limit to what the courts could award in compensation, the Bill held out the prospect of frequent litigation. It made the representatives of the employers more than ever determined to ensure that there was an alternative form of industrial relations available. They insisted that it was not a question of saving themselves expense and accepted more stringent conditions for schemes that would qualify than had been proposed in 1888 and 1890. They agreed to the condition that the employer's contribution had to be at least 25 per cent of the total and to a number of other safeguards.

The previous proposal had been for 20 per cent, and even 25 per cent may not seem much. It was justified on the ground that three-quarters of accidents would be of a kind for which no legal liability would fall on the employer. This was an optimistic assumption in view of the considerable widening of the range of accidents for the consequences of which it was proposed that employers should be liable to pay compensation. On the basis of German statistics Chamberlain had estimated that accidents for the consequences of which no employer would be liable would amount only to 43–7 per cent of the total. This was to calculate accidents, not the amounts to be paid in compensation. If it can be assumed that the employers' liability would relate to the more expensive accidents, the proportion of employer's contribution proposed would seem to be even less adequate. However, there was no criticism of this sort at the time. On the contrary the higher level of the contribution was intended to underline the view that the issue at stake was not one of cost but of the structure through which compensation was provided.

The failure of Asquith's Bill in 1893–4 and the revelation of an irreconcilable conflict between Liberals and Conservatives over the legitimacy of contracting-out schemes strengthened the case for Chamberlain's alternative policy. This was the third time that a government had tried to reform the Act of 1880 and had failed. No one was prepared to defend the law as it stood. It gave the workers a grievance for which they blamed the Conservatives. That grievance would continue even if a future Conservative government were to put a New Employers' Liability Act on the statute book that retained contracting out. It would only attach organized labour more closely to the Liberals, who would be bound to try once more to try to abolish contracting out when they were back in office.

Chamberlain set out at once to persuade the Conservative leadership to commit itself to his policy. In this matter Gorst and he worked in unison, and it was Gorst who first approached Balfour with a proposal for a new Bill. This Bill formed part of the larger packet of social legislation that a few months later Chamberlain tried to persuade Lord Salisbury to introduce into the House of Lords, adding that it was most desirable in the interests of the Unionist Party, as the Conservatives and those Liberals who opposed Home Rule and defended the Union with Ireland were beginning to call themselves, that this question should be finally settled. Salisbury refused in the politest possible way and Chamberlain totally failed, despite repeated attempts, to obtain some form of public commitment from the party leaders.[10] He had to be content with unofficial initiatives. Early in 1895 he backed a private member's Bill, the first to be constructed on the new lines, introduced by A. B. Forwood, who had once been a junior Conservative minister. So did his fellow Birmingham MP, the former Conservative Home Secretary, Henry Matthews. It was no more than a gesture. The Bill was never taken beyond the entirely formal stage of a First Reading. By the time of the general election in July 1895 Chamberlain had not succeeded in obtaining any commitment from the Conservative Party leaders to the new policy.

Gorst's tactics at this time were much the same. In the middle of the general election campaign he had an article published in the *Nineteenth Century* with the provocative title 'The Conservative Programme of Social Reform'. When he referred in it to his and Chamberlain's proposals on employers' liability as 'the rival Conservative programme', he was using the language not of fact but of persuasion.[11]

It is worth noting, however, that when the new 'Unionist' government was formed and the Liberal Unionists at last joined the

[10] Gorst to Chamberlain, 22 Mar. 1894, Birm. Univ. Lib., JC 6/3/3/2: Chamberlain, Memo on Social Reform and correspondence with Salisbury, 29 Oct.–15 Nov. 1894, ibid., JC 5/67/21–24. Some of this is quoted in J. L. Garvin, *Life of Joseph Chamberlain*, ii (1933), 615–17. See also P. T. Marsh, *The Discipline of Popular Government* (Brighton, 1978), pp. 235–6.

[11] *Nineteenth Century* 38 (July 1895), 10.

Conservatives in the Cabinet, it was the Home Office that Lord Salisbury suggested to Chamberlain for his consideration. That would have put him firmly in control of the inevitable legislation on employers' liability. Chamberlain had, however, been assured that he could have almost any Cabinet post and turned down the suggestion in favour of the Colonial Office.[12] Neither Forwood nor Matthews was included in the government, and Gorst became Vice-President of the Council, which gave him responsibility for education. The new Home Secreary, Sir Matthew White Ridley, was far from being a convert to Chamberlain's proposals.[13] In this matter he could not be relied upon, and the student of the surviving records will find the initiative and much of the detail for an Employers' Liability Bill being worked out on Colonial Office stationery.

Up to this point there was really no evidence that proposals to make employers pay the cost of all accidents irrespective of negligence had any chance of being accepted by the employers' interests on whom the Conservatives and Liberal Unionists depended for political support. It was this issue that had to be resolved. In the autumn of 1896 Chamberlain circulated an anonymous memorandum containing the main arguments in favour of his proposals but referring specifically only to Forwood's Bill. It asked manufacturers who were sympathetic to the proposals to take soundings in their own trade and district. Both Ridley and Forwood were consulted over this move. The plan was to send it on an individual basis to influential employers.

By then Ridley had already taken soundings of his own, and, although he had found almost general acceptance of the principle, he was much impressed by the difficulties involved in putting forward any specific proposals. Chamberlain had been thinking of reducing the political risks and administrative complexities by applying the new measure in the first place to a limited range of occupations only. Ridley was told by his parliamentary draughtsman that there was no distinction between trades that was defensible on logical or legal grounds. In any case Ridley had encountered 'a natural fear of putting increased burdens on trades already

---

[12] Garvin, *Life of Joseph Chamberlain*, iii (1934), 5.

[13] MP for North Northumberland and a director of the North Eastern Railway Company, he had been Under-Secretary at the Home Office in 1874–80. See p. 44 above for his views in 1878.

handicapped by our laws and by foreign competition'. He pointed out that Chamberlain's approach to individual employers would provide him with the opinions of advanced and highly organized firms but ignored the great body of employers, who would be really more seriously affected, who had no efficient system of insurance, and who probably did not want to have any. He thought that they should take the prudent course and introduce an Employers' Liability Bill that permitted contracting out.[14] This was as far as he committed the government when he spoke in public in November 1896 and expressed the hope that he would be able to introduce a Bill in the 1897 session.[15] Clearly the two ministers were proceeding on incompatible courses.

In the Home Office there was now a marked interest in the experience of other countries. In July 1896 the Colonial Office was asked to provide details of the law on employers' liability in the self-governing Colonies. This was generally based on the British Act of 1880, but on discovering that several Colonies had forbidden contracting out the Home Office asked for full reports on how this worked in practice.[16]

Nor was this interest confined to the Colonies. The Home Office officials took from the library shelves the voluminous reports on labour laws in foreign countries that had been produced by the Royal Commission on Labour and published early in 1894. There were eleven such volumes, published together with numerous volumes of other kinds of evidence during the course of an enormous exercise in aimless information-gathering. The Home Office also possessed a report of March 1894 on the working of the German law, which had been sent from Berlin to the Foreign Office as part of the routine process of information-gathering through consular and diplomatic channels, and had been passed on to the Home Office.[17] It now asked whether the Foreign Office had anything more up to date, particularly on the German and Austrian

[14] Correspondence between Chamberlain and Ridley, Oct.–Nov. 1896, Richard Webster to Home Secretary, 18 Dec. 1895, Ridley to Chamberlain, 11 Feb. 1897, Birm. Univ. Lib., JC 6/3/3/3–12.

[15] Speech at Perth, *Morning Post*, 27 Nov. 1896. The statement was welcomed in the paper's leading article.

[16] PRO HO 45/9867/B13816H/1,2.

[17] *RC on Labour, Foreign Reports*, vol. v, *Germany*, 1893–4 C. 7063–VII XXXIX, pt. ii; 'Report on the Question of Employers' Liability in Germany, Mar. 1894', listed but not printed in *Foreign Office Reports, Miscell. Series No.* 325, 1894 C7294 LXXXIX. 2.

insurance laws and on those countries that in 1893 had had legislation under consideration. If not, it asked it to circularize the embassies for the latest reports.

In its reply the Foreign Office pointed out that such an inquiry was quite unnecessary, since all the relevant information had been published regularly in the *Labour Gazette* of the Board of Trade. This meant so little to the Home Office that Llewellyn Smith, the head of the Labour Department of the Board of Trade, had to be asked to provide a full list of items relating to the German and Austrian accident insurance published in the *Labour Gazette* since 1893. There were eleven of these and another on the introduction of accident insurance in Norway. For good measure Llewellyn Smith added references to sickness insurance since, as he explained, in the case of Germany the one could not be understood without the other. This incident provides an insight into the way in which information about foreign institutions was being automatically collected and published without ever impingeing on the minds of those responsible for policy in the Home Office. Llewellyn Smith very wisely also drew the Home Office's attention to the Proceedings of the International Congress on Labour and Social Insurance held in 1894 in Milan, and to three authoritative studies of accident insurance in Europe and particularly in Germany recently published respectively by the US Commission of Labour, the French Office de Travail, and the Head of the German Imperial Insurance Office.[18] Copies of all this material were obtained and a barrister was commissioned to digest it and to write a report for the department.[19]

It would be rash to accept this as evidence of any intention on the part of Ridley or his advisers to use the European experience of employers' liability and accident insurance in any significant sense as a model for British legislation. The barrister commissioned to produce the report had obviously allowed his enthusiasm to run away with him when he analysed the German laws very fully 'in order to give some idea of the machinery required for a system of state insurance'. Ridley was chiefly interested in gauging the

---

[18] J. G. Brooks, *Compulsory Insurance in Germany: Fourth Special Report of the U.S. Commission of Labour* (including app. on Compulsory Insurance in Other Countries in Europe; Washington, 1893); Office de Travail, *Études sur les derniers résultats des assurances sociales en Allemagne et Autriche* (Paris, 1895); T. Bödiker, *Die Arbeiterversicherung in den Europäischen Staaten* (Leipzig, 1895). For the Milan Congress see p. 31 above.

[19] PRO, HO 45/9867/B13816H/1, 2, 3, 5.

financial burden that foreign competitors, in particular the Germans, had to bear, so as to meet the charge that new legislation of whatever kind would handicap British industry. When the report became available, he sent a copy to Chamberlain, but dismissed the author's suggestions as matters 'which he was not asked for and which may be taken for what they are worth'.[20]

At this stage Chamberlain was trying to work out the possible cost of compensation for all accidents irrespective of negligence by collecting figures from the few British firms which had kept records, because they ran a general relief fund or for other reasons. If costs drawn from British experience could be shown to be modest, the talk about foreign competition could easily be brushed aside. If the German scheme was expensive, as indeed it was, so much the better. The important thing was to win support where it counted. In December *The Times* printed an article 'from a correspondent' which repeated the argument against a continuation of the old policy and in favour of Chamberlain's proposals in terms that were identical with the latter's anonymous memorandum. What is more, it endorsed the policy in its leading article. Less encouraging was the news that the Liverpool Chamber of Commerce had firmly repudiated the principle of Forwood's Bill. Early in January 1897 Ridley was contemplating the inevitable commitment to employer's liability legislation with the greatest misgivings.[21]

[20] W. G. Clay to K. E. Digby, 5 Nov. 1896 PRO, HO 45/9867/B13816 H/5; Ridley to Chamberlain 24 Oct. 1896, 20 Dec. 1896, Birm. Univ. Lib., JC 6/3/3/5, 8. No copy of the report has survived either in Chamberlain's working papers or in the Home Office files.

[21] *The Times*, 19 Dec. 1896; Ridley to Chamberlain, 20 Dec. 1896, Birm. Univ. Lib., JC 6/3/3/8; *Report of Commercial Law Committee of Chamber of Commerce of Liverpool on Sir Arthur Forwood's Workmen's Accident (Compensation) Bill*, 6 Jan. 1897, PRO, HO 45/9867/B13816H/5; Ridley to Chamberlain, 7 Jan. 1897, Birm. Univ. Lib., JC 6/3/3/9.

3

1897

THE commitment 'to make better provision for the compensation of workpeople who suffer from accidents in the course of their employment' was included in the Queen's Speech on the 19 January 1897 and set the press buzzing with speculation about the form that the promised Bill would take. Particularly interesting at this stage are the views expressed in two Liberal papers sympathetic to the Radical wing of that party.

The *Daily News* reacted to current rumour that the Bill would embody a scheme of universal and compulsory insurance against all accidents, howsoever caused, by organizing an opinion poll of trade union secretaries. These were drawn from a wide range of unions with a total membership of well over a million. By an overwhelming majority they stated that accident prevention was of more importance than compensation, that no proper precautions could be secured under a system of compulsory insurance or otherwise than by a law of employers' liability, and that the trade union proposals embodied in Asquith's Bill of 1893 were the best. In its leading article the paper referred to the German experiment in compulsory insurance, reminding its readers that that had been part of Bismarck's policy of dishing the socialists and had been opposed by the German Liberals. Experience had proved, it went on to say, that the German Liberals were perfectly right and that the effect of the change had been as mischievous as its intention was sinister. It printed the German accident statistics compiled from claims made under the insurance scheme and pointed out that the number of accidents recorded there had substantially increased over the years. Much was to be made of this point in the next few months and its significance was to be widely debated, but to the *Daily News* it was clear evidence that universal insurance had increased the number of accidents by impairing the employers' incentives to carefulness. This article was regarded by Ridley's advisers as important evidence that Chamberlain's proposals would be badly received in trade union circles.[1]

Very different was the reaction of the *Daily Chronicle*. Its editor, H. W. Massingham, was after 1907 as editor of *The Nation* to give firm support to a new Liberal departure in social policy and to exhibit a lively interest in German precedents. The twelve articles which appeared in the *Daily Chronicle* during the first few weeks of 1897 and were published in a revised and extended form as a pamphlet bore the same unmistakable stamp. They examined the state of the law on employers' liability and showed how it worked in practice. Written in simple vivid prose and freely relying on 'human interest' stories, they analysed the position with much acuteness.[2] A large and simple diagram, using German figures 'for lack of our own', demonstrated that as many as 77 per cent of all accidents would not be liable for compensation even if Asquith's Bill were to be enacted. The text argued the moral claims of *all* victims of industrial accidents for maintenance and restoration out of the proceeds of the industry. Using the statistics of the Employers' Liability Insurance Co., it showed that a mere 13 per cent of all accidents reported to the company led to compensation, and contrasted this 'chaos of hopeless thrift, defeated law and casual charity' with general compensation. Its treatment of the evidence that failed to reveal any correlation between general accident insurance, where this existed, and higher accident rates was brisk and to the point. It then turned its attention to the Continent, where the problem 'is not so much whether the injured workman is entitled to honourable provision for his needs at the hands of his industry as by what means it shall be carried out'. As well as drawing attention to the influence that the German insurance system had had on other European countries it devoted careful articles to the German system itself, expounding it simply and vividly by means of interviews with German experts.

A whole section was devoted to the implications of the German

[1] 4 *Hansard* 45 (19 Jan. 1897) 5. *Daily News*, 8 Feb. 1897; copy and minutes in PRO HO 45/9867/B13816H/14.

[2] *The Workers' Tragedy: An account of the Law of Employers' Liability in England and of the Working of the Universal Insurance System in Germany*, by the Special Commissioner of the *Daily Chronicle*, reprinted, revised and extended from the *Daily Chronicle*. There are several copies in the Home Office file PRO, HO 45/9867/B13816H/19. For the original articles, see *Daily Chronicle*, 30 Dec. 1896–5 Feb. 1897.

accident statistics. The continuous increase in the number of reported accidents was explained at least partly in terms of the greater willingness of workers to claim their rights. In this connection attention was drawn to the disproportionate increase in minor accidents reported compared with the relative stability in the figures for serious, particularly fatal, ones. The work of the German insurance organization in encouraging accident prevention was expounded through an interview with a leading member of the German engineering union. The treatment of the whole subject, while kept clear and simple, was not only sympathetic but extremely well-informed. It is rather reminiscent of Matthew Arnold's *Friendship's Garland*, portraying the Germans as absolutely astonished that the British could possibly believe what they did, or behave as they did. Bödiker, the president of the German Imperial Insurance Office, when interviewed, was asked whether compulsory insurance was a necessary corollary of compulsory compensation. On this issue, which was to become so important in the light of Chamberlain's Bill, he replied in the affirmative, and asked the question that was to be constantly reiterated in England by critics of Chamberlain's system over more than thirty years: 'What is [otherwise] to become of the poor man if his employer cannot pay him?'

In its Conclusion the series presented its own proposals for Britain. It advocated universal compensation for industrial accidents and diseases however caused, to be paid for by employers without deduction from wages. Ideally it envisaged employers' associations on a trade basis for the purpose of insurance, as in Germany, but as a concession to English traditions, character, and temperament it firmly rejected compulsion on the part of the State. The State was to provide information and facilities for such combinations and to set up a State Insurance Department using the facilities of the Post Office and the expertise of the Home Office. Employers or trade associations were left free to choose between State insurance and 'the familiar though more expensive agency of the insurance companies'. The latter were to be licensed and closely supervised by the Home Office, so as to avoid the creation of 'a great body of vested interests destitute of public obligations and responsible to no-one but their shareholders'. Similar close supervision was to be exercised over those employers who elected to carry their own risks without insurance. The whole system was to be worked by means of arbitration courts, organized as in Germany on the basis of the principal trades, drawn in equal numbers from employers and workmen with a chairman appointed by the State. The expenses of arbitration were to be borne by the employers' insurance institutions. In such a system, contracting out, 'a discredited cause that finds no champion even in such countries as Russia and Belgium', had no place. As in Germany the system should be introduced gradually, starting with the more dangerous trades. The article predicted that the trade unions would add greatly to their influence by becoming the recognized representatives of the workmen before the arbitration courts. On the implication of these proposals for accident prevention the article predicted that insurance companies would take much the same measures to enforce safety precautions as was the case with the German combinations of employers.

Enough has been said to show the form that a British system strongly and deliberately influenced both by the principle of German law and by its administrative machinery might have taken. It departed from its German model chiefly by refusing to apply compulsion to the establishment of employers' combinations for insurance purposes. This left scope for competition from insurance companies, albeit under strict public supervision.

Chamberlain was greatly encouraged by the attitude of the *Daily Chronicle*, and was to refer to it as a sign of support for his proposals. Not so the Home Secretary, who drew attention to the elaborate machinery of State provision and control that was seen to be a necessary corollary.

Having received the draft Bill on which Chamberlain had been working, Ridley decided that it was time to assert himself. Chamberlain had based his Bill on the principle he had put forward in Parliament in 1893. He proposed to place an obligation on employers to provide compensation for all accidents occurring in the course of employment but to leave it to them to decide how to meet the cost. That cost was to be strictly limited: in the case of death to a maximum of three years' wages or £150, whichever was the larger; in the case of incapacity to a maximum weekly payment of half the previous weekly earnings. In contrast to what he had said in 1893 he now proposed to limit the application of the Bill in the first instance to those trades already regulated in certain other specific ways by Act of Parliament. By this arbitrary but not totally implausible distinction it would be possible to exclude a number of contentious occupations, such as seamen, domestic servants, and agricultural labourers, from whose employers politically embarrassing opposition could be expected.

Ridley returned Chamberlain's draft Bill accompanied by a long letter of objections. He concentrated his attack on the distinction that Chamberlain had always made between the principle of general compensation for accidents and the machinery. He did not deny the attraction and soundness of the principle 'if accompanied with due provision', but Chamberlain was proposing 'to put for the first time in this or any other country this enormous personal liability on employers without any machinery to meet it. Compulsory insurance through such organisations as in Germany is a different thing, but here we leave all to private companies and societies'. He confessed to being afraid of joint opposition from employers and trade unionists and reverted to his own plan of an Employers' Liability Bill which would permit contracting out. He saw this as the only practical way, coupled perhaps with an inquiry of some sort into the best means of effecting general insurance. 'My excuse for not introducing general compensation', he wrote, 'would be (i) that it is not a fair burden to put on industry without providing machinery, and the examination of practice elsewhere, and our present knowledge does not enable us at present to do this, and (ii) that the trade unions do not want it'. Referring to the *Daily Chronicle*, he pointed out that it had coupled its advocacy of general compensation with conditions which it would be difficult to provide. There followed a number of detailed objections including doubts whether the proposed Bill would really put an end to litigation. 'There is a very good American criticism of the German system and I believe the facts show that litigation is not prevented but rather encouraged by it. If this be so the main inducement to the employer falls to the ground'.[3]

Chamberlain replied on the same day. His enquiries among British employers on the cost of general compensation had yielded figures which were much lower than the burden that German and Austrian employers had to carry. His calculations, provided they were credible, made him invulnerable to any argument based on foreign competition, and he was to make a great deal of this point in the debates that lay ahead. Ridley's main objection he met by a

---

[3] Ridley to Chamberlain, 11 Feb. 1897, Birm. Univ. Lib., JC 6/3/3/12. For the source of the American criticism see ch. 2 n. 18.

bland denial. 'I do not know what machinery is required outside the Bill. Of course the German system is more complete but it would require a Bill of 200 clauses and would involve too much interference with private management'. They might make some concessions on this point in committee if necessary 'but even without them the Bill would work'. The objection about litigation he brushed aside rather too easily, as subsequent events were to prove, but his main attack was concentrated on Ridley's alternative legislative proposal, which he dismissed in characteristic fashion for its lack of imagination and boldness. Putting his political reputation on the line, he invited Ridley to produce a rival memorandum and draft Bill and to let the Cabinet decide between them.[4]

This is what Ridley proceeded to do, but even before the Cabinet met he had admitted the strength of Chamberlain's case and had practically accepted defeat. He knew that he was no match for Chamberlain and even apologized for his presumption. The Cabinet decision in favour of Chamberlain's proposal could not have come as much of a surprise to him.[5]

The memorandum that Chamberlain put before the Cabinet in support of his Bill included the favourable comments of twenty-one employer–MPs, who, so he claimed, between them comprised every member on the Unionist side directly interested in the provisions of the Bill.[6] His calculations of the likely cost of the scheme depended on the records kept by a mere seven firms, of whom all but two were in iron and engineering. These showed that the proposals would not significantly exceed the cost of what these firms were already paying voluntarily or under the existing law.

This rather surprising result was to be achieved by a provision in the draft Bill that no payment would be made for any disability lasting less than four weeks. This provision was subsequently made still more restrictive by laying down that no one was to qualify for payment for the first four weeks of their disability, and it was in that form, but with the disqualifying period reduced to two weeks,

[4] Chamberlain to Ridley, 11 Feb. 1897, Birm. Univ. Lib., JC 6/3/3/13.

[5] Ridley to Chamberlain, 12 Feb. 1897, Confidential Memo, 16 Feb. 1897, Ridley to Chamberlain, 21 Feb. 1897, Birm. Univ. Lib., JC 6/3/3/14, 15, 22. The Cabinet met on 4 Mar. and spent a long time discussing the subject, 'which raises many questions of great difficulty': Salisbury to the Queen, 4 Mar. 1897, PRO, CAB 41/246.

[6] *Workmens' Accident Compensation*, initialled J. C., n.d. but printed 17 Feb. 1897, Birm. Univ. Lib., JC 6/3/3/18.

that it became part of the Act. Strangely enough Chamberlain claimed to have taken the idea for this substantial restriction from the practice of the German accident insurance.[7] It is hard to know what to make of this. German accident insurance paid nothing for the first thirteen weeks, a substantially longer period than Chamberlain was proposing. The reason for this was the integration in Germany of accident insurance with sickness insurance, which meant that the first thirteen weeks were covered by sickness-insurance benefits. Such benefits came into force after the first three days. Thus from the fourth day onward the German worker received payment, although for the first thirteen weeks it came from a fund to which he had himself contributed two-thirds of the total, the employers only one-third. Not so in Britain, where it was proposed to launch an accident compensation scheme in isolation from all other statutory provision, leaving the first four weeks to voluntary funds financed entirely by the workers or, failing these, to charity or Poor Law. If Chamberlain had taken the German sickness insurance into account, he had mistaken days for weeks. If he had overlooked it, he provides an extreme example of what can happen when foreign devices are borrowed piecemeal without regard to context. In the Bill as actually presented to Parliament the period before payment began had been reduced from four weeks to two.

The principal features of the Bill presented to Parliament jointly by the Home Secretary and the Colonial Secretary in May 1897 may be summed up under five headings:

1. Workers obtained the right to compensation without being required to establish negligence on the part of anybody (serious and wilful misconduct on the part of the injured workman himself being the one exception).
2. The amount of compensation for injury or death was related to the victim's earnings, and maximum amounts fixed by schedule.
3. It was assumed that these two features together would make compensation largely a matter of routine and cut out the need for litigation. Disputes were to be settled by arbitration.
4. The Bill applied to specified occupations only.

[7] Section 1 (2) (a) of the Act; Chamberlain to Lord Stanley, 14 Jan. 1897, Birm. Univ. Lib., JC 6/3/3/10.

5. Contracting out of the Act was still permitted. This was contrary to Chamberlain's intention; he took the view that employers had been saved from the threat of litigation and therefore from the need to contract out of the Act. However since many Conservative MPs had committed themselves at the previous election to the contracting-out principle, the party's Principal Agent successfully insisted that the right be retained for the sake of party consistency.[8]

The first four of these features were in principle derived from the German law. But that law differed from the Bill in several crucial matters.

1. Employers belonged by law to an association which included all employers in their trade (*Berufsgenossenschaft*).
2. The workers' right to compensation was a claim against the association not, as in the English Bill, against their own individual employer. Appeals were to tribunals composed in equal numbers of workers and employers with a neutral chairman.
3. The association was entitled to impose a levy on its members once a year to meet the cost of compensation.
4. The association was responsible for laying down safety measures to be carried out by its members and had powers to enforce them.
5. Compensation for an initial period of thirteen weeks was paid mainly by the sickness insurance scheme, to which the worker contributed two-thirds and the employer only one-third of the cost.

All this meant that the German employer was compulsorily enrolled in a mutual insurance system administered by its members,

---

[8] See Marsh, *Discipline of Popular Government*, p. 265, for the intervention of Middleton, the Principal Agent. See Memo, *Workmens' Accident Compensation*, and MS Memo, 'Workmen's Accident Compensation', 15 Mar. 1897, Birm. Univ. Lib., JC 6/3/3/18, 28, for Chamberlain's views. As in previous Conservative proposals, contracting out was to be permitted only if the scheme was at least as favourable to workmen and at least as costly to the employer as the provisions made under the Act. In 1888 and 1890 there had been much doubt whether the task of deciding what schemes satisfied these conditions should be undertaken by a government department or left to the courts. In 1897 the more satisfactory course was adopted of giving the responsibility to the Registrar of Friendly Societies, who was accustomed to dealing with a whole range of mutual benefit funds.

which covered his trade and exercised authority over him. The British employer's obligation to compensate his workers was his own and he was left free to make what arrangements he chose. It also meant that the German scheme functioned as part of a wider system of security for the workers, whereas in England that was the case only with a few of the schemes that had contracted out of the Act.

How acceptable were these similarities when they came to be considered in Parliament and what notice did anyone take of the differences? It is the answers to these questions that will reveal how relevant the German precedent appeared to be.

The ministers called their Bill a Workmen's Compensation Bill and emphasized that it was as a compensation Bill that it should be judged. Without denying that it might do something for accident prevention, they did not put it forward for that purpose. If the House wanted to add to the existing arrangements for the prevention of accidents, they argued, it would have to do so through factory legislation or by tightening the criminal law on negligence; it was a mistake to believe that by punishing employers and making them pay it was possible to prevent the majority of the accidents that now occurred.[9]

In this respect the British Bill differed markedly from its German predecessor. Bismarck's policy had been intended as sharp reversal of the plans for future reforms that had been matured in the Prussian Ministry of the Interior. Not only had he been determined to prevent the extension of employers' liability for negligence, he had also been opposed to factory legislation and determined not to permit the proper establishment of what had been until then a mere token force of inspectors. To organize employers in such a way that they could police themselves in preference to State inspection had been one of the objectives behind the establishment of accident insurance on the basis of *Berufsgenossenschaften*.[10] To Chamberlain the effect of his legislation on safety enforcement was quite secondary. While he thought that financial prudence would give employers who decided to carry their own risks an incentive to

[9] 4 *Hansard* 48 (3 May 1897) 1461–5.
[10] Walter Vogel, *Bismarcks Arbeiterversicherung: Ihre Entstehung im Kräftespiel der Zeit* (Brunswick, 1951), pp. 161–9; Lothar Machtan, 'Risikoversicherung statt Gesundheitsschutz für Arbeiter: Zur Entstehung der Unfallversicherungsgesetzgebung im Bismarck-Reich', *Leviathan*, 13. 3 (1985), 420–41.

improve measures of accident prevention, and while he believed, quite wrongly as it turned out, that employers who decided to insure would be put under pressure to do the same by the insurance companies through a policy of differential premiums, this was not the issue to which his legislation was addressed. Unlike Bismarck he exhibited neither lack of confidence in nor animus towards the work of the factory inspectorate, which had been in existence for two generations and whose status, now more firmly defined than once, was not challenged. Its numbers had been substantially augmented only a few years earlier. As the most perceptive comparative study of the British and German systems was to emphasize, the perspective of the British legislation was 'relief for distress'.[11]

This was not of course the contrast of which the ministers were aware. What loomed large in their minds was the contrast between their approach and that of which the British Bill of 1893 had been the culmination.[12] The view that the prevention of accidents formed an integral aspect of the subject was of long standing and not so easily brushed aside. Despite Chamberlain's attempt to shift the focus of attention to matters of compensation for hardship, or perhaps because of it, the debate tended to return repeatedly to the effect of workmen's compensation on accident prevention. In this connection the German example was never far from people's minds. There were constant references to it in the parliamentary debates, and a surprisingly large number of speakers showed themselves familiar with its features. This was not confined to the ministers, who had obviously been carefully briefed, or to a few experts, but extended to a wide range of back-benchers.[13]

[11] F. C. Schwedtman and J. A. Emery, *Accident Prevention and Relief: An Investigation of the subject in Europe with Special Attention to England and Germany* (New York, 1911), ch. 13.

[12] In their 1983 study, *Wounded Soldiers of Industry*, Bartrip and Burman have played down the difference between the policy of 1880–93 and that of 1897. Referring to the statements by which Chamberlain countered the objection that his policy would increase accidents and argued that financial prudence would produce the opposite effect, they have turned what was intended to ward off objections into a major objective of policy-making. Their view that 'improvement of safety was the fundamental reason for introducing . . . both the Employers' Liability Act of 1880 and the Workmen's Compenstion Act of 1897' (p. 213) cannot be accepted. See also ibid., p. 202.

[13] An important source of information was *Report on the Operation of the Insurance Laws in Germany for 1895, Foreign Office Reports, General and Commercial, Miscell. Series*, 418, 1897, recently published as 1897 C. 8278

Speakers paid particular attention to the German statistics of accident claims, being anxious to know whether indiscriminate compensation affected the frequency of accidents. The steeply rising figures for total accidents that the German statistics had revealed ever since the introduction of compensation had been a cause of comment in the *Daily News* and elsewhere. Ridley pointed out that serious accidents, particularly fatal ones, were on the decrease, and like the *Daily Chronicle* he put the increase in the total accident figures down to more accurate notification.[14] A far less favourable interpretation came from Geoffrey Drage, now a Conservative back-bencher but at one time secretary to the Royal Commission on Labour. In that capacity, he had, in 1893, produced a study of the German insurance systems that was highly critical of the cost of administration and of the delays created by the numerous appeals.[15] His expert knowledge enabled him to launch an attack on the government proposal, an attack that he was to press as far as a division. The great increase in the number of those partially disabled both temporarily and permanently could not, he argued, be explained away in terms of better notification. It was evidence of increasing carelessness and malingering on the part of German workmen. He was obviously familiar with the extensive German literature on malingering, but despite his vehemence and knowledge of detail he made little impact on the House.[16]

The principle of compensation for accidents, irrespective of cause, was in fact remarkably well received. Criticism fastened on other matters. The most fundamental and from our point of view the most interesting concerned the basic principle of organization that sharply distinguished the British proposals from the German law. It came from another international expert on labour matters, the Liberal MP Sir Charles Dilke. This former Cabinet Minister, disgraced in 1886 on account of a sexual scandal, had returned to

LXXXVIII. 677. Also useful and accessible were Janet E. Hogarth, 'The German Insurance Laws', *Economic Journal*, 6 (June 1896), 161–266, and Henriette Jastrow, 'Workers' Insurance Legislation in Germany', *Fortnightly Review*, 61 (Mar. 1897), 374–86.

[14] 4 *Hansard* 48 (3 May 1897) 1426. He was using the figures for 1891–5 published in Feb. 1897 in the Board of Trade *Labour Gazette*. There is a marked copy in the Home Office files, PRO, HO 45/9867/B13816H.

[15] *RC on Labour, Foreign Reports*, vol. v, *Germany*, s. III B Workmen's Insurance, 1893–4 C. 7063–VII XXXIX, pt. ii.

[16] 4 *Hansard* 48 (3 May 1897) 1454–6; ibid. 49 (17 May 1897) 636–43.

Parliament in 1892 to become a formidable back-bench expert on labour matters as well as on defence.[17] It was he who drew attention to the fact that at the root of the German system lay the principle of trade responsibility as contrasted with individual responsibility. By placing the obligation to provide compensation on the individual employer, not on the organized trade, the British proposals would fail to obtain the benefits that had flowed from accident insurance in Germany. He drew attention to three consequences. In the first place, the conflict over disputed claims would still be a conflict between the individual employer and his workmen, and although the litigation might in practice be conducted by the insurance company it would be the employer who would reap the ill feeling aroused by the dispute. Secondly, Dilke returned to the subject of accident prevention and drew attention to the powers of the German trade associations to enforce safety by regulation and inspection, by increasing the levy on the firm, and even by fining. Here was a security for safety not to be found within the British Bill. Thirdly, he asked what would happen under a system of individual responsibility if the firm went bankrupt and could not pay the compensation to which its employees were entitled.[18] Each of these were in fact to become major weaknesses of the British system of workmen's compensation and will receive further attention.

Chamberlain was quick to take the point. He readily admitted that it was out of the question in Britain to do what had been done in Germany, to group all firms compulsorily into trade associations obliged to carry responsibility for workmen's compensation. 'The elaboration of the system, its bureaucratic tendency, and the arbitrary interference of officials are all matters which are so objectionable to English people . . . that it is absolutely impossible and absolutely impracticable to attempt any system of operation of that kind. [hear, hear!].'[19] Ridley addressed himself to the same objection a fortnight later, when the problem of the uninsured bankrupt employer was again discussed in the context of collective trade responsibility for compensation. He admitted that there was a risk that the worker would fail to obtain his compensation, but 'it

---

[17] For Dilke's career up to and including the scandal, see Roy Jenkins, *Sir Charles Dilke: A Victorian Tragedy* (rev. edn., 1965); for his later career, see Stephen Gwynn and Gertrude Tuckwell, *Life of the Rt. Hon. Sir Charles W. Dilke*, (1917), ii.
[18] 4 *Hansard* 48 (3 May 1897) 1452–3.   [19] Ibid., 1467.

was hardly to be expected that the Government could have proposed any scheme of compulsory trade responsibility or insurance. Anyone who has studied the details of the German system will feel that it could never be introduced into this country'. He hoped that employers would form trade associations of this kind or make similar mutual arrangements between cognate trades. 'Such arrangements made voluntarily, as is the custom in this country, will be far more effective and economical and in accordance with English feeling than any compulsory system'.[20]

The view that compulsory trade associations were quite out of the question was never challenged in the House. Asquith, the chief spokesman for the Opposition, fully realized the significance of what Dilke had said and subsequently shaped his own criticism along identical lines. Like Dilke he emphasized how different the government's proposals were from what had been done in Germany. Whereas the German system was a perfectly logical attempt to combine absolute assurance of compensation for accidents with methods for raising the standard of safety, the British government's very different Bill made no direct proposals on safety. What was still more remarkable, it departed from the German example by providing no absolute assurance to the workman that he would be able to obtain the compensation to which he was entitled. Such an incomplete proposal could be regarded as nothing more than an experiment, and Asquith expressed his certainty that it would lead to further developments then hardly contemplated. These would not be on the German model, which, as he put it, 'may be very well suited to the economic and social conditions of that country but its adoption here—resting as it does on the double foundations of compulsory grouping and centralised control—would require us to fly in the face of the traditions and the living tendencies of British industry'. The developments that he had in mind were very different. 'When we have passed this Bill into law we shall have practically committed ourselves to a system by which out of State resources you will have to guarantee compensation for accidents'.[21] He repeated these points when the Bill came back for its Third Reading and added:

I conceive it to be an affirmation on the part of Parliament that in future,

---

[20] 4 *Hansard* 49 (17 May 1897) 699–700.
[21] Ibid. (18 May 1897) 747–51.

and at no distant period of time, the charge for making good as far as money can, injury sustained by workmen shall, on grounds of public policy, be thrown on the community at large. I do not shrink from that prospect . . . It is a goal to which our industrial legislation has for a long time been pointing.[22]

No one believed that the principle of compulsory trade associations corporately carrying the onus of compensation, which underlay the German system, could be applied to England. Although Chamberlain described his scheme as laying the burden of accident compensation on the trade in which it occurred, that was merely his way of saying that he expected it to be added to the cost of production. It had no implication for the placing of the legal obligation, which was being placed squarely on the individual employer. It was he who was being left free to decide how he would meet his obligation, and no compulsion was being placed on him to do so in any particular way. Although employers could choose to insure with a commercial company, Chamberlain expected many of the larger firms outside the high-risk occupations such as coal and railways to carry their own risk unaided, thus retaining labour relations under their own control. There was of course nothing to stop the smaller firms doing the same and hoping for the best, thereby saving their insurance premiums. A third course open to employers was, as ever, to contract out of the Act altogether and to make their own arrangements with their workers, provided they were acceptable to them and generous enough. In the context of a relatively generous measure of general compensation, which had eliminated most of the benefits of contracting out while driving up the cost, this course appealed to ever fewer firms.[23] A fourth course was for firms to come together in voluntary associations with others in the same trade to pool their risks on a mutual basis, as Ridley hoped they would.

Such voluntary associations were essentially different from the compulsory bodies of the German law. The latter covered all employers in the trade without exception, and between them covered all relevant trades. Being in this sense comprehensive they could be made to assume corporate responsibility *vis-à-vis* the injured workman, and they could be given an obligation to enforce

---

[22] 4 *Hansard* 51 (15 July 1897) 208.
[23] The decline in the number of contracting out schemes is recorded in Wilson and Levy, *Workmen's Compensation*, i. 201 n. 3.

safety regulations on their members. Disbursing compensation payments for the total work-force in the industry, they could be required to set up arbitration tribunals for the industry as a whole based on joint representation of employers and workers. No such obligations could be imposed where the means to be chosen were left as uncertain as they were by the British law. Even when it came to settling disputes, the Bill provided a choice of means: a joint committee representing employer and workers; a single arbitrator agreed on by both parties; or a single arbitrator appointed by a county court judge—although it is clear from the wording of the Bill and from what Ridley said in the House that joint committees was the method principally envisaged and the intervention of judges seen only as a last resort.[24]

In the absence of prescribed machinery there was little certainty how the numerous individual firms would choose to act, what machinery would be resorted to, and how such bodies as insurance companies, individual firms, and whatever associations might be set up would interpret their terms of reference. It is this uncertainty that is the important point to grasp. 'Will the arrangements work?' is a perfectly normal question to be asked of all pioneering Acts. In this case there was a prior question to be asked: 'What arrangements will be made?'

This lack of prescribed machinery was partly due to the politicians' assessment of what they could expect to steer through Parliament, not least through a House of Commons whose overwhelming Conservative majority had proved unmanageable in the previous legislative session.[25] Chamberlain had said as much to Ridley when the latter complained of the absence of prescribed machinery in his draft Bill, and he was to make much the same point in Parliament, saying that a Bill as big as the German legislation could never have been carried through the House.[26] Nor could it have been carried through Salisbury's Cabinet. It is surprising that Chamberlain achieved as much as he did in spite of both the initial hostility of many employers to the additional burden placed on them and disapproval in influential Conservative

---

[24] 4 *Hansard* 48 (3 May 1897) 1428.
[25] See Marsh, *Discipline of Popular Government*, pp. 247–54, for the problems of the 1896 session.
[26] Chamberlain to Ridley, 11 Feb. 1897, Birm. Univ. Lib., JC 6/3/3/3; 4 *Hansard* 48 (3 May 1897) 1472.

quarters. The Conservative Party made it perfectly clear to Salisbury that it would not tolerate such radical legislation in future.[27] Even those who ideally would have wished for more recognized the magnitude of his achievement. 'Great triumph for J.C. this Bill. This is a great day', wrote Massingham, the editor of the *Daily Chronicle*, after the Bill had survived a critical division.[28]

Such a tactical explanation, true though it is, is also inadequate. It fails to make explicit the fundamental assumptions that governed the political culture within which these tactical decisions were made. At this deeper level the absence of prescribed machinery was due to a belief in the ability of Englishmen to create their own institutions by choice and calculation. In his comparison between the British Bill and the German law Ridley had made this fundamental assumption explicit, and he was not the only one to do so. The *Daily Chronicle* published a letter from one of the German experts interviewed for its original series of articles, who commented favourably on the contrast between the simplicity of the one and the elaboration of the other. In the German Act 'everything is carefully settled from above, every slightest possibility is anticipated and provided for in the minutest detail . . . Your Bill . . . settles the fundamental principle . . . and leaves the administration of the principle entirely to the individual concerned'.

Chamberlain kept this article with the long passage from which this extract is taken heavily scored.[29] Unfortunately the praise was premature. The opportunity to set up joint committees of arbitration to which the writer had confidently looked forward was not taken. Moreover experience was to show that the fundamental principles had not been successfully settled and far too many matters of basic definition were left to be decided by costly litigation in the courts.[30]

---

[27] For the attitude of employers' organizations see PRO, HO 45/9867/B13816L. For the disapproval of the party see Marsh, *Discipline of Popular Government*, pp. 265–8.

[28] Massingham to Dilke, 27 May 1897, BL, Add. MSS 43916, fo. 31. This is the correct reading of the sentence transcribed as 'He is a queer dog' in A. F. Havighurst, *Radical Journalist: A Life of H. W. Massingham* (1974), p. 99.

[29] G. Stoffers, 'The Compensation Bill', *Daily Chronicle*, 11 June 1897; copy in Birm. Univ. Lib., JC 6/3/3/29. Stoffers, editor of the Düsseldorf *Bürgerzeitung* and a member of the Volkspartei, was at this time in gaol for oppositional journalism. He took the opportunity to compare conditions in German prisons favourably with British ones!

[30] 'The Act is drawn in such extraordinary fashion and the methods of arriving at its meaning are so complicated that it is not easy to deal with it on broad grounds of

For the moment what doubts there were about a Bill that left so much uncertain centred on the absence of any guarantee that compensation would actually be paid when due. The fear that firms going bankrupt, perhaps as a result of a major accident, would leave their injured workmen without redress had been voiced repeatedly in the Commons. It was one to which there was no remedy short of making insurance compulsory, with all the implications this might have for State supervision and control, or even, as Asquith had suggested, for a State insurance system. But these doubts were pushed aside for the present; they were raised more to deprive the government of credit than as a commitment for the future. After the passing of the Act, miners' leaders in South Wales made much of this fear and extracted a public admission from Chamberlain that the Act gave workmen no secure protection against a bankrupt colliery company.[31] But for the moment neither the miners' union nor the TUC nor any other labour spokesman was ready to demand compulsory insurance.

commonsense': Lord Justice Collins, qd. in Schwedtman and Emery, *Accident Prevention and Relief*, p. 173.

[31] *The Times*, 11 Jan., 13 Jan. 1898. Details in Birm. Univ. Lib., JC 6/3/3/31–4.

4

The Completion of Workmen's Compensation and the Question of Compulsory Insurance

THE world of organized labour was won over with remarkable alacrity to the radical departure that the 1897 Act represented. After 1898 nothing more is heard at the TUC of the former demands for extending the scope of employers' liability. Schemes for contracting out of the 1880 Act, although they had not been abolished, no longer appeared a threat. The Chamberlain tactics had paid off and the political deadlock had been broken.

Trade union officials had little difficulty in taking on their new duties of claiming compensation on behalf of their members. These fitted easily into the way in which they were accustomed to do business. But with the exception of the Durham and Cumberland coalfields they refused to co-operate with employers in setting up joint committees of the trade to arbitrate in cases of dispute, as had been envisaged in the Act.[1] This device, which Chamberlain had borrowed from Germany and by which he had hoped practically to eliminate litigation altogether, was by the late 1890s unacceptable in trade union circles. Unions preferred to retain their liberty of action in relation to the employers, and in the event of disagreement to appeal to an outside arbitrator, the county court judge or his representative. Despite the intentions of those who framed the Act that jointly agreed administrative procedures should replace litigation, disputes continued to be settled by judges.

The ease with which the trade unions were able to adapt themselves to the new procedures meant that they had few inhibitions in formulating their future demands along the new lines.

---

[1] *Departmental Committee on Workmen's Compensation (Holman Gregory), Report,* paras. 89–91., 1920 Cmd. 816 XVIII.

Already by 1898 the TUC was demanding the extension of the new law to every kind of employment.[2]

The Act of 1897 applied to six branches of employment only, an estimated 50 per cent of the total wage-earning population.[3] Although much criticized in theory, this restriction was on the whole accepted as prudent in view of the uncertainties involved. The Germans, who had also extended their system piecemeal, could be cited as a precedent. There were some rather unconvincing attempts on the part of ministers to pretend that the exclusions were based on consistent principles, such as the inclusion of the most dangerous trades or the exclusion of small employers; these claims do not stand up to examination. Although mines and railways were included, workers in other occupations with high mortality from accidents, such as bargees, sailors, dockers and carters, were not.[4]

The rapidity with which pressure built up for the piecemeal extension of the Act to additional occupations is the best indicator of Chamberlain's political success. The Home Office tried in vain to resist such demands, but after stalling in 1899 the government decided in the following year to yield to pressure from its own back-benchers on behalf of the agricultural labourers. The resultant Act, which had begun as a private member's Bill, was sharply criticized by Home Office officials for adding confusion to the principles of workmen's compensation before these had been properly established. Thereafter all demands for further extension were resisted until May 1903, when the labour representatives obtained a Commons debate on a resolution calling for the amendment of the Act of 1897. Thereupon the Home Secretary promised legislation but suggested a prior need for inquiry into the operation of the system. The result was the appointment of a Departmental Comittee to report on amendments of the law and its extension to other occupations.[5]

[2] TUC, *Proceedings*, 1898, esp. p. 52. For the uncertain and divided attitudes in the previous year see TUC, *Proceedings*, 1897, pp. 22–3, 31.

[3] Railways, Factories, Mines, Quarries, Engineering, and certain kinds of Building: figures from Georg Zacher, *Die Arbeiterversicherung im Auslande*, v. *England (Grossbritannien)* (Berlin, 1899), p. 21.

[4] Table of comparative mortality from accidents, in *Departmental Committee on Compensation for Injuries to Workmen, Report*, app. viii., 1904 Cd. 2208 LXXXVIII. 487.

[5] For Home Office policy of resisting piecemeal extension see PRO, HO 45/9942/B29142; HO 45/9943/B2914A/1; HO 45/10223/B36188. For Labour

Since the state of affairs which the investigations of the Departmental Committee revealed was almost at once to be transformed by legislation, it is better to postpone any consideration of its working until later and for the moment to concentrate on the legislative thrust that was to transform the tentative and fragmentary beginnings into the full-blown system established by the Act of 1906 and was to prove so surprisingly long-lived. In that story of legislative development the Departmental Committee is important more for its recommendations than for the full range of its investigations.

Chaired by a Home Office official, and in addition composed of a further Civil Servant, a judge, a representative of the insurance societies, and a trade unionist, it was a cautious body. Its members found it impossible to forecast the ultimate cost of the scheme to employers, since every year new claims were being added to those payments to the permanent or long-term disabled which had originated in previous years. This was bound to make for annually rising costs for many years to come. Deeply impressed by this uncertainty they recommended that nothing be done at this stage to increase the burden that the 1897 Act had placed on employers who came within its scope. They confined themselves to recommending minor amendments of procedure or definition.[6] Turning to the extension of the law to further occupations, they took the view that an extension generally to all employment was unworkable, even if some particularly difficult cases were excluded. Instead they nominated certain specified occupations for inclusion.

Nevertheless they were worried that even such a limited extension would increase the number of uninsured employers and that the bankruptcy of such employers would deprive injured workers of their lawful compensation. Such risk, they pointed out, was inseparable from the principle on which the Act of 1897 had been based.

This difficulty, and indeed many other difficulties to which the system gave rise, could only be solved, they argued, by placing the liability for compensation on a collective fund, to which all

demands for extension and amendment and government response see TUC, *Proceedings*, 1903, pp. 43, 78–81; 4 *Hansard* 122 (13 May 1903) 647–51.

[6] The most substantial procedural amendment, the appointment of salaried medical referees in place of medical men in private practice, was to be ignored by Parliament.

employers were compelled to contribute. Although they felt that their terms of reference obliged them to accept the principles of the Act, imperfect though it was, and not to embark on proposing a system of compulsory insurance, they made it clear beyond doubt that, unless Parliament was prepared to contemplate compulsory insurance, no amendment of the Act would be satisfactory. It was impossible to regard the Act of 1897 as anything more than a step towards a more comprehensive system, and they looked to Parliament to give the fullest consideration to proposals for National Insurance. The trade union member, G. N. Barnes, less inhibited than his fellows by constitutional niceties, came out firmly 'in favour of compulsion, provided insurers were offered national insurance as an alternative to that with the ordinary Companies'.[7]

By 1904 no investigation such as this was complete without a survey of foreign and colonial methods. With the help of an official from the Board of Trade, the Committee published a wide-ranging survey but repeatedly came back to the German system as the most complete. It contrasted the provisions for medical treatment and rehabilitation with the lack of anything of the kind under the English law, and ascribed this to the absence in England of anything resembling the highly organized system of compulsory insurance that was found in Germany. Similarly, in reviewing the provisions for accident prevention abroad, it found 'that the more completely the system of compulsory insurance is developed, the more thorough-going and effective is that part of the legislation which deals with the prevention of accidents'.[8]

There was no mistaking the message, however restricted the actual recommendations of the Committee might have been. It was a message to which the government of the day had no desire to pay attention. Recently weakened by divisions over tariff reform and actually within a year of total collapse, it was in no position to embark on ambitious reform. Yet exactly because it was weak and its electoral future uncertain there was good reason to offer something in response to the constant parliamentary pressure for the amendment and extension of the Act. It accepted the specific

---

[7] *Departmental Committee on Compensation for Injuries to Workmen, Report*, pt. iii esp. para. 318. Also ibid., *Memo*, by G. N. Barnes.

[8] *Departmental Committee on Compensation for Injuries to Workmen*, vol. iii, *Memo on Foreign and Colonial Laws*, pp. 23, 33, 1905 Cd. 2458 LXXXV. 897.

recommendation of the Committee but also accepted the view expressed by the Home Secretary in his submission to the Cabinet:

At the end of their Report, they express the view that many of the difficulties to which the present system of compensation gives rise could only be solved by some form of compulsory insurance, whereby all employers would be required to insure their workmen in some Association under state regulation. This, however, would be a radical alteration of the principle of the personal liability of the employer, which was adopted by Parliament in 1897; and I do not think that so great a change should be made until further experience has been gained.[9]

The resultant Bill was introduced into the House of Lords in March 1905 and debated in April. This highly unsuitable venue made Lord Ripon, the Liberal leader in the Lords, the spokesman for the views of organized labour. He was in close touch with the Parliamentary Committee of the TUC throughout. That body had criticized the Bill for making no provision for compulsory insurance which would guarantee the injured person his compensation, and Ripon in debate drew attention to the views of the Departmental Committee that, as he put it, 'the great question of national insurance for accidents is one that ought to be further considered by the Government, with a view, if possible, to adopting some system such as that which exists in Germany and, I believe, in other countries'.[10]

The government Bill got only as far as the committee stage before being withdrawn, and by the end of the year the government itself had fallen. The enormous Liberal majority that resulted from the general election in January 1906, and the return of fifty-four labour representatives, of whom twenty-nine belonged to the Labour Party and followed their own whips, signalled the moment for bolder and more far-reaching labour legislation than anything contemplated in the previous Parliament. In view of the commitment of the TUC to compulsory accident insurance in 1905, and of the attitude taken by Lord Ripon in his official capacity as Liberal leader in the Lords, the moment for that full consideration of proposals for National Insurance hoped for by the Departmental Committee seemed to have arrived. If the Conservatives had had

---

[9] Cabinet Memo, *Workmen's Compensation*, by A[retas] A[kers-] D[ouglas], 21 Nov. 1904, PRO, CAB 37/73/148.

[10] 4 *Hansard* 144 (4 Apr. 1905) 279; TUC, *Proceedings*, 1905, pp. 80–3.

good reason in 1905 quickly to offer organized labour a Compensation Bill, however limited, the new Liberal government, with several years ahead of it, could have been expected to take a different line. It was inevitable that it would have to introduce a Bill to reform the law on trade unions to meet the overwhelming grievance created by the Taff Vale case. One major piece of labour legislation might have been enough for the opening session.

Yet the government decided to make a Workmen's Compensation Bill one of the first measures to come before Parliament, together with a Trades Disputes Bill and one on education. The suggestion had come from Asquith, writing to Campbell-Bannerman on 20 January in the wake of the election. It 'ought to be quite easy to carry' was his only comment in explanation. Campbell-Bannerman accepted the suggestion and passed it on to Herbert Gladstone, the new Home Secretary, asking him to get in touch with the Law Officers.[11] They worked fast. The Bill was introduced to the House on the 26 March, only two months later. It repealed the Acts of 1897 and 1900 and put the whole law on Workmen's Compensation into a single consolidated Bill.

The Liberal Bill was certainly no mere copy of its immediate predecessor. On the contrary, whereas the Conservatives had kept close to the cautious and limited recommendations of the 1904 Departmental Committee, the Liberals had clearly drawn their inspiration from elsewhere, and on a range of fundamentals were deliberately ignoring that body's recommendations.

The new Bill was to apply to employers generally with only a few categories explicitly excepted. Of these the most important were workshops employing five people or fewer, shopkeepers, and outworkers. It was to apply to injury from industrial diseases as well as accidents. Moreover, it was to apply to all injuries lasting more than a week, thus halving the waiting period introduced in 1897. Each of these far-reaching proposals had been considered and rejected by the Departmental Committee in 1904. The last was a

---

[11] Asquith to Campbell-Bannerman, 20 Jan. 1906, BL, Add. MSS 41210, fo. 259; Campbell-Bannerman to Herbert Gladstone, 21 Jan. 1906, ibid., Add. MSS 45988, fos. 213–14. He was, however, unhappy at having 'two sops for Labour' unless balanced by some other Bill of general interest besides education. Otherwise colour might be given to the Opposition's assertion 'that we are in the hands and at the mercy of Labour'. Campbell-Bannerman to Asquith, 21 Jan. 1906, Bodl., Asquith Papers, Box 10, fos. 200–1. This letter is quoted in Gilbert, *Evolution of National Insurance*, p. 203.

mere matter of greater generosity to workers at the expense of employers, and in committee it became more generous still, but the other two had a direct bearing on the questions of compulsory insurance and trade-based liability respectively.

On introducing the Bill, the Home Secretary justified the exclusion of the small employer on practical grounds while adding that the ultimate solution to the problem was probably to be found in a scheme of compulsory insurance. 'But we have not reached that point yet'. The House largely shared his view on the need for compulsion, but not his willingness to defer the issue. The introductory debate gave evidence of so widespread a demand for the inclusion of the excepted categories, especially the small employer, that it was unlikely that the government would be able to stand out against it, and this ultimately proved to be the case. At the same time most of the speakers were in favour of compulsory insurance as the only safeguard for the worker.

Sir Charles Dilke roundly attacked the principle of the government Bill. He was by far the best-informed critic, with a detailed knowledge of European labour legislation. There was no need to hanker after German precedents, he argued. 'That this country was not likely to adopt the German scheme had been very clearly seen before the introduction of the original Bill and had been more clearly seen since'. But there were now many other models available, for 'we were hopelessly in the rear of every country in Europe in this matter, and owing to the fact that we never attended any of the international conferences we did not know that all the problems which were being inquired into today had been inquired into and solved by every foreign country'. This reference to the Congress on Workers' Insurance held the previous year at Vienna, whose Proceedings included reports on workers' insurance in sixteen different countries which he appears to have seen, was followed by a somewhat vague reference to the latest French proposal. He left the House in no doubt that a great deal of experience was already available on methods of compulsory insurance and that there was no reason for regarding such a step as premature.[12]

On the Second Reading of the Bill, Dilke moved a critical

---

[12] 4 *Hansard* 154 (26 Mar. 1906) 906–8; Congrès International des Accidents du Travail et des Assurances Sociales, *Rapports et procès-verbaux* (2 vols.; Vienna, 1906). For the lack of interest on the part of government departments, see p. 31.

amendment, which was seconded by W. A. McArthur, a Liberal MP closely connected with the insurance industry. Although McArthur disclaimed the role of official spokesman, his remarks show that at least some insurance people were not frightened of compulsory insurance because of the prospect of closer State control over insurance companies that such a step was bound to bring with it. He welcomed State supervision that would exclude unsound companies from competing for the business. From Labour came demands for State insurance as an alternative to the commercial companies. The debates revealed a diversity of emphases but such a widespread demand for compulsory insurance that the Home Secretary was definitely put on the defensive. 'As the House is well aware, the time at our disposal is somewhat limited', he explained, but after speaking at length in order 'to show that there is a great deal to be considered before you definitely decide what system of insurance you are going to have' he promised an inquiry into the question of a general scheme of compulsory insurance either that year or the next.[13] There was every reason to assume that, having decided to enlarge the scope of workmen's compensation, the Parliament of 1906 was also about to move to compulsory insurance in some form or other.

What that form would be was still very unclear. With the wide range of foreign precedents then available, it is far from certain that the German model of insurance through compulsory trade associations would have been the most attractive. It was precisely the relationship between voluntary trade associations, commercial insurance companies, and a system of State-enforced accident insurance that would have been the crucial issue in the construction of any British scheme.

The first step towards a possible State alternative to existing forms of insurance had in fact been taken by the government during the Third Reading of the Bill. Pressed to allow post offices to act as agents for insurance companies in selling workmen's compensation policies, so as to make them easily available to small employers everywhere, Sidney Buxton, the Postmaster-General, refused to agree, but promised an inquiry to see whether the Post Office might not sell such policies in its own right. Here could have been the

---

[13] 4 *Hansard* 155 (4 Apr. 1906) 523–42. He repeated that promise again explicitly with reference to workmen's compensation on 1 Aug., ibid. 162 (1 Aug. 1906) 1107.

basis for that State-provided alternative to existing agencies for which some Labour spokesmen had been pressing. Buxton's alacrity to redeem his promise was in striking contrast to the procrastination that was to mark Gladstone's action at the Home Office. In March 1907 a Departmental Committee was set up under the chairmanship of Lord Farrer, and by early June it had rejected the idea. The insurance industry, which had been massively represented among those called to give evidence, had fought off the threat of competition. To judge from the way in which the Committee pursued its inquiry and the wording of its report, the insurance companies had had an easy task.[14]

The upshot of the parliamentary session of 1906 was a Workmen's Compensation Act which covered a range of occupations that was more extensive even than in Germany,[15] but which added no form of compulsion to what had been established in 1897. Yet by 1906 the need for some sort of compulsory insurance had been widely acknowledged. The Home Secretary had explicitly committed the government to guaranteeing to workers as far as possible their statutory right of compenstion and to setting up an early inquiry into methods of compulsory insurance.

However, what had been promised under pressure would in the nature of politics be redeemed only if that pressure persisted. One of the most obvious sources of such pressure was organized labour. In 1905, in the wake of the 1904 Departmental Committee Report, the TUC had adopted a resolution in favour of compulsory and even of State-provided insurance. In April 1908 the Parliamentary Committee of the TUC reminded the Home Secretary of the promise he had given during the 1906 debates. Gladstone replied that he was prepared to advise the appointment of a Committee but added that a Royal Commission, though slower, would be preferable. Yet when the Parliamentary Committee proceeded to send a questionnaire to trade unions to discover what their experience had been of the shortcomings of the Workmen's Compensation Act, it had so few replies and these so unsatisfactory that it did not feel it was in a position to insist on the appointment of a Royal Commission. It asked for the appointment of a Departmental Committee instead.[16]

[14] Ibid. 166 (29 Nov. 1906) 329–37; *Departmental Committee on Life Insurance through the Post Office, First Report*, 1907 Cd. 3568 LXVIII; *Mins. of Ev.*, 1907 Cd. 3969 LXVIII. Wilson and Levy, *Workmen's Compensation*, i. ch. 6.

[15] Unlike the German scheme it included domestic servants.

[16] TUC, *Proceedings*, 1905–9.

Between 1906 and 1908 politically effective pressure for compulsory insurance from organized labour seems to have drained away. The main explanation is almost certainly that unemployment posed the more urgent challenge and that any attention that could be spared from the Right-to-Work campaign was given to the demand for old age pensions. A further explanation may be that in 1909 the Accident Offices Association, i.e. the principal insurance companies in the business, ceased to charge additional premiums for physically defective workers, including the elderly. This removed one of the principal grievances of trade unionists regarding the operation of workmen's compensation.[17] Whatever the explanation, it is apparent from the TUC Proceedings that the enthusiasm for radical reform of workmen's compensation had passed.

The other sources of possible pressure proved even less effective. The Association of Chambers of Commerce showed a passing interest in 1907 in off-loading some of the cost of workmen's compensation on to some form of insurance against sickness, invalidity, and old age to which the workers would themselves contribute. They were told to wait for the promised Royal Commission, but do not appear to have pressed their case a second time.[18]

That leaves the insurance industry itself to be considered. In 1906 the proposal to introduce compulsory insurance had been seconded by William McArthur, a director of two insurance companies. Although making it clear that he spoke in a private capacity, he had welcomed the State regulation of insurance companies which such a proposal would inevitably have brought in its wake. What he had in mind was the elimination of companies with inadequate assets, and one can well imagine that the introduction of compulsory insurance would have been welcomed by the bigger companies operating through the Assurance Offices Association, not only as a way of boosting business but also as a way of keeping out difficult

[17] W. A. Dinsdale, *History of Accident Insurance in Great Britain* (1954), p. 285. For the specific link between this grievance and the demand for a government inquiry see TUC, *Proceedings*, 1909, pp. 154–5.

[18] J. R. Hay, 'Employers and social policy in Britain: The Evolution of Welfare Legislation 1905–14', *Social History* 4 (1977), 448–50. This article is valuable for its information on the Chambers of Commerce, but its suggestion that government policy in 1907 embraced ideas for sickness and invalidity insurance is entirely speculative. I have found no evidence that Gladstone was interested in anything more than a Royal Commission into compensation for industrial accidents and diseases.

competition.[19] But the Board of Trade was in any case prepared to take the initiative in dealing with unsound companies. It introduced a Bill which gave it powers to require a £20,000 deposit as security from any company taking on workmen's compensation and employers' liability business and to demand regular returns in a form that made supervision possible. This became law in 1907 and appears to have given the established companies the sort of protection for which they had been asking.[20] Certainly there is no further demand from the insurance industry for legislation on compulsory insurance.

Little could be expected from the government in the absence of outside pressure. Gladstone himself was overwhelmed by Home Office routine and quite unable to take any serious policy initiative himself. At the same time labour pressure was proving highly effective over old age pensions and unemployment. It was the action of Lloyd George and Churchill in deflecting this pressure away from policies to which they were opposed that was to generate the significant initiatives in 1908–9. These will be examined in Part II. The briskness with which in the autumn session of 1908 these two began to interest themselves in schemes of compulsory insurance against infirmity, sickness, and unemployment left no time or space for a leisurely Royal Commission on such a cognate subject as workmen's compensation. Gladstone's promises were quietly forgotten.

In 1906 it could reasonably have been assumed Parliament was about to insist on compulsory insurance for workmen's compensation. In that case it would have had to deal with the problem of grafting compulsion and comprehensiveness on to institutions that had so far operated on a voluntary and fragmentary basis. This did not happen. Instead it was in relation to health and unemployment insurance that the respective roles of voluntary associations, commercial undertakings, and the State bureaucracy were to be balanced against each other within a system of compulsion. It was Friendly Societies not mutual indemnity associations, industrial insurance companies not accident insurance companies, the Treasury

[19] 4 *Hansard* (4 Apr. 1906) 529–33. On McArthur see *Post Magazine and Insurance Monitor*, 21 Apr. 1906, p. 293.

[20] Employers' Liability Insurance Companies Act 1907, superseded by Assurance Companies Act 1909. For details see Dinsdale, *History of Accident Insurance*, p. 154.

and the Board of Trade, not the Home Office, that bore the brunt of that difficult reconciliation of divergent interests.

In such a situation the wisest course was to leave workmen's compensation severely alone. From the first the Treasury decided that no benefits would be payable under the proposed health insurance if an allowance was already being received under the Workmen's Compensation Act. Although it did not prove quite as simple as had at first been thought to keep the two separate subjects apart, for approved societies under health insurance would clearly have an interest in seeing that employers paid up under workmen's compensation, there was never any intention to include accident insurance in the insurance proposals.[21] Beveridge, working at the Board of Trade, had considered the possibility but only in order resolutely to turn his back on the idea. 'Given a clear field,' he wrote, after analysing the advantages of the German system of statutory associations of employers as carriers of insurance,

it is likely enough that something after this German model would prove to be the best plan also in this country. The field, however, is as far as possible from being clear, and the defects of the system set up by the Acts of 1897 and 1906 hardly appear sufficient to justify heroic measures in the way of displacing the enormous established interests of the insurance companies.[22]

What the defects of the system as established in 1906 actually were and whether they called for accident insurance under the control or supervision of the State was a question which there was no opportunity to investigate until after the end of the 1914–18 War. In 1919 the Home Office appointed a Departmental Committee with just those terms of reference, under the chairmanship of Holman Gregory, a Coalition Liberal MP and Recorder of Bath.

After a detailed investigation the Committee rejected the idea of a State system of accident insurance in any form, and made detailed proposals for State control of the existing institutions. In addition it turned its attention once again to the problem of the uninsured employer and the consequent lack of any guarantee that injured

[21] *Insurance against Sickness, Invalidity, etc., Provisional Scheme*, submitted to the Actuaries, 20 Apr. 1909, in *Report of the Actuaries*, p. 51, *LPES*, Braithwaite Papers II. 4. The clash of interests between employers and approved societies focused on clause 11 of the original Bill (I owe this information to Dr J. L. Melling).

[22] *Accident Insurance*, by W. H. B[everidge], 8 June 1909, LPES, Beveridge Papers III. 39/25.

workers would always obtain the compensation to which they were legally entitled. Among those uninsured employers were certain large companies, particularly railway companies, which it was reckoned had quite enough reserves to meet their liabilities. It was the small employers too careless or too improvident to cover themselves who, as in 1906, were the focus of unease. The Holman Gregory Committee estimated on the basis of very inadequate statistics that they amounted at the very least to a quarter of a million. It was, however, the extent of the injustice suffered by injured workers through the loss of their rights that alone would give grounds for action, and on this the evidence was not statistical but fragmentary and anecdotal.

That cases occur where a smaller sum than is due is accepted by the workman, owing to the employer's threat of bankruptcy if the full amount is insisted on, or where claims are not pressed because the employer is not worth fighting, is beyond dispute. To ascertain their number is quite impossible.

The Committee had no doubt that such cases led to hardship, but in the absence of any assessment of the extent of the problem it was the strong sense of grievance voiced by workers' representatives that it cited as the ground for its view that insurance should be made compulsory for all but the really large employers.[23] Its view was shared by the whole body of county court judges, who, since they were responsible for arbitration in disputes and the registration of all compensation agreements arrived at, had a better knowledge of the problem than anyone else, and it was accepted by not a few employers who had given evidence.

The detailed administrative implications of this far-reaching change were left rather vague, but the Committee recommended the appointment of a Commissioner with detailed powers of obtaining information and of approving all insurance companies and mutual indemnity associations. In other words a system of 'approved societies' would have been created under the supervision of a bureaucratic authority.[24]

The weakness of the Committee's proposal was that it rested on

[23] It also excepted public authorities, statutory companies, and householders in respect of domestic servants.

[24] *Departmental Committee on Workmen's Compensation (Holman Gregory), Report,* 1920 Cmd. 816 XXVI. 1. For a very full analysis of this investigation see Wilson and Levy, *Workmen's Compensation,* i. chs. 7–11.

an alleged sense of grievance. Whether that was great enough to induce the government to take action was quite another question, and one that largely depended on political factors. In fact like so many other far-reaching reforms put forward in the heady days of post-war reconstruction the vast bulk of the Holman Gregory proposals of 1920 were to be ignored. Although there was legislation in 1923 and again in 1925, no Commissioner was appointed and insurance remained voluntary as before.[25]

What hardship there was tended to be found in occupations into which trade union organization had penetrated least effectively; the vast bulk of it continued to go unrecorded and it never became more than a minor political issue. Only when it affected so articulate and well-represented an occupation as coal-mining did the logic of compulsory insurance finally acquire a political appeal.

Between 1927 and 1933 the falling domestic demand for coal and the loss of overseas markets led to a drastic series of bankruptcies of collieries, as the industry tried to rationalize and reduce output. Many of these firms had insured only exceptional risks and carried ordinary risks themselves. There were 280 liquidations during those years in the coal-mining industry and in 30 cases those entitled to compensation under the Workmen's Compensation Act lost out altogether. This affected 1,600 men or their dependents, amounting to a total loss of £200,000. But in a far larger number of liquidations, although liabilities were ultimately covered, there were delays in payment and major uncertainty whether the position could be salvaged. The bankrupt employer problem, so often referred to since 1897, had well and truly struck the very industry whose work-force was most liable to industrial injury. The result was a private member's Bill that became law in 1934 and made full insurance against all claims under the Workmen's Compensation Acts compulsory throughout the coal-mining industry.[26] It was as an *ad hoc* response to a particularly acute problem that compulsory insurance finally entered the statute book, but that was typical of the way that the social services were developed in those years. There was no attempt to draw out the implications of this step for the system as a whole. General

---

[25] Ibid., i. chs. 12, 13.
[26] *RC on Workmen's Compensation, Mins. of Ev.*, Home Office Memo, paras. 284–93; copy in Beveridge Committee Papers, PRO, CAB 87/76/305. Wilson and Levy, *Workmen's Compensation*, i. 258–62.

compulsion did not come until 1946 after another war had finally created the will for systematic reform.[27]

[27] W. Beveridge, *Report on Social Insurance and Allied Services* (1942), pp. 35–48; National Insurance (Industrial Injuries) Act 1946.

5

Mutual Associations

IN focusing on the question of compulsory insurance, the previous chapter has largely concentrated on what did not happen, at least not in the years with which this study is primarily concerned. It is time to ask, what did happen? Left to themselves what steps did British employers take to meet the obligations imposed on them by the legislation which we have discussed?

Basically they could take one of the four courses already indicated. They could insure with a commercial insurance company, they could associate with other employers to share the risk by means of a mutual indemnity fund, they could carry their own risk without insurance, or they could induce their workers to take part in a jointly financed benefit fund in exchange for contracting out of the rights guaranteed them by employers' liability and workmen's compensation laws. The last alternative was the least used since it required the consent of the workers and would have had to be financially more generous than what would otherwise have been required from the employer. By 1920 there were only twenty such schemes, covering 63,000 workers out of an estimated total of fifteen million.[1]

These figures are at least reliable and informative. The information relating to the other three possible courses is neither. Until 1906 government attempts to monitor the operation of the Workmen's Compensation Act of 1897 were perfunctory. The strictures of the 1904 Departmental Committee induced the Liberal government to strive for some improvement in that respect. By the Act of 1906 the Home Secretary acquired power to demand regular returns giving the number of cases of compensation, the amount paid, and other such particulars. In 1908 he exercized these powers in respect of seven major branches of industry: shipping, factories, docks, mines, quarries, constructional works (i.e. civil-engineering works but not

[1] *Departmental Committee on Workmen's Compensation (Holman Gregory)*, Mins. of Ev., Q. 22827, vol. ii. 1920 Cmd. 909 XXVI. 605.

building), and railways. These were mostly industries that were already under some form of State regulation or else, as in the case of docks and apparently constructional work, were concentrated enough for the attempt to be worth making. That left building, agriculture, inland transport, sea fishing in sailing vessels, domestic service, workshop production, and a miscellany of other occupations to escape the net. As the Home Office explained, these were too scattered and too unknown to be realistically included. In consequence the statistics of compensation related to fewer than half the employers who came under the law.[2] Nor was this a temporary piece of statistical caution due to Edwardian conditions. The same continued to be the case right up to the 1940s. The effect of this on the appreciation of the seriousness of the problem posed by the small uninsured employer has already been noted.

To judge from these statistics the most important result of the Workmen's Compensation Acts was the formation of employers' mutual indemnity associations, confined to one or to several related trades. In other words employers responded to their obligations by means of voluntary associations, that characteristic British expedient. The figures show that the proportion of compensation paid by, or handled with the assistance of, mutual indemnity associations continued to increase throughout the period 1908–38, and these figures can be assumed to understate the actual situation.[3] According to the best estimates available to the Beveridge Committee in 1942, close on 70 per cent of all compensation was paid by mutual associations or mutual companies.[4]

If there was one matter on which there had been widespread agreement in the years before 1914 it was that the German practice of forming trade-based employers' associations (*Berufsgenossenschaften*) by compulsion and imposing on them the duty of compensation for industrial injury was thoroughly unacceptable in Britain. It is therefore of some interest to discover to what extent the form of organization that had been rejected as compulsion had in practice been adopted voluntarily.

    [2] *Workmen's Compensation Statistics for 1908*, 1909 Cd. 4894 LXXX. 949. For detailed and scathing comments on the inadequacy of the statistics see Schwedtman and Emery, *Accident Prevention and Relief*, pp. 173–4; Wilson and Levy, *Workmen's Compensation*, i. 307–15.
    [3] *Workmen's Compensation Statistics, Annual Series*.
    [4] *Workmen's Compensation in Relation to a General Social Security Scheme*, Notes by Government Actuary, 20 June 1942, LPES, Beveridge Papers VII. 32.

Table 5.1 Workmen's Compensation Statistics 1928

| Industry | Workers Covered | | Compensation Paid | | Compensation paid by or through* | | | | | |
| | | | | | (i) Mutual indemnity associations | | (ii) Insurance cos. | | (iii) Uninsured employers | |
	No.	% of total	Amount (£)	% of total	Amount (£)	%	Amount (£)	%	Amount (£)	%
Factories	5,455,652	73.4	2,360,982	36.6	862,705	36.5	1,049,622	44.5	448,655	19.0
Docks	142,835	1.9	283,700	4.4	100,997	35.6	68,372	24.1	114,331	40.3
Quarries	73,691	1.0	93,288	1.4	16,699	17.9	60,544	64.9	16,046	17.2
Constructional work	125,762	1.7	146,864	2.3	16,302	11.1	101,630	69.2	28,932	19.7
SUB-TOTAL	5,798,076	78.0	2,884,834	44.7	996,703	34.5	1,280,168	44.4	607,964	21.1
Shipping	193,568	2.6	240,411	3.7	194,732	81.0	6,732	2.8	38,947	16.2
Mines	944,666	12.7	3,026,678	46.9	2,139,861	70.7	184,627	6.1	702,189	23.2
SUB-TOTAL	1,138,234	15.3	3,267,089	50.6	2,234,593	71.5	191,359	5.9	741,136	22.7
Railways	497,350	6.7	305,350	4.7	0	0	305	0.1	305,045	99.9
GRAND TOTAL	7,433,660	100	6,457,273	100	3,331,296	51.6	1,471,832	22.8	1,654,145	25.6

* Some mutual associations did not make returns on behalf of their members, but left it to them to make their own returns. These would have been included under uninsured employers in column (iii). However, those associations that did make returns normally also included the compensation paid by their members individually and not covered by mutual indemnity. Hence only the figures in column (ii) actually mean what they say.

Source: constructed from *Workmen's Compensation Statistics*, 1928, 1929–30 Cmd. 3481 XXIX. 1163.

The answer is that it had not been adopted to the extent that the figure of 70 per cent would at first suggest. In those sectors of the economy which experienced the highest rate of industrial injury and therefore contributed a disproportionate amount to the total compensation paid, the principle of mutual association had been adopted very much more completely than elsewhere. In terms of organization, therefore, mutual associations covered rather less of the ground than figures based on compensation payments would at first suggest. This can be demonstrated from Table 5.1, which is based on the returns for 1928, the first years in which relevant statistics are available. In that year shipping and mining relied on mutual indemnity associations for over 70 per cent of all their compensation payments. These two groups of industries accounted for about 50 per cent of total compensation paid by all the seven groups, yet employed only about 15 per cent of the relevant labour force. Railways were unusual too, since they covered their own risk practically without exception. But as the table shows, the remaining four groups covered by the statistics, with 78 per cent of the labour force and less than 45 per cent of compensation payments, almost certainly relied on mutual associations to a lesser extent than they did on commercial insurance companies.

These figures indicate only the extent to which associations existed, they tell us nothing about the degree of protection that they offered their members. But unlike *Berufsgenossenschaften*, which were responsible by law for compensation payment and could not escape the obligation, British associations tended to cover only the exceptionally heavy liabilities, leaving it to their members to be responsible for more normal risks.[5] In practice this blurred the distinction between mutual insurance and non-insurance and it was this that caused the hardship in the coal-mining industry which led to the imposition of full compulsory insurance in 1934.

Being merely off-loading expedients with an incomplete membership and a limited commitment to their members, the British associations developed medical rehabilitation and enforcement of safety measures to a much smaller degree than was the case with their German counterparts. It must be remembered that the German bodies were collectively responsible for the provision of

---

[5] *Departmental Committee on Workmen's Compensation (Holman Gregory), Mins. of Ev.*, vol. i 1920 Cmd. 908 XXVI. 87; vol. ii 1920 Cmd. 909 XXVI. 605, *passim.*

compensation, a responsibility that presupposed compulsory membership. It is the absence of these two features of collective responsibility and compulsory membership that is the crucial difference between the provision in the two countries and largely accounts for the less dynamic role that the British associations played in the development of services.

There were however some matters for which voluntary association was just not adequate and it was their awareness of this that pushed British reformers repeatedly in the direction of the *Berufsgenossenschaft* model. The problems raised by the inclusion of industrial diseases as grounds for compensation are a case in point. There had been no precedent for this in the German scheme despite the latter's thoroughness in other respects. The Germans were not to include the principle of compensation for industrial diseases into their insurance system until 1925. In England the distinction between accidents and diseases had been broken down by a decision of the House of Lords, acting as a court of appeal, that a worker who contracted anthrax while sorting wool imported from the East had been injured 'by accident'.[6] Once such a ruling had been made, it was not difficult to place the liability on the employer whose wool had been responsible for the infection.

The Act of 1906, once again ignoring the recommendations of the 1904 Departmental Committee, drew the logical conclusion and generalized the principle of the Lords' decision. It specified certain industrial diseases, known to arise from specific industrial processes, as grounds for compensation claims and gave powers to the Home Secretary to include others in the light of expert advice. Yet some diseases, while undoubtedly arising from employment in a particular industry, did not strike suddenly, like anthrax, but were gradual in their onset. It did not seem just to lay the burden of compensation entirely on one employer, and the Act gave the victim's last employer a complicated and burdensome right to claim part of the cost of compensation from his earlier employers. A better alternative would have been to make compensation the collective responsibility of the industry, expressed by means of a compensation fund to which all employers were obliged to contribute. The logic of compulsory association and collective responsibility was hard to resist. In the case of the pottery industry

---

[6] *Brinton's Ltd.* v. *Turvey* [1905] AC 230.

a compensation fund for sufferers from lead poisoning had been set up on a voluntary basis already. If compensation was henceforth to be compulsory, the pottery manufacturers pressed for compulsory insurance through a mutual trade organization and had a clause to this effect inserted in the Bill. This gave discretionary powers to the Home Secretary to introduce a scheme limited to a single industry where a majority of employers in that industry were already insured in a mutual trade insurance company or society. Even then the Home Secretary could act only with the consent of the society.[7] It was a complicated formula hammered out in a debate in which some of the issues inevitably raised by the introduction of compulsory organization were given an airing. The pottery industry's principal spokesman in the Commons, Josiah Wedgwood, the Radical MP for Newcastle under Lyme, was well aware of the implications of what he was doing. With an eye to the investigation into compulsory insurance which the Home Secretary had promised, he presented the proposal as 'the seed of the German system, which he was anxious to see introduced all over the country. His main object was not merely to fulfil the wishes of his constituents . . . but to provide a model on which future extensions of insurance might be based'. Dilke was quick to distance himself from any such tactics and hoped 'that there was no intention in advance of the enquiry which was to be made of treating this as a stereotyped form to be adopted'.[8]

This clause of the Act was never acted upon. Yet even if the pottery employers were in the end to fight shy of collective action, the same problem existed wherever there was an industrial disease clearly connected with a particular work process but gradual in its development. In 1918 the matter was raised at the insistence of the Yorkshire Mining Federation in connection with silicosis, and the Workmen's Compensation (Silicosis) Act of that year gave the Home Secretary power to make a scheme for the establishment of a general compensation fund in a specified industry. This would require all employers to subscribe to the fund and all compensation under the scheme to be paid out of it. The fund was to be administered either through an employers' mutual trade insurance company or society, or 'in such other manner as may be provided by the scheme'. In spite of that final mealy-mouthed alternative,

[7] Section 8 (7) of the Act, continued as Section 45 of the Act of 1925.
[8] 4 *Hansard* 166 (5 Dec. 1906) 1031–4.

here was the *Berufsgenossenschaft* model once more in evidence and accompanied by another German precedent that had frequently appealed to British social reformers, the committee representative of both employers and workmen with an independent chairman for the settlement of claims.[9]

The first of such schemes was the Refractories Scheme of 1919, with further compensation schemes for silicosis set up for the metal-grinding industries in 1927 and the sandstone industry in 1929. In 1930 similar powers were given for asbestosis compensation schemes, and in 1931 all these were reviewed and revised. Such use of mutual indemnity associations for the purpose of compulsion involved the State in the kind of control that had always been so conspicuously absent when they were merely voluntary bodies. As a Home Office memorandum put it in 1939, 'the companies are thus in the nature of compulsory mutual indemnity associations, but their operations are largely under the control of the Secretary of State'.[10]

[9] Section 3 of the Act.

[10] *RC on Workmen's Compensation, Mins. of Ev.*, Home Office Memo, para. 268., PRO, CAB 87/76/305. This document provides the best description of the schemes in question. See also Wilson and Levy, *Workmen's Compensation*, i. 264–5.

6

Conclusion

IT is significant that the two great issues that more than any other distinguished the British approach to accident compensation from the precedent set by the Germans were both concerned with compulsion. In both cases it will have become apparent that the legislation of 1906 gave rise to problems which the politicians were not willing to resolve, because they were not willing to accept the necessity of compulsion. This is true of compulsory insurance, the great issue that contemporaries recognized as such. It is also true of compulsory association by trades. If that matter loomed less large to contemporary reformers, it was not because they preferred the alternative of a single State fund but because they still understood only very dimly what they had taken on when they made industrial diseases grounds for compensation. Section 7 of the Act of 1906, with its powers left to the discretion of the Home Secretary and never invoked, is a pointer to an ignored agenda, and in that respect is analogous to the Home Secretary's commitment to proceed to an investigation of the means of compulsory insurance.

In 1897 Asquith had stated the grounds on which the government had rejected German precedents.

The German system may be very well suited to the economic and social conditions of that country, but its adoption here—resting as it does on the double foundation of compulsory grouping and centralised control—would require us to fly in the face of the traditions and the living tendencies of British industry. . . . The Government were perfectly right in discarding that feature of the German system, although it must be admitted that in doing so they have been obliged to deprive the workman of a security which, under the German system he does undoubtedly enjoy.[1]

What Asquith said then was still true in 1906. In contemporary perception what distinguished the British from the German way was freedom. Yet, as Asquith had recognized, the price of freedom

[1] 4 *Hansard* 49 (18 May 1897) 749.

was lack of absolute security. Partial protection and lack of universal coverage had been an acceptable price to pay in 1897. By 1906 this was no longer quite so obvious. Here was the new agenda. If henceforth universal provision was to become of primary importance, the question of freedom versus compulsion would need to be reviewed and new priorities established. In the case of workmen's compensation these new priorities never were established. Universal provision did not matter enough to overcome the resistance to compulsion.

Why did it not matter enough? We know that only a few years later, in the case of the wage-earner disabled by illness, resistance to compulsion was no longer acceptable. If that case was significantly different we need to know why. I would suggest two answers: a lack of information and the absence of political mobilization. I shall refer to the first at length before returning briefly to the second.

There was no lack of vague disquiet over the shortcomings of existing provisions. That it was never turned into a sense of shock by the discovery of how large the gaps actually were was due in part to the failure to insist on complete statistics and indeed to the tardy and inadequate interest in monitoring the operations of the Act. This has already been touched on, but, since the lack of statistics is of considerable importance, it deserves a fuller explanation.

Information on the operation of the system came from three sources. The first was the county courts, which dealt with disputed cases, and could appoint medical referees where there was disagreement on medical matters. Decisions made in the courts were registered as a matter of course. After 1906 some attempt was made to insist that all agreements, however arrived at, were registered, but this certainly never happened. Hence the information that was available on the terms of the settlements was fragmentary, and the wider question of the means by which settlements were made and the adequacy of what was paid remained in the realm of accusation and anecdote.

The second series of figures were the ones required by the Home Office. Their limitations have already been exposed. Precisely because they did not concern themselves with those parts of the economy in which the small employers predominated, they were of little value in resolving doubts about the small employer's willingness or ability to cover his risks.

The third source of information was the insurance companies.

Under an Act of 1907, soon superseded by a further one in 1909, all insurance companies transacting employers' liability business had to deposit £20,000 with the Board of Trade and to file their revenue account with the board, which was published.[2] From 1923 onwards the Home Office began to take an interest in the profit made by the commercial companies and negotiated an agreement to limit this. But mutual indemnity associations, being non-profit-making, escaped the attention of the Home Office, just as they had been excluded from the Acts of 1907 and 1909. This made it impossible to know anything about the cost of the system and ruled out comparison of their operation with that of commercial companies. The Board of Trade knew little about them, and what little it knew it failed to publish.[3] Although the Holman Gregory Committee had suggested that they too should be required to file their accounts, the suggestion was never carried out. Indeed, so little notice did the State take of the operation of mutual indemnity that it was not until the investigations of the Beveridge Committee in 1942 that the mutual associations found it expedient to set up a Mutual Insurance Companies Association to represent them in public and to collect their own information for that purpose.[4] It is significant that the Accident Offices Association to represent the bulk of the commercial companies was first established in 1906.[5]

Such a haphazard collection of information by different government departments might have been replaced by an attempt to identify the information needed for a view of the operation of the whole system, had the Holman Gregory Committee's proposal for a Commissioner to supervise the operation of workmen's compensation not been ignored. In consequence there was no centre of administrative initiative and therefore none of the administrative momentum which could often lead to the further development of an existing service.

The frequency with which suggestions for the greater systematization of the available information was ignored does, however, suggest that lack of knowledge was as much a symptom as a cause

[2] See ch. 4, n. 20 above.

[3] See evidence of W. J. Smith, *Departmental Committee on Workmen's Compensation (Holman Gregory), Mins. of Ev.*, QQ. 11770–899, vol. i 1920 Cmd. 908 XXVI.

[4] Memo of Ev., Mutual Insurance Companies Association to the Beveridge Committee, 6 May 1942, PRO, CAB 87/79/50.

[5] Dinsdale, *History of Accident Insurance*, pp. 284–8.

of lack of interest. If there had been political pressure, the information to prove or to disprove hostile assertions would soon have been forthcoming. It is this consideration that leads to the second point. A deeper reason why universal provision did not matter enough is provided by the lack of such political pressure after 1906. In its absence workmen's compensation was not on the agenda for anything but tinkering. In such a situation the German experience of compulsion had little to offer to anyone, except to a few experts beating their heads against a wall of indifference.[6]

---

[6] Two such frustrated experts were Sir Arnold Wilson and Hermann Levy, whose 2 vol. study *Workmen's Compensation*, undertaken in the later 1930s, has proved invaluable.

PART II

From Total Rejection to Acceptance
of the German Precedent
Old Age Pensions and National Insurance

7

The 1880s

JANUARY 1881 saw the publication of the first version of Bismarck's proposals for workers' insurance, accompanied by a long explanatory memorandum of justification for the policy. Although the measure was strictly limited to insurance against the consequences of accidents at work, it was presented as the first step towards a far-reaching system of insurance against many of the hazards that could deprive a worker of his livelihood. In April a slightly amended draft Bill began to be debated in the Reichstag, and in the same month the *Contemporary Review* carried an article by Canon W. L. Blackley, in which Bismarck's scheme of compulsory insurance was roundly condemned as 'mistaken in principle, faulty in detail, hurtful in method, and almost demonstrably certain to prove disastrous in result'.[1]

As the chief advocate of universal compulsory insurance in England at the time, Blackley's opinion is of considerable significance. In 1878 he had proposed that every man between the age of 18 and 21 should be compelled to pay £10 into an annuity fund which, Blackley declared, would suffice to provide him with sick-pay when needed and a pension of 4s. a week at the age of 70. The idea caught on; it was elaborated in pamphlet form, and this led to the formation of the National Providence League, which campaigned in the early and mid-1880s for legislation along these lines.[2]

Blackley was a good German linguist and had been able to follow the German developments in the specialist literature and the press.[3]

[1] W. L. Blackley, 'Prince Bismarck's Scheme of Compulsory Insurance', *Contemporary Review*, 39 (1881), 610–28. The quotation is on p. 614.

[2] Idem, 'National Insurance: A Cheap, Practical and Popular Means of Abolishing Poor Rates', *Nineteenth Century*, 4 (1878), 834–57; idem, *Collected Essays on the Prevention of Pauperism* (1880); idem, *Thrift and National Insurance as a Security against Pauperism: With a memoir of the Late Rev. Canon Blackley and Reprint of his Essays by M. J. J. Blackley* (1906).

[3] He was co-author of a *Practical Dictionary of the German and English Languages* (1866), and his article quoted from *Concordia*, the periodical of the Academic Socialists, and other reforming literature.

He lost no time in distancing himself from Bismarck's proposals to turn the German worker into a pensioner of the State by means of generous State contributions to an insurance system. In the case of many lower-paid workers Bismarck was at this early stage proposing that the cost should be shared entirely between the employer and the State, the worker himself contributing nothing. The essence of Blackley's own scheme was to use the coercive power of the State to compel men to provide for themselves. His views on the German proposals were forthright. 'The true name of this measure, by which . . . the State . . . provides for one class . . . at the cost of another . . . is Pauperism and not Philanthropy'. Englishmen knew all about this Bismarckian blessing, he declared, for they had experienced it for a long time now as a curse. It was nothing more or less than the principle of the English Poor Law. Yet it was worse even than its English counterpart, for it gave the German working man no choice but to be forced into a pauper's role, 'a recipient of forced alms, a pauper from his first day of earning to his last'.[4]

With a few bold strokes Blackley had reduced the German scheme to terms that Englishmen could understand. It became an item in the perpetual debate that the Victorians conducted among themselves over the uses and abuses of the English Poor Law. It was in that debate that Blackley had become a leading protagonist. Universal compulsory insurance as he understood it was for 'the prevention of pauperism' or, as he put it on another occasion, a 'means of abolishing poor rates'.

So crucial a place did the Poor Law and its various institutions occupy in the lives of Englishmen who owned no property, that neither they nor anyone concerned with their condition could ignore it. Most people were agreed that it was a necessary evil. An evil both for the burden it imposed on property and for the effect it had on the character of the recipient and of all who might be influenced by his example. But necessary, too, since it was neither safe nor humane to let people starve, no matter whether negligence or misfortune had brought them to the state of destitution. Its importance was far greater than could be reckoned from the mere numbers who had recourse to it. For the effort to escape from that necessity inspired a whole range of institutions for mutual help,

---

[4] Blackley, 'Prince Bismarck's Scheme of Compulsory Insurance', p. 626.

while the desire to save the deserving from its chill clutches gave impetus to many of the charitable gestures, whether regular or spasmodic, whether well- or ill-informed, that emanated from the well-to-do. In particular, the institutions of working-class thrift stood in so symbiotic a relationship to the Poor Law that no major change in its scope or operation could leave them unaffected.

The major developments in social policy in twentieth-century Britain have been prompted by a revulsion against the Poor Law and a determination to provide services free from its associations. In this way the Poor Law has exercised a profound and pervasive influence over the history of social policy in Britain, shaping the new developments by the force of negations and denial. The desire of social reformers to turn their back on institutions that they found offensive has been largely shared by historians of social reform. They too have preferred to deal with the new institutions in which the hopes of the reformers were enshrined and to have as little dealing as possible with the confusing, infuriating, and embarrassing network of Poor Law institutions. Yet without a knowledge of this it is impossible to understand the context of the innovations.

These remarks are prompted in particular by the way in which historians have frequently written about the origins of old age pensions.[5] Only when the movement for old age pensions in England is restored to its Poor Law context can we begin to understand why so little interest was taken before 1908 in the German model of social insurance, and why the opposite is true once the Old Age Pensions Act was out of the way.

These are the two matters that require explanation. For this

[5] An exception is Pat Thane, 'Non-Contributory versus Insurance Pensions 1878–1908', in Pat Thane (ed.), *The Origins of British Social Policy* (1978), the emphasis of which differs somewhat in this respect from her 1970 London University Ph.D. thesis, P. M. Williams, 'The Development of Old Age Pensions in Great Britain 1878–1925'. It is the best and most balanced treatment of the subject. For some reservations, see ch. 9 n. 39 below. Gilbert, *Evolution of National Insurance*, ch. 4, treats the movement for old age pensions prior to 1898 almost entirely as part of the history of Friendly Societies. R. V. Sires, 'British Legislation for Old Age Pensions', *Jour. of Econ. Hist.*, 14 (1954), 229–53, treats the demand for old age pensions and most misleadingly as a conversion to a collectivist political philosophy; Sir Arnold Wilson and G. S. Mackay, *Old Age Pensions: A Critical History* (1942), as a revival of Tory paternalist political philosophy. Doreen Collins, 'The Introduction of Old Age Pensions in Great Britain', *Historical Journal*, 8 (1965), 246–59, is perceptive but treats the controversies over rival pension schemes as abstract exercises in political theory.

subject as for so many other aspects of the history of British social reform, it is 1908 that marks the decisive turning-point.

There was a sense in which Blackley had been too quick off the mark. The features of Bismarck's proposals which had especially aroused his scorn did not survive the political conflicts from which the legislation of 1883 and 1884 was finally to emerge. Sickness insurance received no State subsidy, except indirectly in the form of administrative support. All beneficiaries had to pay contributions and indeed the worker's contribution was twice that of his employer. But the protracted process that led to the creation of the actual system appears to have aroused little interest in Britain. When in 1885 Blackley again wrote about German insurance, he was able to claim that he had been the only man to have dissected the German measure and exposed its fallacies. On this occasion, far from paying any attention to the difference between what he had originally condemned and what had been established, he was merely concerned to distance himself from what had been done in Germany and to insist that his own proposals should be judged in their own right.[6] His renewed interest in German insurance was entirely defensive, for the National Providence League had finally persuaded the House of Commons to appoint a Select Committee on National Provident Insurance. The Committee had been appointed in May 1885, not a time when MPs found it easy to give their single-minded attention to the subject. Within a month the fall of Gladstone's government had set in motion that chain of political crises which was to lead to the break-up of the Liberal Party in the face of Irish demands for Home Rule.

In those turbulent years the Committee, twice reappointed by newly elected Parliaments, examined its witnesses and finally reported in August 1887. It had concerned itself first and foremost with Blackley's scheme and its feasibility. But it had also stepped aside to enquire about the system of compulsory insurance against sickness that had been in force in Germany since 1883. Its informant was Dr Aschrott, a member of the Prussian judiciary, who happened to be in England at the time to investigate the English Poor Law.[7] Aschrott, like the good Prussian civil servant

---

    [6] W. L. Blackley, 'Mr. Goschen on National Insurance', *National Review*, 5 (1885), 490–503.
    [7] *SC on National Provident Insurance, Mins. of Ev.*, QQ. 1690–1794, 1884–5 (270) X. Dr P. F. Aschrott, who published *Das englische Armenwesen* (Leipzig,

that he was, had prepared his evidence carefully, but when cross-examined on matters that he had not thought about in advance, he occasionally had to confess ignorance. Although it sat for three years, the Committee made no effort to obtain fuller information. Aschrott presumably did not know enough about the procedure of Select Comittees to submit a systematic description of the scheme in the form of a written memorandum, and no one on the Committee thought it worth the effort to procure it from any other source.

The reason for this relative lack of interest emerges clearly from the questions that Aschrott was asked by the Committee members after he had ended his exposition. Blackley had assumed, when designing his scheme, that the two principal causes that drove men on to the rates were temporary sickness and infirmity resulting from old age. To deal with them was to deal with the overwhelming proportion of pauperism. This was the common-sense assumption of someone familiar with the lives of the poor. There might be other causes of pauperism as well, indeed the Report was to complain that Blackley had neglected to pay any attention to unemployment, but nothing that failed to deal with old age could have been expected to reduce the poor rates to any significant degree. The Committee was quick to note that Germany had at that time no scheme for insurance against old age. Insurance against industrial accidents had just been introduced, but Aschrott could tell them nothing about provisions for old age that was of any interest to them. He gave it as his personal opinion that there would never be any compulsory insurance against permanent incapacity for work. The distinction was one that his English questioners might usefully have pondered, but it meant nothing to them. Instead they pressed him to explain what was to happen in old age, and when they got a reply that was obviously irrelevant to the condition of the English rural labourer, they dropped the matter.

Even sickness insurance did not at that time cover agricultural labourers in Germany, although it was to be extended to them before the Committee reported in 1887. Nor did it cover the self-employed, such as costermongers and their like. The Committee

1886) and *Die Entwicklung des Armenwesens in England seit dem Jahre 1885* (Leipzig, 1898), was to be in his day the leading German authority on the English Poor Law. A translation by H. Preston-Thomas of *Das englische Armenwesen* was published in England in 1888 as *The English Poor-law System*, and ran to an enlarged second edition in 1902.

was quick to recognize the difficulty of levying contributions on people such as these. What struck them most about the German scheme was that, compulsory though it was, it failed to include the entire working population. Its irrelevance was summed up for them in the answer to the one crucial question: 'This scheme has not abolished your Poor Law at all?' 'Certainly it has not', replied Dr Aschrott.[8]

When the Committee reported in 1887, it briefly described the German scheme and pointed out where it differed from what Blackley was proposing. There was no suggestion that the German scheme might be a model in its own right. On the contrary. 'The insurance is solely against accident and sickness', ran the Report, 'and thus what appears to your Committee to be the most desirable part of any scheme for National Provident Insurance is unprovided for'.[9]

This distinction between sickness insurance and insurance against old age had come to appear important to the Committee. It is true that it rejected Blackley's scheme altogether, referring to ideological objections to its compulsory nature and to the protests of the Friendly Societies against dangerous competition by the State, but adding that its actuarial shortcomings and the administrative difficulties that it presented were sufficient obstacles in themselves. It did point out, however, that the objections which the financial experts and the vested interests had raised against sickness insurance did not apply in anything like the same degree to the proposals for old age pensions.

In view of this distinction, its members might have been expected to follow the lead of their chairman and show a positive interest in compulsory insurance for old age. In fact they refused to accept his suggestion on this point and went no further than to recommend voluntary insurance either through Friendly Societies or with the help of benevolent employers. It is therefore not hard to see why the German scheme should have evoked no interest. When the Report suggested that Parliament should keep an eye on the future development of compulsory insurance in Germany, this was more a way of dismissing the subject of compulsion from the agenda than of recommending it.

The common verdict on the agitation of the National Providence

---

[8] *SC on National Provident Insurance, Mins. of Ev.*, Q. 1781.
[9] *SC on National Provident Insurance, Report*, p. vii, 1887 (257) XI.

League in the 1880s was that it had fallen foul of the opposition of the Friendly Societies, whose political power it appears to have greatly underestimated. Blackley had been much influenced by the evidence of financial instability and incompetence presented by the Royal Commission on Friendly Societies in 1874. This had convinced him that the voluntary institutions of working-class thrift, conventionally regarded as the alternative to the Poor Law, did not and could not fulfil that role. He brushed them aside as irrelevant.

At least one member of the National Providence League understood the danger of such an attitude and tried to give the Friendly Societies an incentive to co-operate with the objects of the league. James Rankin's proposals to entrust the larger societies with the management of the insurance scheme, compelling everybody to join one of these approved societies, who in return would provide a minimum scale of benefits laid down by Act of Parliament, was in many essentials like that which Lloyd George persuaded the Friendly Societies to accept between 1909 and 1911. Moreover, since the compulsory contributions were to cease at the age of 21 or possibly 25, his scheme gave the societies the most favourable conditions imaginable for the recruitment of life-long adult members to the voluntary side of their work. There was only one obstacle. When Rankin submitted his scheme to the Friendly Societies 'a good many' of them rejected it. This rebuff by those on whose co-operation he had relied cut the ground from under his feet, as it was subsequently to do to Joseph Chamberlain. Rankin failed in 1887 to persuade the Select Committee on National Provident Insurance, of which he was a member, to include even a reference to his proposals in its Final Report.[10]

The effect of a national scheme of compulsory insurance on the existing voluntary organizations was one of the major issues that the Committee had to consider. Dr Aschrott had claimed that

[10] James Rankin, Conservative MP for Leominster 1880–5, Leominster division of Herefordshire 1886–1906, 1910–12. A member of the Select Committee on National Provident Insurance, 1884–5, he was defeated at the general election in 1885 and only returned to the House of Commons in July 1886. He was once more a member of the Select Committee in 1887, but in the interval he had appeared before it as a witness. He belonged to the minority on the Committee who were consistently defeated in the drafting of the Report. A Herefordshire landowner, he was the hon. treasurer of the National Providence League and subsequently its president. He was created a Baronet in 1898.

Bismarck's scheme had solved this problem by leaving similar voluntary bodies in Germany with scope for their continued operation. This was confirmed by a British witness, a railway contractor with experience of working in Germany. When it was suggested to Rankin that his proposals were in many respects closer to the German scheme than to Blackley's, he merely replied that he could not remember the details of the former sufficiently to comment.[11] This is the crucial point. The level of attention that the German initiatives received at this stage was not high. In no sense did those who advocated national compulsory insurance in the England of the 1880s consider that the German initiatives had anything positive to offer.

[11] *SC on National Provident Insurance, Report and Mins. of Ev.*, QQ. 1744–49, 1884–5 (270) X; Q. 449 1887 (257) XI; QQ. 917–980, 1886 (208) XI. Sess. 1.

8

The Old Age Pensions Debate 1890–1905

Insurance of sickness and insurance against old age are two separate objects to be kept apart and considered each on its own merits. The lumping of the contribution for these two purposes into one fund is open to great objections from the actuarial and administrative point of view and is not commended by consideration of general policy.[1]

This was how the young journalist, J. A. Spender, writing from the perspective of 1892, reproached Blackley for creating a prejudice among Friendly Society leaders against proposals for old age pensions. Had these proposals been kept strictly separate from those for sickness insurance, such prejudice, he thought, might never have arisen. Certainly the most important consequence of the Report of 1887 was to split apart what Blackley and his supporters had originally thought of as a single matter, the provision of insurance against sickness and against old age. In so far as he had made any distinction at all Blackley had originally regarded insurance against sickness as the more important of the two, since all working men were liable to sickness while only some survived into old age. But in future the National Providence League decided to concentrate on the needs of the aged poor.

Blackley had tried to collect some evidence of the close connection between pauperism and old age by appealing to parish clergy to examine their burial registers with the help of the local relieving officer and his records. He obtained replies from twenty-six rural parishes scattered fairly widely over the country. From a total of 12,000 cases, 42½ per cent of all those who died aged 60 years and over had been in receipt of poor relief at the time of their death. Sir Henry Maxwell, Chairman of the 1887 Select Committee, called these figures both new and very startling. He thought it most unsatisfactory that this inquiry should be so fragmentary, and wanted an official return from every parish, but

---

[1] J. A. Spender, *The State and Pensions in Old Age* (1892), pp. 124–5.

on this as on so much else the majority of the Committee refused to follow his suggestion.[2]

Nobody really knew how large a proportion of the population was forced to turn to the Poor Law in old age, or how large a proportion of pauperism was accounted for by the needs of different age groups. The copious statistics on poor relief compiled and published each year by the Local Government Board had nothing to say on this. They distinguished the 'aged and infirm' from the 'able-bodied', the children, and the lunatics, but there was no classification by age.

In 1890 this information became available for the first time, as a result of a parliamentary question from Thomas Burt, Liberal working-man MP for Morpeth. Burt's Return, as it was called, gave the number of over-60-year-olds in receipt of poor relief on 1 August 1890, dividing them into five-yearly age groups. The figures that it gave, when set against the age distribution of the population provided by the Registrar-General, showed that 30 per cent of the total population aged 65 and over was dependent on the Poor Law.[3] This could only mean that a very large proportion of the elderly paupers had kept themselves clear of the Poor Law until overtaken by old age.

To one politician these figures conveyed a political message which he was quick to take up. Previously politicians concerned with Poor Law legislation had tended to look to the ratepayers for their support. Those on the verge of pauperism were unlikely to have the necessary qualifications to be put on the electoral register in significant numbers, while those in actual receipt of poor relief were *ipso facto* disfranchised. Politicians with an eye on working-class support had pursued other causes, such as the sort of labour

[2] *SC on National Provident Insurance, Mins. of Ev.*, QQ. 2786–825, 1886 Sess. 1 (208) XI; *Report*, pp. xiv–xv, 1887 (257) XI.

[3] *Return . . . of the Number of Persons . . . in Receipt of In-door relief and of Out-door Relief Aged over 60 Returned in Quinquenniel Groups on 1 August 1890 (Burt's Return)*, 1890–1 (36) LXVIII. 563. Burt's Return, being the count of paupers on a single day only, was not easily turned into a percentage figure relating to the number receiving poor relief in any year. The figure of 30% quoted in the text was arrived at only in 1892 after the figures based on a whole year's count were published in, *Return . . . of the Number of Persons . . . over 65 Years and Upwards . . . in Receipt of In-door Relief and Out-door Relief on 1st Jan. 1892 and at Any Time during the 12 Months Ended Lady Day 1892 (Ritchie's Return)*, 1892 Sess. 1 (265) LXVIII. 619. In 1891 Chamberlain referred to 1 in 7 of the population over the age of 60, then to 1 in 2 of the working classes; Charles Booth estimated 38.4% of the population over the age of 65, subsequently revising this to 26%.

legislation favoured by the Parliamentary Committee of the TUC.

Burt's Return showed that this distinction no longer held good. If these figures meant anything, then a significant proportion of working-class voters, men whose way of life was far removed from that of the habitual clients of the relieving officer, were living under the threat of ultimate degradation. The word is not too strong to describe the attitude of respectable independent working men towards the Poor Law. These were the men capable of organizing and delivering valuable political support, and to save them from the pauper taint was not only good social policy, it was also good electoral politics.

Joseph Chamberlain believed that the labour leaders had no monopoly in understanding the needs and wants of the working class. He had striven since the early 1880s to make himself the politician to whom it would look. In 1886, when President of the Local Government Board, he had already reacted to the occurrence of cyclical unemployment with a policy to save the regularly employed workman from the pauper taint. Since then the débâcle over Home Rule had separated him from the Liberal Party and he was looking for a cause that would re-establish him as the champion of working-class aspirations. The figures on aged pauperism showed him what that cause could be. In March 1891 during a by-election at Aston in his Birmingham area of political influence he launched himself as an advocate of pensions for the respectable, and he did so by expounding the moral of Mr Burt's Return.[4]

He returned to the subject on several occasions within the next few weeks. In May he was approached by the National Providence League, who recognized him as the ideal leader of its cause. He agreed to chair an informal all-party committee of members of both Houses of Parliament, which in turn set up a sub-committee under his chairmanship to devise a suitable scheme. With his energy and flair to aid it, and the prospect of a general election not far off, the subject of old age pensions soon became a general political talking point. Chamberlain expounded his views in the *National Review* in February 1892, and this was followed by replies in the March issue of the journal. In May 1892 the all-party committee published a definite scheme.[5]

[4] *The Times*, 18 Mar. 1891.
[5] Speeches at Plymouth, 2 Apr. 1891; Birmingham, 21 Apr. 1891. For the co-

What Chamberlain was proposing was some kind of public subsidy for those prepared to save for an annuity through the Post Office Savings Bank. There is no point in expounding the details of his proposals for, as he was at pains to explain, those details were nothing if not flexible. That is very understandable under the circumstances. Chamberlain's political need was to renew his contact with the working-class voter. Any scheme, however defective, that would positively appeal to a significant section of the electorate would serve. What mattered was to convince the working-class electorate that a policy was 'within their reach if they will but stretch their hands to it, but that it required this cordial support'. He realized that the politics of social reform was primarily a matter of building up the momentum needed to make a start, and that once a measure, however unsatisfactory, had been enacted it could always be improved.[6]

Hence, while he was infinitely flexible within the limits of his political objective, he was not interested in anything that looked like a political liability. That consideration determined his attitude to the German scheme of old age and invalidity insurance that had been enacted amid much publicity in 1889.

He mentioned the existence of the scheme in his first speech in order to show that it was not impossible for something to be done, and added that it was on a very large scale with good results. In his third speech he again referred to the German scheme as a precedent, telling his audience quite erroneously that the German State added a proportionate contribution to what the workman saved, that is, did what Chamberlain was suggesting should be done in England. But he pointed out that the German scheme was compulsory, whereas he went on to suggest a voluntary one. He was convinced that the English working classes were not ready for compulsion, and steadily fought off any suggestions in that direction.

As he became increasingly immersed in responding to detailed suggestions and in constructing a common denominator of policy, so his tendency vaguely to refer to the German law as a precedent disappeared. Instead he dealt with it merely in order to point out

operation with the National Providence League see memoir in Blackley, *Thrift and National Insurance as a Security*, and Garvin, *Life of Joseph Chamberlain*, ii. 508–13.

[6] Speech at Plymouth, *The Times*, 3 Apr. 1891. Speech at Birmingham, *The Times*, 19 Nov. 1891.

objections to it which did not apply to his own proposals. These objections featured prominently in the article published in the *National Review* in February 1892, which was his most important policy statement up to then.

The basic issue was compulsion, which he was determined to fight off, since whatever a few enthusiasts might say, he believed that it would be fatal to the political success of any scheme. In order to do this he developed the argument that compulsion would be unjust unless it covered literally everyone, and he concentrated on the fact that the German scheme was unable to include either the casually employed or the self-employed.[7] There are of course even more objections to be made to his own proposals if completeness of cover were really the criterion, nor is it obvious why compulsion should not have been applied where this was administratively possible. But by emphasizing these *administrative* shortcomings, he was able to argue forcefully that compulsion was *politically* quite unacceptable, without pinning the blame for this on the very people he was out to woo.

Yet oddly enough he totally failed to achieve his objective. What had looked like a winner in 1892 was a dead duck by 1898, if not before. We know that he was right to think that he had found a cause on which the political energies of the organized working class could be focused. The fear and hatred of an old age under the Poor Law was an emotion with which the active members of the working class could identify themselves. The statistics carried a menace against which the aspirations of even the most striving and energetic working man were not proof. Nor was his failure due to the hostility of the Friendly Societies, as has often been suggested. They were not always so totally opposed nor so united in their disapproval of his proposals.[8] But he needed more than the absence of hostility. Strong positive support was necessary to overcome the built-in obstacles to the spending of public money, and to give the cause sufficient political momentum.

Paradoxically enough that support from the organizations of the working class which was withheld from Chamberlain, who had trimmed his sails for the sole purpose of obtaining it, was to be given in full measure to that most unpolitical of animals Charles

---

[7] J. Chamberlain, 'Old Age Pensions', *National Review*, 18 (1892), 722–3.

[8] The best analysis of Friendly Society opinion is in Williams, 'Development of Old Age Pensions', and in Thane, *Origins of British Social Policy*.

Booth. Since this fact was to dominate the politics of old age pensions, it is necessary to understand the attraction that Booth's approach held for organized labour. His interest in the subject was a by-product of his famous survey of poverty in London. His knowledge of the vulnerability of the elderly was drawn in the first place from an analysis of the causes of pauperism in the Poor Law unions of Stepney and St Pancras, which he was studying just as the figures from Burt's Return became available. He estimated that nearly eight-ninths of the pauperism of those of 65 and older was either directly or indirectly due to old age, in the sense that the person concerned would not otherwise have been a charge on the rates. To anyone who believed, as Booth did, that strict deterrence was the only safe basis on which the Poor Law could be administered, the obvious unsuitability of a deterrent approach to such a large amount of undeserved misfortune was a problem. Far from advocating, as most other Poor Law reformers were to do, the granting of generous out-relief on a non-deterrent basis to these deserving old people, Booth believed that only by removing the whole category completely from the scope of the Poor Law could what he considered to be the pernicious spread of out-relief be arrested. 'Out-relief', he wrote,

is not deterrent and it is only on the side of deterrence that our Poor Law encourages economic virtue. Here we have the weak place and hence the demand for some pensions system which, for most of the aged poor, shall take the place of either indoor or outdoor relief and which, [even] if it does not positively encourage thrift, shall at least not discourage it by making the exhaustion of all savings a first qualification for aid, as is the case under the present law.

He was subsequently to add that, provided the pension was not so large as to meet all possible desires of the recipient, it would indeed be an encouragement to thrift.[9]

It was the logical thoroughness of Booth's approach that caused him to reject a means test or a character test and to argue firmly for universal pensions, to be financed from general taxation, administered in ways that totally separated them from the Poor Law, and claimed as of right by all citizens at 70 years of age. Such a

---

[9] Charles Booth, 'Enumeration and Classification of Paupers and State Pensions for the Aged', *Jour. Royal Statistical Soc.*, 54 (1891), 600–43; idem, *Pauperism, a Picture and Endowment of Old Age: An Argument* (1892).

simplification of the task of the Poor Law administration would make it possible to enforce a strict and deterrent system. 'The principles involved would be more clear when disentangled from old age, and their application might be made more uniform and more strict'.[10] The consequence of such logical thoroughness was estimated by him at £20 million per annum, by his critics at £26 million. The latter sum was a little over one-sixth of the total public revenue in 1899. Logical it might be, but it was also of a staggering naïvety on his part to think that any Cabinet would have been prepared to contemplate such an additional burden of taxation.

This sort of approach was of course totally ruled out for an active politician such as Joseph Chamberlain. There was no point in taking up a policy that would have made him a political leper when he was hoping for acceptance in the Unionist camp. 'Impossibilism' was not one of his options.[11] He assumed that it would also be dismissed by those whose votes he wished to attract. That is where he was wrong. Cabinet ministers, whether actual or potential, had to think about how to raise the money. But the leaders of organized labour did not see themselves as potential ministers, nor did they necessarily identify with those who did. The same was largely true of the leaders of the Labour Party in its very early years.

The irony is that the initiators of the National Committee of Organized Labour for Promoting Old Age Pensions (NCOL), one of the most formidable pressure groups of early twentieth-century politics, were political innocents, not much concerned to calculate the relation between means and ends. The NCOL was founded in 1898 by a conjunction of Charles Booth, who provided the programme, with the leaders of organized labour, who were to provide the numbers. The cost of a central office and an organizing secretary was shared between them with additional help from George Cadbury, the Quaker philanthropist-businessman.[12] Booth's non-political attitude has already been touched upon. F. H. Stead,

[10] Booth, 'Enumeration and Classification of Paupers', p. 641.
[11] In 1899 the Chancellor of the Exchequer was to refer to Booth's contribution as 'proposals which could never have been recommended by a government to parliament': *Old Age Pensions*, by Sir Michael Hicks-Beach, 20 Nov. 1899, PRO, CAB 37/51/89.
[12] The annual reports and occasional publications of the NCOL are to be found in its *Ten Years' Work for Old Age Pensions 1899–1909* (1909). See also F. H. Stead, *How Old Age Pensions Began to Be* (n.d. [1909]) and Frederick Rogers, *Labour, Life and Literature* (1913).

warden of the Browning Hall Settlement in south London, who
took the initiative and was the essential mediator between the two
worlds of academic statistical investigation and labour activism,
came to political impossibilism by a different route. Booth followed
the logic of his mind, Stead the promptings of his heart. His
passionate concern for the dignity of old age came from his
sympathy for the poor and the weak in Walworth among whom he
lived. Since he firmly believed in divine guidance and the power of
prayer, he did not much concern himself with calculations of
political probability.

None of these men cared a jot for the worries of cabinet
ministers, although the organizing secretary, Frederick Rogers,
proved to have a shrewd understanding of the tactics of pressure
groups. The formidable organization that was built up by the
dedication of labour politicians had by 1902 obtained the support
of the TUC, the Co-operative Movement, the Independent Labour
Party and the Labour Representation Committee.

It is not hard to see why Booth's policy of non-contributory
pensions for all should have appealed to organized labour. It was
not Booth's advocacy of a deterrent Poor Law, but his total
rejection of the Poor Law machinery for the aged that provided the
common ground. So did his total rejection of contributory pensions
at a time when organized labour distrusted all offers to subsidize its
own benefit schemes, as liable to lead to interference with the
affairs of its societies. The basis of the alliance is well revealed in the
formula used after the first mass meeting of the new movement in
1898.

It unanimously approved the idea of a universal non-contributory system
of old age pensions. This, it was pointed out, would not invite any
governmental interference with Trade Unions or supervision of them. All
contributory schemes were held to be incomplete and unsatisfactory. They
would not, it was maintained, cover the most necessitous cases, and they
would tend to take away the independence of trade unions.[13]

The general election of January 1906 provided the NCOL with
its long-awaited opportunity. It issued a manifesto, held meetings,
and put test questions to the candidates, and so ensured the return
of a sizeable body of support for old age pensions. Although the
Liberal Party leaders refused to commit themselves, it was a

[13] Stead, *How Old Age Pensions Began*, p. 28.

different story with Liberal MPs: 59 per cent of Liberal candidates mentioned the need for pensions in their election addresses, and in the London area alone out of the 37 Liberals returned 21 were pledged to old age pensions. In addition the return of 29 Labour MPs provided a solid phalanx, all pledged to the programme of the NCOL.[14]

[14] For the figures on candidates see A. K. Russell, *Liberal Landslide: The General Election of 1906* (Newton Abbot, 1973), p. 71. Unfortunately this study makes no distinction between successful and unsuccessful candidates. For the more fragmentary but more significant figures see John Brown, 'Ideas Concerning Social Policy and their Influence on Legislation in Britain 1902–11', Ph.D. thesis (London, 1964), p. 54.

9

Old Age Pensions and the
Liberal Government 1906–1908

THE newly elected House soon gave the government notice of the need to pay attention to the demands for old age pensions. In this connection the existence of a Labour contingent independent of the Liberal Whips was of the greatest tactical importance. There were more Liberal back-benchers pledged to old age pensions than the total of the Labour Party in the House, but the Labour members had an incentive to demonstrate their independence from the government and could more easily take the lead.

On 14 March 1906 James O'Grady, Labour MP for East Leeds, moved a resolution in favour of old age pensions out of general taxation. It was seconded by a Liberal back-bencher, and after a debate in which Asquith, the Chancellor of the Exchequer, took part the resolution was carried without a division. Nor did the old age pension lobby intend to leave the matter there. Systematic pressure was applied through the Liberal and Labour back-benchers, and in June representatives of the Liberal, the Liberal–Labour, and the independent Labour sections interviewed the Chancellor, who professed himself 'entirely sympathetic'.

When pressed to include pension provisions in the next budget, he used the fact that a Select Committee was then investigating the possibility of a graduated income tax as an excuse for not committing himself.[1] He received a deputation from the NCOL on 21 June, and assured them that not only he himself but the government was anxious to satisfy the desires and demands of his supporters and to give effect to his own feelings in the matter. He stressed his agreement with the NCOL on the principle of universal pensions but was obviously trying to find out how far it would be prepared to compromise. When told that the full scheme of

[1] Stead, *How Old Age Pensions Began*, pp. 202–14.

pensions at 65 would cost £15 million 'after making the proper deductions', Asquith pointed out that this meant 6*d.* on the income tax. He left the deputation in no doubt that the obstacle was a financial one.[2]

By August he had decided to investigate the pensions problem with a view to legislation. The shape of the government measure was determined by the way in which ministers and their advisers investigated the evidence and narrowed down the issues during the course of the next twenty months. Yet from the very outset there was one consideration that could not be ignored. No policy would serve its object that did not remove the pressure from the government. This is not to say that the NCOL was in a position to impose its own policy on the minister. Far from it. Like all pressure groups that operated from outside the Cabinet it was extremely vulnerable. All that the Cabinet had to do was to produce a measure that would take the wind out of its sails.

In November the Prime Minister and the Chancellor confronted a huge delegation of Liberal and Labour MPs and committed themselves to old age pensions, 'as soon as time and money permitted'. They ruled out contributory pensions or anything associated with the Poor Law, and managed to satisfy the delegation that they intended to provide pensions out of taxation on a universal basis with certain exceptions which they left vague. Not long afterwards the Prime Minister, who had previously shown no interest in such matters, sent Asquith suggestions for the introduction of universal old age pensions by instalments.[3]

In addition to the direct pressure from the formidable pensions lobby there were other reasons why the government was prepared to contemplate old age pensions in November/December 1906. Nonconformist opposition to the 1902 Education Act had been one of the most prominent aspects of the general election campaign, and one important item in the programme for the 1906 session was an Education Bill. That Bill was thrown out by the House of Lords in November 1906, and it began to look as if the same treatment would be given to any of the other measures distinctively associated with Liberalism. An Old Age Pensions Bill, provided that the

[2] NCOL, 'Seventh Annual Report July 1905–July 1906', in NCOL, *Ten Years' Work for Old Age Pensions*.

[3] Stead, *How Old Age Pensions Began*, pp. 218–24; H. Campbell-Bannerman to H. H. Asquith, 2 Dec. 1906, Bodl., Asquith Papers 74, fo. 25.

money could be found without drastic new taxation, would be a popular social reform. What is more, it might be presented as a money Bill and therefore beyond the constitutional power of the Lords to reject.

By then the work in Asquith's office was well under way. Meiklejohn, Asquith's personal private secretary, had begun by trying to discover the scope of existing Friendly Society provisions for old age. He requested the Chief Registrar of Friendly Societies to send out questionnaires, and by November the staff of the Registrar's office were sending him the first and somewhat inadequate replies.[4]

By 14 December the Treasury had worked up the subject sufficiently to submit a memorandum to the Cabinet.[5] This was a survey of previous investigations and proposals from the days of Canon Blackley onwards. Although it made no recommendations, it is of interest for the way in which it presented the subject. The memorandum commended Blackley's scheme as a good type of an old age pensions scheme founded on compulsory contributions. It regarded the investment of a lump sum before the age of 21 as preferable on the ground of administrative simplicity to the German scheme, in which compulsory contributions continued practically throughout adult life. It also pointed out the difficulty of 'reaching the migratory population in irregular employment'. But from the point of view of practical politics the fatal objection to Blackley's scheme, the authors added, was that it could not come into operation for close on half a century. This was indeed true of the scheme proposed by Blackley, who had disapproved of State subsidies and had insisted on complete payment of contributions by the age of 21. But it was not an objection that applied to the German scheme. The reference to Germany had been inserted into the analysis for the sake of making a single point and no more. Yet we shall find that Meiklejohn's way of putting this matter was to create strange confusions in Asquith's mind.

Apart from this passing reference the memorandum displayed no interest at all in the experience of other countries, a subject on which there was at this stage considerable ignorance in official

    [4] R. Meiklejohn to J. D. Stuart Sim, Aug. 1906, J. D. Stuart Sim to R. Meiklejohn, Nov. 1906, Bodl., Asquith Papers 74, fos. 11, 18.
    [5] Memo on Old Age Pensions, by R. M[eiklejohn] and M. S[turges], 14 Dec. 1906, 25 pp., Bodl., Asquith Papers 74, fo. 30; also in PRO, CAB 37/85/96.

circles. 'An analysis and report on the German system would be interesting', wrote the Chief Registrar of Friendly Societies on receiving a copy, and added some very garbled information that he had obtained the previous day in conversation with 'a man who knew it'. One of his subordinates had written a month previously saying that he was briefing himself on old age pensions and asking where he could find any recent information on the working of the German law or the French State annuities.[6]

The Treasury had in fact already sent a request to the Foreign Office at the beginning of August for information on the operation of old age pensions schemes abroad. At that time it possessed nothing more recent than a Blue Book of 1899.[7] In November the Treasury received a copy of a despatch from Berlin extracting information from an article in a German newspaper. This had been occasioned by the twenty-fifth anniversary of the inauguration of the Bismarckian policy of social insurance, and gave figures of the scope of the scheme in terms of both people covered and money involved.[8] The silence of the memorandum of 14 December would suggest that the more systematic information had not yet been received by the time that some of the basic issues arising from the government's recent commitment had begun to clamour for attention.

The missing overseas dimension to the subject was supplied four months later in a memorandum dated 4 April 1907. This dealt with the provisions made in seven countries and devoted a little over one folio page to Germany.[9] We shall see later what use Asquith was to make of it.

Meanwhile the pressure of the pensions lobby had been kept up in the country at large. When the parliamentary session opened in February without any reference to pensions being made in the King's speech, the Labour Party moved a hostile amendment. Asquith's persuasiveness only just managed to divide the forces

---

[6] J. D. Stuart Sim to R. Meiklejohn, 20 Dec. 1906, J. H. Hall to R. Meiklejohn, 23 Nov. 1906, Bodl., Asquith Papers 74, fos. 52 and 16.

[7] Edward Hamilton to FO, 8 Aug. 1906, PRO, T12/28/504–5. I am grateful to Valerie Cromwell for drawing my attention to this item.

[8] Despatch No. 363, J. de Salis to Sir Edward Grey, 19 Nov. 1906, Bodl., Asquith Papers 74, fo. 14. The embassy had translated most of the financial figures into English values, but where it had omitted to do so someone in the Treasury took the trouble to add them in pencil in the margin.

[9] Denmark and Iceland, France, Belgium, Italy, Germany, New Zealand and Australia; see Memo on Foreign and Colonial Systems, by R. M[eiklejohn] and M. S[turges], 4 Apr. 1907, 11 pp., Bodl., Asquith Papers 74, fo. 79.

against the government and stave off defeat. When he introduced his budget in May he therefore announced that the government was committed to old age pensions, and set aside £4½ million for a pension fund. There was at this stage no government policy at all. It is quite clear that the government had been hurried into its announcement well in advance of any legislative project by the political pressure under which it found itself. This pressure was to continue both in the country and in the House itself throughout the following year.[10]

The required policy was subsequently hammered out, between April 1907 and April 1908. This job was given in the first place to Reginald McKenna, President of the Board of Education but until recently Financial Secretary to the Treasury, and subsequently to a Cabinet Committee consisting of Asquith, McKenna, and Burns.[11] They reported to the Cabinet early in April, and in his budget speech on 7 May 1908 Asquith indicated for the first time what kind of scheme the government meant to introduce later in the session. He made it clear that pensions would be financed out of general taxation, as the NCOL had demanded, and given to those over 70 years of age. By not entering into the details of the grounds for disqualification he managed to give the impression of a more generous measure than was actually intended.[12]

Two remarkable features of Asquith's statement were the ease with which he dismissed any form of compulsory insurance as totally unsuitable, and the amazing ignorance of the German insurance scheme which his remarks revealed. Nor are these matters unconnected. This is not to suggest that the Cabinet failed to appreciate the relevance of compulsory insurance for old age out of ignorance of the German system. On the contrary, ministers were happy to remain in ignorance, since compulsory insurance of whatever kind was patently ruled out for them as a political option.

The Report of the Cabinet Committee had established in its very first recommendation that all 'contributory' schemes were ruled

---

[10] Stead, *How Old Age Pensions Began*, pp. 224–37; NCOL, 'Annual Reports', in *Ten Years' Work for Old Age Pensions*.

[11] Williams, 'Development of Old Age Pensions', pp. 194–5, 205. John Burns was President of the Local Government Board. Lloyd George became a member when he was appointed Chancellor of the Exchequer in April 1908.

[12] *Old Age Pensions, Report of the Cabinet Committee*, Apr. 1908, Bodl., Asquith Papers 75, fo. 200; also in PRO, CAB 37/92/54; 4 *Hansard* 188 (7 May 1908) 463–76.

out. Asquith in his budget speech was less direct. He adopted a historical approach and dealt with the stages by which old age pensions had become a major issue. In the course of this he referred to the German scheme 'which is one of compulsory State-aided insurance' as having been in existence since 1889, and dismissed it with a few belittling statistics. There were, he said, not more than 126,000 persons in receipt of old age pensions in 1907 out of a population of over fifty-two million. German pensions averaged a little over £6. 13s. 0d. a year, that is about 2s. 2d. a week, compared with the 5s. a week that was generally considered necessary by British old age pensions advocates, and the State contribution amounted to less than 40 per cent of the whole. 'More instruction, I think, for our purposes is to be derived from the legislation initiated in Denmark in 1891, in New Zealand in 1898, and subsequently in New South Wales and Victoria'. Later in his speech he explained why compulsory insurance was ruled out. There was 'the hostility of many other competing bodies like the Trade Unions, Friendly Societies, insurance companies and a host of others. Moreover—and this in itself . . . is conclusive . . .—none of its benefits would come into actual enjoyment until after the lapse of twenty or more years'.[13] The Report of the Cabinet Comittee had made the same two points.

To those who knew anything about the working of the German scheme of compulsory insurance these assertions seemed extraordinarily silly. Asquith's figures were nonsense; they ignored the fact that in Germany old age pensions and pensions for impaired earning capacity, known as invalidity or infirmity pensions, were administered as part of one and the same scheme. Infirmity pensions were the more generous of the two, and those who qualified for them received them instead of old age pensions. To quote figures for German old age pensions, as Asquith had done, without mentioning those for infirmity pensions was therefore grossly to mislead.[14] Not that this was a sinister plot; it was the

[13] Ibid. (7 May 1908) 464, 467.
[14] The number of people in receipt of pensions on 1 Jan. 1907, the date Asquith was referring to, was 962,277, viz. old age 125,603, permanent invalidity 814,575, provisional invalidity, i.e. due for review at a later stage, 22,099. That was close on 2% of the population, not ¼% as Asquith's figures had suggested. The average pension as granted in 1906 was £8 a year, or 3s. 1d. a week. Calculated from *Return of Workmen's Insurance in Germany against Sickness, Invalidity and Old Age*, 1908 (102) XCVI 1189.

result of incompetent briefing. Asquith had used the figures and the conclusions provided in the memorandum on foreign and colonial systems produced by Meiklejohn and Sturges in April 1907. That memorandum had in turn been based on the information collected by the Foreign Office. The Treasury request had been for information on old age pensions and this was what it received. No one inquired long enough into the actual system to discover that for Germany information on old age pensions alone was irrelevant. Meiklejohn and Sturges had noticed that the number of German old age pensions was declining steadily over the years, but they never inquired why. For them the moral was obviously that the proportion of pensioners to population was very small.

Even sillier was Asquith's claim that a compulsory insurance scheme would not be able to provide any benefits for the first twenty years or more. The memorandum of April 1907 had in fact explained the arrangements for transitional provisions which had enabled the German scheme to come into operation at once for the benefit of the older population. But this information had made no impression on Asquith, who had relied for his arguments on the more recent document, the Report of the Cabinet Committee of April 1908. The myth that contributory schemes inevitably involved a substantial delay before they could provide any benefits had had a continuous existence in British discussions of old age pensions ever since it had been raised as an objection against Blackley. The Chaplin Committee in 1899, which took no evidence on the matter, had given it as one of the objections to adopting anything like the German scheme. The other objection, significantly enough, had been the opposition of the working class, and the Chaplin Comittee had expressed the opinion that either of these was fatal to any such proposals. It is reasonable to infer from its lack of interest in the evidence that it was not its objection to delay that had led the Committee to recommend the provision of pensions out of general taxation for the aged deserving poor.[15] When Chamberlain had spoken in support of the Chaplin Committee's proposals in the Commons the same alleged objection had been prominent among the reasons he gave for abandoning his previous advocacy of contributory pensions. He had claimed that there would be no benefits for forty years, and the same point had

---

[15] *SC on the Aged Deserving Poor, Report*, para. 47, 1899 (296) VIII.

been repeated in the Treasury memorandum of December 1906. Asquith, who had had a transcript made of the speech, quoted the relevant passage for the sake of its effect on the Opposition party. The belief that a politically fatal delay was inevitable with a system of contributory pensions appears to have been firmly impressed on Asquith's mind.[16]

There were those who knew better, and it was not long before they said so. Of these one of the first was William Beveridge, who was at the time writing regularly on social questions in the *Morning Post*. This was a Tory paper, but Beveridge was given freedom to write as he wished in his own field. The previous February he had described the German system as a model for compulsory insurance against old age, his second article on the subject within five months.[17] He drew the obvious conclusion from Asquith's performance. 'The Government have put the German system out of court without acquiring even the most superficial knowledge of it'. 'Is it too late', he asked, 'to suggest that the Government should, even at this late hour, reconsider their determination to have none but a non-contributory scheme. They have clearly reached their determination without adequate study of the alternatives'.[18]

Over the next two weeks he followed up with two articles on 'Old Age Pensions by Contribution'. The first dealt in detail with Asquith's references to Germany, explained the importance of infirmity pensions, correcting his figures, and describing the nature of the transitional provisions. 'The essential point to notice is that the German old age pensions scheme is a contributory scheme which started as a non-contributory scheme'. One main lesson to be learnt from it was that it was possible to find a better use for the money now available than that of starting a scheme that would always be non-contributory. 'Could not the money be used to

---

[16] Transcript of Chamberlain's Speech of 22 Mar. 1899, Bodl., Asquith Papers 74, fo. 1; 4 *Hansard* 188 (7 May 1908) 467. Sidney Webb, who strongly disapproved of all contributory schemes, did at least realize that a 20-year delay was not inevitable. His long memo on old age pensions had been sent by Haldane to Asquith on 17 Dec. 1907, but this particular item of information obviously made no impression. See *Suggestions as to Old Age Pensions*, by S. Webb, 29 Sept. 1907, R. B. Haldane to H. H. Asquith, 17 Dec. 1907, Bodl., Asquith Papers 75, fos. 137, 131.

[17] *Morning Post*, 8 Feb. 1908; see also 'Social Reform: How Germany Deals with It, iii', *Morning Post*, Sept. 1907. Copies of all Beveridge's *Morning Post* articles are preserved in LPES, Beveridge Papers XII.

[18] *Morning Post*, 14 May 1908.

confer immediate benefits on those who are already old, while for those still young the benefits for which they would have to contribute were maturing?'[19]

Even these few extracts demonstrate that Beveridge was not just correcting Asquith's misstatements for the sake of accuracy. He had been engaged for some time in a fundamental exploration of alternative ways of dealing with the problem. The government project of providing gratuitous pensions of 5s. a week or less at 70 to those who could prove both poverty and desert seemed to him the worst of all possible policies. 'Here is a scheme not of social reform but of doles', was his comment on the Bill when it was published.[20]

Much as in any case he disliked non-contributory pensions provided out of general taxation, he was convinced that to hedge them around with restrictions, as the government proposed to do, was even worse. The proposal to confine pensions to those with less than £26 a year was, he thought, a discouragement to thrift and an encouragement to lying. Like many other commentators he regarded the proposal to exclude some applicants by a thrift or character test as unworkable, as well as being demoralizing both to the applicant and to those who were to make the decisions. Finally he recognized that there was no justification for delaying the grant of a pension until the age of 70. Ever since 1891, when the first statistics on aged pauperism had been published, 65 had been regarded as the suitable age for pensions.[21] Beveridge showed that those few trade unions that gave superannuation allowances to their members no longer able to earn the ordinary rate of wages found themselves paying out on average already at 63.[22] 'In other words the scheme is still utterly incomplete. It does not make the provision for old age which social conditions undoubtedly require ... The beginning made is so insignificant that it cannot possibly be regarded as laying down the permanent lines of treatment in the future'.[23]

Unlike many other critics of the government's proposals Beveridge

[19] *Morning Post*, 21 May 1908.   [20] *Morning Post*, 4 June 1908.
[21] The government had originally intended to give pensions at age 65 and changed its mind quite late on in the planning of the Bill, because it did not think it had enough money to go round. See Williams, 'Development of Old Age Pensions', p. 208.
[22] 'The Age for Pensions', *Morning Post*, 4 June 1908.
[23] *Morning Post*, 4 June 1908.

did not think that the logic of the case pointed inevitably to non-contributory pensions for all. This had been his position once,[24] but by April 1907 he had changed his mind and was stressing the merits of compulsory insurance. What appealed to him about the German system of insurance was that it already protected the wage-earner against many of the principal hazards of industrial life. Although still incomplete, it held out the hope that it would one day be able to give protection against the whole range.[25] Such completeness was far removed from hurried *ad hoc* expedients to meet a particular political pressure. Even when considering old age pensions Beveridge could not get away from his overriding preoccupation at the time, which was with the problems of casual work, under-employment, and unemployment. He considered these to be the consequences of the defective organization of society. The contribution that the State should make towards the removal of these evils was not to hand out doles to the workless, nor yet to hand out doles disguised as wages in exchange for artificially created 'public works'. It was to 'banish disorganisation', both by creating the institutions that were lacking, such as labour exchanges, and by using its powers of regulation, as for instance towards the decasualization of labour.[26]

He was therefore always looking beyond the immediate question of old age pensions towards a wider range of issues. 'The merit of the contributory system . . . is that it makes it possible to treat the incapacity of old age as only one among other forms of incapacity; . . . to do away with all specific provisions for old age—the rough and ready test—in a general scheme based upon the essential fact of inability to work'. It was for this reason that he thought the German system of combining old age and infirmity pensions within the same scheme vastly superior to pensions at a fixed age. They could be taken up at any age by those no longer fit for work. And as early as April 1907 he was drawing the further moral that 'this completeness is a thing that cannot be got by rough and ready methods. It depends upon organisation and the willingness to submit to organisation'.[27]

Far from fearing the growth of State power, Beveridge welcomed

[24] See *Morning Post*, 16 Feb. 1906.

[25] 'Social Reform: How Germany deals with It, i', *Morning Post*, Sept. 1907.

[26] Throughout 1907 and 1908 he was expounding in articles and lectures the views which were to appear in book form in 1909 as *Unemployment: A Problem of Industry*.

[27] *Morning Post*, 20 Apr. 1907.

it. What really mattered to him was that it should proceed on the right principles. He was therefore not content merely to correct the inaccuracies in Asquith's budget speech, but attacked his objections to compulsory insurance on the widest possible front. 'It cannot be too strongly laid down', he wrote in a passage very reminiscent of the Webbs,

that every step towards social reform nowadays means more government, and that to embark upon social reform while grudging thought and money to the construction of administrative machinery is to court disaster. In some way or other the State must get hold of its individual citizens, must know much more about them, must make them consciously and actually part of the social organisation.

A non-contributory pension scheme sets up the State in the eyes of the individual as a source of free gifts. A contributory scheme sets up the State as a comprehensive organism to which the individual belongs and in which he, under compulsion if need be, plays his part. Each view involves abandonment of traditional *laissez-faire*. The first, however, represents a change for the worse which it will be hard to retrieve. The second is a natural recognition of the growing complexity and interdependence of industrial life.[28]

The danger of non-contributory pensions lay in the precedent they created and in the attitude they fostered. To the objection that they were what the public overwhelmingly demanded, Beveridge had two answers. Of course getting something for nothing, he said, is popular with the workman. 'But it is infinitely better for him . . . that he should not get into the habit of looking to the State as a Lady Bountiful with a Fortunatus purse'.[29] As for the fears of trade unions and Friendly Societies that compulsory insurance would necessarily interfere with their own insurance business, Beveridge pointed out that once again Germany had something to teach. The German sickness insurance had managed to accommodate existing voluntary associations, and there was no reason why the same principle should not be applied in England to contributory old age pensions.[30]

[28] 'Old Age Pensions by Contribution: Mr Asquith's Objections, ii', *Morning Post*, 29 May 1908.
[29] 'Compulsory Insurance against Old Age: The German Model', *Morning Post*, 8 Feb. 1908.
[30] 'Old Age Pensions by Contribution: Mr Asquith's Objections, ii', *Morning Post*, 29 May 1908.

The weakness of all this lay in the quiet authoritarianism with which he disposed of the well-known political unpopularity of a contributory pensions scheme. There is no recognition anywhere of the existence of the formidable political power that had been mustered in support of non-contributory pensions in the House of Commons and outside. Beveridge's wider vision seemed to be peculiarly blind to the political dimensions of social reform.

He had visited Germany in the summer of 1907 to investigate labour exchanges and social insurance at first hand. The last of several articles written on that occasion for the *Morning Post* had ended with a great panegyric of German statesmanship.

The German system of industrial insurance does not simply dispense benefits. Its elaborate machinery brings men of all sorts into co-operation with one another, in accident insurance associations, in the arbitration tribunals, in the management of sick funds, and in countless other ways. It increases the opportunities of public service. It impresses upon all the sense of the reality of the State and of the claims of the community upon each man's time and thought. It does this just because it is in itself the expression of a very real expenditure of constructive thought upon social problems. The governors of Germany have done and do many things which would make them very unpopular as governors of England. They have at least not been idle. They have recognised that it is the business of statesmen to fashion a State worth living in and have had the courage to throw to the winds all narrower arbitrary definitions of the functions of Government.[31]

Such an attitude was as far removed as anything could be from the one that prevailed in the Cabinet at the time. With the single exception of Haldane, ministers did not want to embark on the task of constructing far-reaching forms of social organization. Least of all did they wish to impose unpopular kinds of regimentation on the people for the sake of constructing a machinery that might ultimately be used for further highly controversial social reforms. Their conflict was with the House of Lords, which was currently engaged in destroying every one of the measures that were closest to the heart of their traditional supporters. They wished to bring forward legislation that enjoyed political support so overwhelming that the Lords would not dare to touch it. By those tests Beveridge's ideas were most unattractive, and his interpretation of German

[31] 'Social Reform: How Germany Deals with It, iv', *Morning Post*, Oct. 1907. See José Harris, *William Beveridge: A Biography* (Oxford, 1977), for further comments on the cast of Beveridge's mind and his views at this period.

statesmanship irrelevant at the one point that really mattered to a government, namely its political base.

No wonder they did not bother about the details of the German system of social insurance as much as Beveridge had done. The attention paid to the German schemes by the Cabinet and those who briefed it was undoubtedly perfunctory in the extreme. This was due not to contempt for the experience of other nations but to the conviction that the German model was irrelevant.[32]

The carelessness displayed towards Germany was in sharp contrast to the interest that Asquith had shown in New Zealand and in Denmark. These countries' old age pensions schemes were non-contributory, limited to those whose income or property was below a prescribed figure, and they imposed some test of character and desert.[33] The New Zealand scheme featured most prominently in the discussions. The memorandum on foreign and colonial systems, produced in April 1907 by Meiklejohn and Sturges, had devoted two closely printed pages to it and to the variants more recently introduced in New South Wales and Victoria. The copy in the Asquith papers is copiously annotated in Asquith's hand.[34] In September 1907 he queried whether it was up to date and gave Sturges a book on the subject to summarize. He was then sent the latest report of the New Zealand Old Age Pensions Department, and two further detailed memoranda on the working of the scheme were produced for his benefit.[35] The same file contains the reports of the department going back to 1900, regulations issued in 1906, and copies of the relevant Acts, a total of twelve printed items.

Of course it was easy to regard the colonial experience as an extension of British political culture, but a similar interest was shown in the Danish precedent. Not content with the memorandum of April 1907 Asquith had a very clear and detailed description of the Danish system drawn up, leading to three conclusions, all of which were politically unpalatable and two of which he was careful

[32] It is a remarkable fact that the files relating to old age pensions in the Asquith Papers, which contain at least one press cutting from the *Morning Post*, contain none of the many articles that Beveridge wrote on old age pensions in that journal during 1907 and 1908.

[33] Asquith, in 4 *Hansard* 188 (7 May 1908) 464.

[34] In contrast to the rest of the memo, which is unmarked.

[35] Bodl., Asquith Papers 75, fos. 1–106. The second of the two memos is dated 13 Jan. [1908].

to suppress when referring to the Danish scheme in public.[36] It was the details of the system that interested him, for the Danes were in fact operating a strict character test and limiting the grant of pensions to the deserving poor.

In discussing how to fix the qualifications for a British pension the practices in Denmark and New Zealand were very much in the Cabinet Committee's mind, and in Asquith's budget speech there are copious references to these precedents.[37] As early as April 1907 McKenna had described the government's intentions to Mrs Webb, who referred to them as 'something between the New Zealand and Danish plan'.[38]

All this serves to show that the government was not suffering from insular myopia in general, but had made its choice and knew what it was after. This being so, the statements about the administrative shortcomings of the German compulsory insurance system, wrong though they were, had the advantage of providing respectable explanations for a course of action whose real grounds it would have been embarrassing to avow. It was patently obvious that no one really liked the scheme that was being concocted. It was financially inconceivable that the government should follow the only logically satisfactory course and provide non-contributory pensions for all, as Booth had advocated, at a notional cost of £26 million. But any limited scheme was bound to be open to innumerable objections, and it was not hard to see that the government's proposals were as full of holes as a sieve. Since it was better not to confess that the government was embarking on a rash

[36] *Old Age Relief in Denmark*, by Alan Johnstone (n.d. but probably late 1907), pp. 7, Bodl., Asquith Papers 74 fo. 123. The memo concluded on the strength of the Danish experience: (i) that the cost of such pensions is likely to increase annually; (ii) that old age pensions diminish little, if at all, the cost of poor relief; (iii) that once the system of old age pensions has been commenced demands will be constantly forthcoming for the extension of the system. In his Budget speech Asquith admitted the first of these facts, which applied also to New Zealand, but quickly added that the cost of administration was very low: 4 *Hansard* 188 (7 May 1908) 465.

[37] *Old Age Pensions, Report of the Cabinet Committee*, Apr. 1908, Bodl., Asquith Papers 75, fo. 200; 4 *Hansard* 188 (7 May 1908) 468–9. See also *Old Age Pensions, Points on Draft Clauses*, 30 Apr. 1908, Bodl., Asquith Papers 98, fo. 67. When the relevant clauses of the Bill were being drawn up, the wording of the New Zealand legislation served as a model: A. T. Thring to J. Bradbury, 28 Apr. 1908, asking for the New Zealand statutes (letter endorsed 'sent'), Bodl., Asquith Papers 75, fo. 310.

[38] Diary entry, 27 Apr. 1907, in Beatrice Webb, *Our Partnership*, ed. Barbara Drake and Margaret Cole (1948), p. 379.

and dangerous course because it could not resist political pressure, the political arguments were discreetly veiled by the use of bogus administrative ones.

Where administrative objections could not be found, the alleged implacable resistance of Friendly Societies to all conceivable forms of contributory insurance was regularly brought up instead. To have explored the possible ways of removing that opposition would merely have removed a politically convenient fig leaf. In fact the Friendly Society movement by this time was far from presenting a solid front on the issue of old age pensions. Few Friendly Societies provided specific superannuation schemes, and those which did found little demand for them. Their habit of paying what were in fact superannuation benefits disguised as sickness benefits to their elderly members was seriously affecting their solvency. But the support of the Friendly Society movement for the claims of the NCOL was half-hearted. In 1902 the National Conference of Friendly Societies had certainly endorsed a scheme of State-provided old age pensions linked to insurance through Friendly Societies, but right up to 1907 it was not difficult to find statements by leading Friendly Society officials taking up almost any position along the spectrum.[39] Between 1908 and 1911 Lloyd George was able to persuade them to participate in a State-subsidized scheme of compulsory sickness insurance, which affected their business far more closely than any contributory old age pensions would have done.

Thus when in September 1907 Lord Avebury, Sir Edward Brabrook, former Chief Registrar of Friendly Societies, and others put forward a scheme whereby the Treasury would subsidize voluntary contributory old age pensions, carefully designed to meet all possible objections from the Friendly Societies, and to come into effect immediately, Meiklejohn reported unfavourably to Asquith.

---

[39] Williams, 'Development of Old Age Pensions', pp. 154–8, and *passim*. Most of this evidence is utilized in Thane, *Origins of British Social Policy*. Unlike earlier historians she recognizes that the rejection of a contributory pensions policy cannot have been due to the political opposition of the Friendly Societies. She therefore finds the explanation mainly in the administrative difficulties that would have prevented the provision of contributory pensions for vulnerable groups not in regular paid employment. I am not so impressed with the administrative coherence of the 1908 Act, nor with the attention paid by ministers, either then or at other times, to considerations of coherence when devising a brand-new policy. Such matters tend to become more important subsequently, when amending legislation is introduced as a result of the practical experience of administering an existing law.

The Times, too, thought it was an impossible project. It pointed out that the demand for old age pensions was already for something much more comprehensive and, it added, much more questionable. 'In *republica Platonis*' Avebury's proposals might well be held to be an excellent solution to the problem. 'It remains to be seen whether in *faece Romuli* it is likely to be accepted as any solution at all'.[40] There is none of this frankness in Meiklejohn's report. There the scheme is criticized, unjustifiably as it turned out, on actuarial grounds, and wrongly described as bound to compete very seriously with Friendly Society business and as not meeting the needs of those already over 40. The administration, Meiklejohn added, would be difficult and costly, the calculations uncertain, and the proposed accumulated pension funds difficult to invest. The only political objection mentioned was the fear of opposition from Friendly Societies, opposition which the scheme was especially designed to avoid, and which it was unlikely to arouse. The real political reasons are not even touched upon.[41]

Enough has been said to show that old age pensions based on compulsory insurance could be regarded as a political lost cause, interesting perhaps in theory to academically minded systematizers like Beveridge, but repudiated in practice on inescapable political grounds. Campbell-Bannermann and Asquith, on committing themselves in principle to old age pensions in November 1906, had ruled out contributory schemes from the first, and during the Commons debate in February 1907 Asquith had repeated that he regarded all contributory schemes 'as altogether inadmissable'.[42] Was there anyone in the world of actual politics willing to champion such a lost cause?

What view did the Opposition front bench take? It was certainly pleased to be able to discredit Asquith's handling of the facts. A few days after the publication of Beveridge's article, Henry Chaplin, former Conservative Cabinet Minister, tabled a parliamentary question for the Chancellor of the Exchequer which, after pointing out the close connection between the German invalidity and old age pensions, asked for the total numbers of such pensions on 1 January 1907. Lloyd George provided the information and was

[40] *The Times*, 3 Sept. 1907.
[41] R. S. Meiklejohn to H. H. Asquith, 12 Sept. 1907, Bodl., Asquith Papers 74, fo. 152.
[42] Stead, *How Old Age Pensions Began*, pp. 221, 226.

immediately bombarded by further explanations in the form of a supplementary question. The same points were taken up later in the day by Austen Chamberlain, the Opposition spokesman.[43]

Austen Chamberlain's position at this time is worth attention. The stroke that had removed his father from active politics had laid on Austen the burden of fighting for the causes dear to the elder Chamberlain's heart. This meant tariff reform first and foremost but also such reforms as old age pensions. He had tried in October 1907 to persuade Balfour to come out in favour of a general tariff and a corn tax and to couple this with social reform. He was at that stage under the impression that Asquith had committed himself to a non-contributory scheme of old age pensions that was universal in scope. 'I believe this to be vicious in principle and impossible on account of the cost,' he wrote to Balfour. 'May we not say that we are prepared to propose a contributory scheme, somewhat on the German model—one-third from the workman, one-third from the employer, one-third from the State?'[44] Of course Balfour, who was about to move cautiously somewhat nearer to the tariff reform position, had no intention of complicating his careful balancing act within his party by responding to bold proposals for social reform.

Austen Chamberlain owed this favourable view of the German system as a model for future policy almost certainly to discussions which he and other leading tariff reformers were holding at this time on a social reform programme for the future. The group included the editor of the *Morning Post*, for which Beveridge was writing his articles on German social insurance and its implications. In early May 1908 Asquith revealed the details of his pension proposals, and it became clear that they were far from impossible. At that stage Chamberlain explained that he himself would have preferred a compulsory contributory system on the German model, since with a given sum of Treasury money one could reach three times as many people as with a non-contributory one. He conceded that, once the government had committed itself the other way, a contributory scheme became impossible not only in the present but in the future. But by 25 May he had changed his mind and was making proposals similar to those that had appeared in the

[43] 4 *Hansard* 189 (25 May 1908) 771–2, 794.

[44] Austen Chamberlain to A. J. Balfour, 24 Oct. 1907, qd. in Alan Sykes, *Tariff Reform in British Politics 1903–1913* (Oxford, 1979), p. 137, which provides a good guide to the relation between Austen Chamberlain and Balfour at this time.

Morning Post four days earlier. In view of the inadequacies of the government proposal, not least the fact that it did not come into effect until the age of 70, he suggested that a compulsory contributory scheme to provide pensions at an earlier age might well be the way forward in the future.[45]

As on so many other occasions Chamberlain failed to take his colleagues all the way. On 4 June the Conservative leaders decided to bow to the inevitable and not to oppose the Bill at the Second Reading. They went along with Austen Chamberlain in distancing themselves from the principle on which it was based, accepting it merely as a temporary bridge to a complete scheme on a contributory basis. But complete apparently did not mean compulsory. Chaplin, on behalf of the Opposition, was careful to make that clear.[46]

The real challenge to the government came, therefore, not from the Conservative leadership but from a Liberal back-bencher, one of those independent-minded persons whom no party Whip was able to subdue. Harold Cox, Liberal MP for Preston, played a crucial role in this story exactly because he did not calculate political probabilities, or at least was not prepared to let such calculations muffle the expression of his opinions.[47] He was the first person in the House to correct Asquith's statement that contributory pensions could not be introduced without a twenty years' delay, and he did so by drawing attention to what had been done in Germany.[48] When the actual Bill was introduced, Cox tabled a hostile amendment which led to a major debate on the rival merits of the government's scheme versus a compulsory contributory one.

Cox regretted that the government had not taken the trouble to send someone to Berlin to find out how the German system worked.

[45] 4 *Hansard* 188 (7 May 1908) 482; ibid. (25 May 1908) 793.

[46] Austen Chamberlain, *Politics from Inside* (1936), p. 118; 4 *Hansard* 190 (24 June 1908) 1761–6.

[47] Harold Cox, born 1859, educated Cambridge, Cambridge University extension lecturer on political economy, agricultural labourer, founded a communistic farm that failed. He taught mathematics in India, read for the Bar, but then went into journalism. Secretary of the Cobden Club, the body that propagated orthodox political economy and free trade, 1899–1904. Liberal MP for Preston 1906–9. Broke with the government over old age pensions, worked closely throughout 1909 with the Unionist free traders. He stood as Independent Free Trade Liberal in Jan. 1910, representing the 'Free Traders of Preston who were either Conservative or moderate Liberals', and was defeated. LCC alderman 1910–12, editor *Edinburgh Review* 1912–29, died 1936.

[48] 4 *Hansard* 188 (25 May 1908) 811–12.

He himself had gone in 1907, strongly prejudiced against it, and had been converted by the experience.[49] He spelt out what he thought were its advantages and made some points of which much was to be heard in the future.

1. Invalidity pensions were given when the workman needed them, not at some arbitrary age.
2. The cost of the whole scheme to the State was less than £3 million per annum. Asquith had sneered at this as a mean contribution; his successor at the Treasury was to think differently.
3. The Germans provided sanatoriums in which disabling diseases were treated at an early stage and prevented from bringing the whole family into destitution.[50]
4. The insurance institutions were directly interested in identifying, and working towards the improvement of, conditions in unhealthy trades.
5. The accumulated pension funds were available for such socially desirable investment as improved housing for the working classes.

There was an even better system coming into operation in Austria, he added, which combined the various German insurance schemes into a single administration and added a benefit for widows and orphans.

Like Beveridge, Cox explained that the German sickness insurance scheme had permitted the use of voluntary societies as an alternative to payment into the State system, and had been careful not to destroy the voluntary bodies. Aschrott had said the same thing in 1885, but during the preoccupation with old age pensions

[49] There was an element of exaggeration here. In May 1907 after his visit to Germany he praised the German system as 'sound in equity as well as economics' and infinitely preferable to forcing the taxpayer to provide other people's pensions. But he still felt that 'the English people would be content when they examined this question more closely, to rely on their natural system of private effort combined with their historical system of Poor Law'. 4 *Hansard* 174 (10 May 1907) 491–2, debate on W. Lever's Old Age Pension Bill.

[50] A Report commissioned by the Medical Department of the Local Government Board had recently emphasized the importance of German insurance arrangements for the early treatment of tuberculosis. See *Report on Sanatoria for Consumption and Certain Other Aspects of the Tuberculosis Question*, by H. Timbrell Bulstrode, MD, *Supplement to Local Government Board, Annual Report of the Medical Officer for 1905–6*, 1907 Cd. 3657 XXVII. 1.

since 1891 little attention seems to have been paid to the German sickness insurance scheme. The point had certainly not been stressed recently until Beveridge drew attention to it.

Finally Cox turned to the widespread notion that compulsory insurance systems required regulation and regimentation of a kind that Englishmen would find intolerable. He reminded the House that English workmen by the thousands submitted to weekly levies on their wages by trade unions. Many even allowed employers to deduct a contribution from their wages in support of the local hospital. 'There was absolutely no reason why the system should not be extended'.[51]

Even as hostile an observer as F. H. Stead called Cox's performance brilliant and incisive. It gained from contrast with the apologetic and half-hearted speech with which Lloyd George had opened the debate, and it easily dominated the proceedings. Since, however, it had been made in support of a wrecking amendment on a matter which the vast majority of MPs wished to see tackled, its immediate political effectiveness was nil. The Opposition leaders were glad to make political capital out of the fact that the government had obviously never considered the advantages of the German system with any care, but they were not prepared to vote for an amendment that would have destroyed the Bill.[52] The only support for Cox came from political mavericks like himself.[53]

The importance of his intervention was not tactical but pedagogic. For listening to his exposition of the advantages of compulsory insurance on the German model was Lloyd George, the recently appointed Chancellor of the Exchequer. He had taken over the task of piloting through the House what had really been Asquith's Bill, but had not previously had much to do with it.[54] His speech indicates that he was ill at ease and on the defensive in the face of

[51] 4 *Hansard* 190 (15 June 1908) 604–9.

[52] See the statements by Chaplin, Balfour, and Walter Long, in 4 *Hansard* 190 (15–16 June 1908) 590–1, 714, 816–22.

[53] The amendment was seconded by the Tory frondeur Lord Robert Cecil. It was lost by 29 to 417 votes.

[54] Campbell-Bannerman's resignation in Apr. 1908 had led to Asquith's appointment as Prime Minister. Lloyd George, who had been President of the Board of Trade, succeeded him as Chancellor of the Exchequer. Until then he had not been a member of the Cabinet Committee on Old Age Pensions. There is no indication in the Asquith Papers, the Lloyd George Papers, or the Treasury Papers that he had taken any personal interest in the making of pensions policy, in contrast to Haldane for instance.

the many criticisms that had already been made.[55] He defended it as an admittedly inadequate first step, but was clearly not keen to see the particular principles on which the Bill had been constructed become the basis of future policy. Instead he gave notice that he would greatly prefer in future to use public funds for the support of those who were not yet past work, rather than to add more generous provisions for the old.

The old man has to bear his own burden, while in the case of a young man who is broken down, and who has a wife and family to maintain, the suffering is increased and multiplied to that extent. These problems of the sick, of the infirm, of the men who cannot find means of earning a livelihood . . . who are out of work through no fault of their own . . . are problems with which it is the business of the State to deal; they are problems which the State has neglected too long.[56]

For the moment he was merely concerned to ward off demands for the lowering of the pensionable age to 65 and for the removal of the various disqualifications that had been written into the Bill. There are no grounds for thinking that he had a policy along the lines that he was indicating. His attitude to contributory schemes was at this stage entirely negative, and he was no better briefed than his predecessors on what was being done in Germany.[57]

Lloyd George always found it easier to pick up knowledge by ear than from the printed page. While sitting on the front bench listening to Cox, he was learning fast. On the second day of the

---

[55] According to *The Times* that morning (15 June 1908) the Bill 'shows no sign of having been framed with any particular consideration of the great issues involved, but on the contrary bears every appearance of having been hastily flung together with a contemptuous dismissal of all alternative proposals as impracticable. It has no definite principle of any kind . . . It must render it extremely difficult if not impossible for the country to revert to any scheme based upon scientific and economic principle.' But in other quarters there were loud complaints at the restrictive nature of its provisions.

[56] 4 *Hansard* (15 June 1908) 585.

[57] He thought that the German insurance scheme included unemployment benefits. The House had, however, recently had a memo presented to it on old age pensions in New Zealand and on the German scheme of insurance against invalidity and old age. The German section contained a short description of the administrative machinery and some basic figures of numbers and expenditure since the previous publication in 1899. Lloyd George used it to show that the British scheme involved a far greater expenditure of public funds: 4 *Hansard* (15 June 1908) 574; *Memo on the Old Age Pensions Scheme in Force in New Zealand and the Scheme of Insurance against Invalidity and Old Age in Force in the German Empire—Ordered 1st June 1908*, 1908 (159) LXXXVIII. 391.

debate he announced that his total rejection of any contributory system on the previous day applied only to old age pensions, and that a contributory system for infirmity or sickness was 'a totally different thing', on whose merits or demerits he had never expressed himself. Asquith on winding up the debate followed the Chancellor's lead in keeping future options open, but with a marked lack of enthusiasm on his part. Indeed he felt it necessary to add to his defence of the non-contributory principle of the present Bill a strong attack on the German system, specifically including a reference to the provision against sickness as well as old age.

The Member for Preston knows a great deal about many things; but . . . there is one subject in regard to which his knowledge is in need of improvement, and that . . . is the character, the disposition, the habits and the motives of the average British citizen. His argument . . . was founded on his observation of the German system . . . The German system has great merits, though I think in some respects they have been much exaggerated, but it could not be transplanted here, for one simple and sufficient reason—that it is founded on the two pillars of inquisition and compulsion.

When the Bill was in committee the government once again had to fight off an amendment in favour of contributory pensions. When the issue was raised yet again on the Third Reading, Charles Masterman weighed in with a sweeping condemnation of German insurance, little guessing that he would soon be assisting the Chancellor to construct a scheme on very similar lines.[58]

But for Lloyd George the Second Reading debate had been decisive, and he was careful to condemn insurance schemes only in connection with the particular problems of old age to which this Bill addressed itself. Indeed his experience of piloting the measure through the committee stage brought home to him the dangers of a government policy that consisted of handing out free grants in response to political pressure. In 1911 he was repeatedly to refer to that experience. He claimed to have added up the total cost of the various amendments that he had been urged to accept. According to Lloyd George these came to £62 million, compared with the £6–7 million for which provision had been made and the £200 million that constituted the entire public revenue. It was to this that

[58]   4 *Hansard* 190 (16 June 1908) 736, 826–7, 1763; ibid. 192 (9 July 1908) 142.

in retrospect he ascribed his interest in contributory insurance.[59]

In the face of this spate of demands the government refused with one solitary exception[60] any concession that would have saddled it with further immediate expenditure. This was achieved, however, at the expense of mortgaging the future. It experienced the greatest difficulty in defending its proposal to disqualify all applicants for a pension who had been on poor relief subsequent to 1 January 1908. Nor is that surprising, since this extraordinary clause penalized the very people whom the old age pensions advocates were most concerned to help, i.e. the respectable poor who had been forced by advancing age to resort to the Poor Law. The government finally gave way and agreed to allow the clause to lapse by the end of 1910. This concession cost no money for the present but piled on the liabilities for the future.[61]

The government's explicit statement that the Act constituted merely a first step, limited for the moment by the resources available, created the assumption that more of the same kind would be forthcoming after a while. The TUC wasted no time in thanking the government for what it had provided, but insisted that the Act would not be satisfactory until a 5s. pension was given to all men and women unconditionally at 60. The Annual Conference of the Labour Party did the same, and added a demand for infirmity pensions irrespective of age.[62] The NCOL concentrated in the short term on the immediate removal of the pauper disqualification. When it was disbanded in 1909 its work was in effect taken over by the Labour Party, whose commitment to the full pensions programme was assured. The NCOL's secretary, Frederick Rogers, who had acquired a well-founded belief in the squeezability of the Liberal ministers, thought that the Act was so framed and based that the NCOL's further demands would grow naturally out of it, 'if those who have been a potent force in causing it to be passed, I mean the

---

[59] H. N. Bunbury (ed.), *Lloyd George's Ambulance Wagon: The Memoirs of W. J. Braithwaite C.B. 1911–1912* (1957), p. 71.

[60] It removed the provision whereby married couples living together received less than the full pension per head.

[61] It was assumed that the action to be taken after the Report of the Royal Commission on the Poor Law, which was then sitting, would provide an opportunity of dealing with this matter as part of a general reorganization.

[62] TUC, *Proceedings*, 1908, pp. 57, 194. *The Times*, 30 Jan. 1909. Both resolutions are quoted in Williams, *Development of Old Age Pensions*, p. 242 n. 1, 246 n. 3.

Labour Party, continue alert and awake to future developments'.[63]

In view of the government's handling of the issue and of the political conditions under which it lived, old age pensions were unfinished business, and promised to be most expensive unfinished business, when Parliament adjourned in 1908 for the summer recess.

For the Chancellor of the Exchequer the immediate problem was to find some way of dealing with demands for the indiscriminate reduction of the pensions age. To limit any further benefits to those who were prevented from working by infirmity might be one way of doing that. Lloyd George had learnt enough to wish to see the German administration of invalidity pensions at first hand, and in August 1908 he set out for a working holiday in Germany, combining the pleasures of a motor tour with an inspection of the national insurance system. In Berlin he was entertained by Bethmann-Hollweg, soon to be Imperial Chancellor, but then Minister of the Interior responsible for the insurance system, and he was shown over the Central Insurance Office. He spoke on the burning issue of naval disarmament at a banquet in Hamburg, thereby causing some anxiety in London, before embarking on a German boat for his return to England.[64]

He talked to the press on the boat-train between Southampton and London.

I never realised before on what a gigantic scale the German pension system is conducted. Nor had I any idea how successfully it works. I had read much about it, but no amount of study at home . . . can convey to the mind a clear idea of all that state insurance means to Germany . . . It touches the

---

[63] *Report of the Proceedings at a Public Presentation made to Mr. Frederick Rogers at Browning Hall on November 5 1909*, qd. ibid. p. 246 n. 2; for Roger's views of the ministers, see ibid., p. 215.

[64] Lloyd George's host was Charles Henry, a wealthy Liberal MP, and he was also accompanied by Harold Spender, the radical journalist, whose biography of Lloyd George, *The Prime Minister* (1920), ch. 12, describes the journey. Spender's assertion that 'Lloyd George had already publicly promised to round off the British pension system by a general scheme of national insurance' (p. 155) is presumably an inaccurate reference to the speech of 15 June 1908 quoted on p. 146 above. The book is of course a blatant piece of myth-making and includes endearing passages such as the following. 'After a long day spent in the Central Insurance Office at Berlin, the men who went round with us were very enthusiastic. "He grasps the system more rapidly than any student we have ever had." Mr. Lloyd George indeed made a very exhaustive study of the German system' (p. 164). The passage provoked Braithwaite to some acid comments in his memoirs: see Bunbury, *Lloyd Geroge's Ambulance Wagon*, p. 82.

great mass of German people in well-nigh every walk of life. Old-age pensions form but a comparatively small part of the system. Does the German worker fall ill? State insurance comes to his aid. Is he permanently invalided from work? Again he gets a regular grant whether he has reached the pension age or not.[65]

Lloyd George appears to have gone to Germany to find out about infirmity pensions but discovered during his visit that the German old age and invalidity scheme presupposed the existence of a scheme of sickness insurance, using its machinery and relying on it to make provision for the first thirteen weeks.[66] Although he continued to refer to his plans as concerned with pensions, the scope of the German scheme, its connection with provisions both financial and medical in times of sickness, had obviously enlarged his ambitions. He spoke enthusiastically to the press of the provision of hospitals and sanatoriums out of the insurance funds, and of the plans for health education which German insurance committees were planning to undertake.

The other points that he particularly stressed were aimed at smoothing the political path. 'The thing that impressed me most', he explained, 'was the general satisfaction expressed by every class. Employers assured me it made for efficiency. Socialist workmen said they welcomed it. The official classes spoke well of it.' The trade unionists even wanted to see the workers' contributions increased for the sake of higher benefits and were convinced that insurance had raised the general standard of life and comfort in Germany. 'I wish some of our trade union friends would study the question on the spot.' He was also quick to repudiate the view that universal compulsion had undermined voluntary effort, and briskly asserted the opposite: 'All kinds of things are done to supplement the sick and invalidity grant.' Finally, he turned to the considerations that were bound to weigh heavily on a Chancellor of the Exchequer who had just accepted a large and growing commitment to the old age pensioners:

The surprising thing is that all this elaborate and wonderful machinery for insuring the workers against sickness, invalidity and old age only costs the

[65] *Daily News*, 27 Aug. 1908.
[66] See Gilbert, *Evolution of National Insurance*, pp. 231–2. There is evidence that even in Oct.–Nov. 1908 those to whom Lloyd George spoke of his plans thought of them as being for infirmity pensions. George Allardice, Baron Riddell, *More Pages from My Diary 1908–1914* (1934), p. 6; Webb, *Our Partnership*, pp. 417, 418.

German exchequer some £2½ million a year. These £2½ million are supplemented by about £31½ million contribued by employers and workmen.[67]

There were plans to increase this total to £53 million by adding widows' and orphans' pensions and generally widening the range of the insured population, but even then the State contribution was not intended to exceed £5 million.

Although he had declared himself 'profoundly impressed with German methods', he decided to commission studies of the Belgian and Austrian pensions systems also. Investigators were despatched within a few weeks and reports on the two countries were available by December.[68] They did nothing to influence subsequent events.

[67] *Daily News*, 27 Aug. 1908.
[68] P. A. Chance, *Report upon the Provision Made in Belgium for Old Age Pensions, Infirmity, Sickness and Unemployment*, Dec. 1908, A. F. Whyte, *Report on the System of Workmen's Insurance in Austria-Hungary*, Nov. 1908, both in LPES, Braithwaite Papers, II. 1. Chance was sent to Belgium around 12 Sept., Whyte left for Austria on 26 Oct.: see PRO, T 12/29/747; T 12/29/814.

10

A New Strategy for the Unemployed

LLOYD George's visit to Germany attracted favourable comment from the veteran journalist W. T. Stead. 'As might have been expected,' he wrote in a leading article on the Chancellor's visit, 'he has come back awe-struck at the marvellous scientific thoroughness of the German system.'[1] In 1905 Stead himself had vainly tried to interest the public in the subject which he regarded as one of the 'coming questions' of the day.[2] 'The question of questions', he now wrote,

is whether thirteen million British workingmen will consent to contribute to such a national system of insurance . . . They certainly will not until they have satisfied themselves that they cannot compel the State to make any further non-contributory payments, and until they can be convinced that it is only by such a contributory system that they can adequately deal with the question of non-employment.[3]

It was no red herring that Stead was dragging across the path of contributory insurance when he tied it so closely to the unemployment problem. For that was the quarter where the political storm clouds were now gathering. In mid-August Churchill, as President of the Board of Trade, had warned the Cabinet that the unemployment figures were disquieting and would become worse during the course of the winter.[4] That month the unemployment

---

[1] *Review of Reviews*, 38. 225 (1908), 206.

[2] He had commissioned an article, 'The Insurance of the Working Classes in Germany', from Percy Ashley, a Board of Trade official, and persuaded Sir John Gorst, the Conservative MP famous for his advocacy of social reform, to sponsor it. It was published in the series 'Coming Men on Coming Questions' in the *Review of Reviews*, July 1905, and the whole series was republished in book form just before the general election. A proof copy of this article is the first item in the file that the Treasury accumulated and passed to W. J. Braithwaite in Dec. 1910: LPES, Braithwaite Papers II. 1. 1.

[3] *Review of Reviews*, 38. 225 (Sept. 1908), 206.

[4] Cabinet Memo by Churchill, 8 Aug. 1908, circulated 17 Aug., qd. in Churchill, *Winston S. Churchill*, ii. *Companion*, pt. 2, p. 834.

returns from the trade unions reached 8.5 per cent, the highest figure since 1893, and they continued to rise.[5]

The government was ill prepared to take a suitable initiative in this situation, for it had allowed itself to be boxed in by popular pressure in ways that were reminiscent of its position *vis-à-vis* old age pensions in 1906–7. Like the plight of the aged, that of the unemployed made a strong appeal both to organized labour and to the humanitarian sentiments found widely diffused in English political culture and particularly strong among those committed to a democratic Liberalism. In this instance organized labour itself was under pressure from the small but energetic groups of the Marxist Social Democratic Federation, who saw in unemployment the breakdown of capitalism and in the unemployed the shock troops of revolution. The result had been the creation of a political alliance round the problem of the unemployed which operated both in the House of Commons and, by means of demonstrations, outside. It was an alliance that had already forced a reluctant Conservative Cabinet in 1905 to enact its Unemployed Workmen's Act.

That Act created distress committees representing sanitary authorities, Poor Law authorities, and local charitable bodies, which were compulsory in London and the larger provincial centres, optional elsewhere. These were to organize public relief works for the temporarily unemployed outside the deterrent aegis of the Poor Law. The policy had been pioneered in London, where it was to be under the co-ordinating umbrella of a Central Unemployed Committee. The administrative costs of the scheme could be paid for out of the rates, but after some initial disagreement the Cabinet had refused to permit the public works themselves to be financed in this way. It regarded distress committees rather as a more effective way of organizing the use of voluntary contributions of the kind raised in periods of distress by Lord Mayor's Funds and similar appeals. Yet the inadequacy of such voluntary finance was obvious, and from the beginning demands for rate-financed public works had been loud and clear. The Unemployed Workmen's Act had all the hallmarks that were soon to characterize the Old Age Pensions Act. It was a well-

---

[5] Figures from Board of Trade, *Seventh Abstract of Labour Statistics*, 1901 Cd. 495 LXXIII; idem, *Seventeenth Abstract of Labour Statistics*, 1914–16 Cd. 7733 LXI.

intentioned gesture to deal with an acknowledged evil, but one that had been extracted from a reluctant government anxious to limit the commitment on the public funds. It comprised a bundle of contradictions that it was impossible to justify in detail.

The Liberals who came into office shortly afterwards were committed to amending the Act, but they remained studiously vague in the face of Labour demands. Basically they were playing for time, and in July 1906 decided to postpone any action until the appearance of a Report of a Royal Commission then sitting. That body had been set up late in 1905 to investigate the entire operation of the Poor Law and the other means for meeting distress due to unemployment, and it provided a classic excuse for delay. No one knew how long it would be sitting. On the other hand, the Labour MPs elected in strength to the new Parliament knew what they wanted, namely the provision of public works paid for out of public funds. Their Unemployed Workmen's Bill was the result of close liaison with the trade unions. It was introduced by Ramsey MacDonald in July 1907 and proposed the establishment of unemployment committees in counties and county boroughs, and a central authority with its own expert staff. If a local committee designated an area as suffering from exceptional unemployment, the government was to be obliged to finance emergency schemes out of the Exchequer. Under Clause 3 of the Bill the local authority had a duty to supply anybody registered as unemployed with work or maintenance. The Right-to-Work Bill, as it was popularly called, aimed therefore at removing the hardship caused by unemployment by means of extensive provision of funds out of taxation and by creating employment whose effect on the normal labour market was not too carefully considered.[6]

The Bill made no progress in the Commons when first introduced, but when reintroduced in March 1908 on behalf of the Labour Party by a sympathetic Liberal back-bencher it could not be so lightly brushed aside. It embodied a clear-cut policy at a time when the government had none. No one held a brief for the existing Act, which had been a temporary expedient due to lapse in 1908 unless renewed. In the face of this challenge the Cabinet was divided. Asquith, then acting Prime Minister, regarded the right to work as quite inadmissible but felt that it would not look good if nothing

[6] For details, see José Harris, *Unemployment and Politics* (Oxford 1972), pp. 241–3.

was done at all. Other ministers also felt, in Sidney Buxton's phrase, that if they were to oppose the Bill they ought at least to have an alternative. On the other hand, John Burns, who had the departmental responsibility at the Local Government Board, was content to wait for the impending Report of the Royal Commission, and he got his way. The Labour Bill was defeated on the Second Reading by 267 to 118. Sixty-five Liberals had voted for it, including such able and forthright back-benchers as Charles Masterman.

Lloyd George, who had wanted Asquith to take over responsibility from Burns and had been overridden, was conspicuously absent from the House.[7] Even under favourable conditions the government's position was hardly tenable for long. With rapidly worsening unemployment Asquith thought it necessary in September to send an open letter to the Liberal candidate at a by-election in Newcastle, where shipbuilding had been seriously affected, promising 'the early presentation of practical legislative proposals'.[8] The government was bound to have to make major concessions to the Labour demands, unless it could quickly take the initiative along other lines.

After all the Labour Bill, sweeping though it was, was no more so than the Old Age Pensions Bill sponsored by the NCOL and modelled on Charles Booth's proposals. Its advocates had a case whose strength must not be underestimated merely because things ultimately did not go their way. The normal workman temporarily thrown out of employment through no fault of his own had been regarded as a person to be protected from the stigma of the Poor Law for even longer than the respectable aged poor. Since 1886 it had been assumed that this could be done, if the municipal authority made itself responsible for public relief works in times of exceptional distress. The difficulty had been that such public works were an expensive form of investment and not easy to pay for through the normal channels of loan finance. Yet if they were to be provided on the scale necessary, and regarded as relief rather than investment, where was the money to come from? By 1908 it was

---

[7] Harris, *Unemployment and Politics*, pp. 243–4. K. D. Brown, *Labour and Unemployment 1900–1914* (Newton Abbot, 1971), p. 90. Burns's Diary for 11. Mar. 1908 does not support Brown's statement, however, that Lloyd George had been in favour of the Labour Bill: BL, Add. MSS 46326.

[8] Harris, *Unemployment and Politics*, p. 274.

obvious that voluntary relief funds were inadequate and that even the local ratepayers were not able to shoulder all the burden. Unemployment even more than aged pauperism tended to be greatest in the localities least able to pay for its relief. Like aged pauperism it seemed to call for treatment on a national scale out of general taxation. That was the object of the Labour Party Bill. It was constructed on the same basic principles that had been accepted for old age pensions in 1908, that of taking a deserving group of the needy out of the Poor Law and making provision for them by grants out of general taxation.

Like the old age pensions agitation, the so-called Right-to-Work movement was easy to combine with demands for radical policies of taxation, such as a progressive income tax and land taxes, which seemed to those who advocated them to have vast potential for the redistribution of wealth. This was a policy of social reform which provided the common ground on which the Labour Party and humanitarian Liberals could co-operate.[9] Its pressure had been irresistible over old age pensions. There was every likelihood that it would be equally irresistible over unemployment.

On 14 October Burns was outvoted in the Cabinet, and a combined Cabinet Committee on Unemployment set up. Masterman, who had become Burns's Under-secretary at the Local Government Board, was already having confidential discussions with Arthur Henderson, the secretary of the Labour Party. Henderson was urging the government to take the plunge and use the rates to pay the wages of men on public relief works, adding that he was having the greatest difficulty in restraining his supporters. But at a crucial Cabinet meeting in the following week Burns once more succeeded in preventing what he rightly regarded as an open-ended concession. Those ministers including Churchill, who were prepared to yield to the Labour Party demands in the face of the difficult economic situation, were outvoted. The Treasury merely increased the money available for loans to public authorities.[10]

More important in the long run than Burns's stolid resistance

---

[9] H. V. Emy, *Liberals, Radicals and Social Politics 1892–1914* (Cambridge, 1973); A. Offer, *Property and Politics 1870–1914* (Cambridge, 1981), pt. 5.

[10] Lucy Masterman, *C. F. G. Masterman* (1939), pp. 110–12. Harris, *Unemployment and Politics*, pp. 274–5. Burns, who called the Labour proposals the Right-to-Shirk Bill, was congratulating himself in December on having 'stemmed the tide of Pauperisation, let loose by that King of Cadgers, K[eir] H[ardy] MP': Diary, 4 Dec. 1908, BL, Burns Papers Add. MSS 46326.

were the other initiatives that had been taken during the second half of 1908, for it was these that were to provide the government with a policy of its own. This policy consisted of three components, a national system of labour exchanges to organize the labour market, State-subsidized unemployment insurance for those trades most exposed to fluctuations, and the creation of central funds to promote the development of national resources.[11]

The minister responsible for the first two of these was Winston Churchill, who had been appointed President of the Board of Trade in April. He brought to his task a restless energy and a mind recently influenced by some of the leading experts in the field of social reform. One of his first acts in office was to brief himself on the theory of labour exchanges. In practice this meant the writings of William Beveridge, the indefatigable advocate of these institutions. By early July Churchill had decided to embark on a labour exchange policy. Beveridge, to whom he had first been introduced by the Webbs in March, and who had been working as a freelance expert for the Board of Trade since the previous year, was offered a permanent post.[12]

Churchill's new adviser was a convinced opponent of public relief works. The Labour Party's policy rested ultimately on the assumption that these were an effective means of helping the men whom the Labour Party and the trade union movement were championing, the workers normally in employment but temporarily displaced by a trade depression. Beveridge's membership of the London Central Unemployed Committee, the body responsible for putting the Unemployed Workmen's Act into effect, had given him the opportunity to study the operation of public relief works in practice. It had convinced him that such schemes did not in fact serve the kind of working man for whom they were intended, and that it was misguided to expect them to do so. As long as there was a pool of chronically under-employed casual labourers, these would be the principal clients of any scheme of public relief works. Yet under-employment could not be remedied by the provision of temporary work, only by the more efficient organization of the labour market through a network of labour exchanges.

By 1907, when the Labour Party produced its first Right-to-Work Bill, Beveridge was arguing that it was essential to distinguish

[11] Harris, *Unemployment and Politics*, p. 278.
[12] W. H. Beveridge, *Power and Influence*, (1953), pp. 64, 66–9.

between remedies for unemployment on the one hand and the relief of distress on the other. To combine these two objects, as they were being combined in public relief works, was to create confusion. The real remedies for unemployment were to be found elsewhere. One was to reduce to the minimum the necessary 'reserve army of labour' by the more efficient organization of the labour market. Another was to prevent the abuse of cheap juvenile labour in dead-end jobs, which created a constant supply of 'youths so brainless and demoralised as to be almost unemployable'. To these should be added other efforts of this kind aiming at a more purposeful regulation of industrial life. Turning to the relief of distress, he argued that it was not helped by the duplication of the work of the Poor Law authorities through the creation of more lenient distress committees. He wanted to see a single distress authority able to classify those who came to it and to treat them 'according to their need'.[13]

Originally Beveridge's interest had focused on the problem of casual labour, and on the use of labour exchanges for dovetailing jobs and rationalizing the practices of employers. He now began to pay closer attention to the problem of relief for the unemployed, which he regarded as a distinct and separate matter altogether. By the end of July 1907 he was arguing that for the normal workman the most suitable form of relief was a simple money payment and that the system of mutual insurance provided by the trade unions did this in the cheapest and most effective way. Mutual insurance of this kind depended, however, on two prior conditions, which the trade unions had been able to ensure for their members, and without which no extension of unemployment insurance by the community was feasible. The first was steady employment at wages which made regular contributions possible. Casual earnings and the erratic way of life that they produced were in his opinion now a greater obstacle to this than low wages. The second was some way of ensuring that the claimant took a job as soon as one became available. The trade unions had their house-of-call, at which claimants had to sign on daily and to which vacancies within the trade were more or less systematically reported. This was what a public labour exchange could provide for the community as a whole. Although Beveridge had originally advocated a system of

---

[13] *Morning Post*, 6 July, 10 July 1907. See also the subsequent criticism of the Labour Party policy in *Morning Post*, 20 Jan., 14 Mar. 1908.

public labour exchanges for the purpose of reducing the amount of casual employment, he now recognized that it was also the essential prerequisite for a workable system of unemployment insurance.[14]

For the passionate advocate of labour exchanges this was a most satisfactory conclusion to have reached. Even more pleasing was his discovery that a German committee of inquiry into unemployment insurance had said the same thing less than a year before. When he read the report issued by the German Imperial Statistical Office and found there his own insistence on labour exchanges as a prerequisite for unemployment insurance, he was 'quite overcome'. Recording his discovery on 22 August 1907, he added: 'If the Germans and I can understand one another at all our unanimity will be quite wonderful. It really *is* rather encouraging.'[15] Within a few days he had set out for Germany to inspect both the well-established German labour exchanges and the system of social insurance.

His impressions were set down shortly in three articles published in the *Morning Post* and at greater length in a memorandum that he submitted to the Royal Commission on the Poor Laws as a supplement to the detailed exposition of his views that he had presented already before his German tour. The combined effect of these documents and his handling of the questions which the Commissioners put to him was overwhelming. The Commissioners, who disagreed on so many issues, were unanimous on the need for a national system of labour exchanges.[16]

It was, however, not quite in this form that Beveridge's views were to be given widespread publicity in the months immediately following. He was at the time a protégé of Sidney and Beatrice Webb, whom he had interested in his ideas and whom he saw continually from December 1906 onwards. The Webbs were hammering out a policy for the unemployed to be presented by Beatrice to the Royal Commission, of which she was a member. They regarded unemployment insurance as of very marginal

[14] 'Trade Unions and Unemployment: A great System of Insurance', *Morning Post*, 20 July 1907; 'Insurance against Unemployment: The Possibility and Conditions of its Extension', *Morning Post*, 23 July 1907.

[15] Beveridge, *Power and Influence*, p. 61. The report referred to was Kaiserliches Statistisches Amt, *Die bestehenden Einrichtungen zur Versicherung gegen die Folgen der Arbeitslosigkeit im Ausland und im deutschen Reich* (3 vols.; Berlin, 1906).

[16] 'Labour Exchanges in Germany', *Morning Post*, 5 Oct., 5 Nov., 13 Nov. 1907. *RC on the Poor Laws, Mins. of Ev.*, QQ 77831–8370, 1910 Cd. 5066, XLVIII; *Majority Report*, pp. 396–405, *Minority Report*, pp. 1180–9, 1909 Cd. 4499, XXXVII.

importance but saw labour exchanges as a valuable tool in their wider strategy of government intervention and regulation of the labour market. They believed that all job vacancies should be registered compulsorily, and so went considerably further than Beveridge, whose focus of interest did not really coincide with theirs. But Beveridge was happy to have labour exchanges 'boomed by an arch-strategist like Sidney Webb', even if the proposals were being put out in the form that suited the Webbs. Like him they were insisting on labour exchanges as part of the necessary organization of normal economic life at a time when these were still being regarded primarily as part of the machinery of distress committees and relief schemes. That was the point that mattered most to Beveridge at the time.

It was the Webbs who introduced these proposals to Balfour and to the leading members of the Labour Party; it was they who arranged for the Christian Social Union to bring out a pamphlet on the same lines. Above all it was they who re-established close contact with Winston Churchill, when they met him on 10 February 1908 at Haldane's house, and thereafter supplied him with their ideas. 'He had swallowed whole Sidney's scheme for boy labour and unemployment and had even dished it up in an article in *The Nation* the week before', Beatrice wrote triumphantly in her diary for 11 March. It was the day on which she gave a dinner for Churchill and introduced Beveridge to him.[17]

The article mentioned by Beatrice had appeared in *The Nation* on 7 March in the form of a letter to the editor, congratulating him on the first anniversary of the founding of this Radical, social-reform-orientated paper. Entitled 'The Untrodden Field in Politics', it signalled Churchill's emergence as a social reformer. Although still an Under-Secretary of State at the Colonial Office, he was earmarked for promotion to a Cabinet post in the reorganization that was due to occur on Campbell-Bannerman's impending retirement. His frequent contact with the Webbs and obvious willingness to be coached by them is easily understandable under the circumstances. He had turned his attention to these domestic matters first in December 1907, as a long African tour drew to an end and he began to contemplate his return to active politics after a rest of more than six months. He had been looking for a mentor

---

[17] Beveridge, *Power and Influence*, pp. 61–7; Webb, *Our Partnership*, pp. 399–404.

and the Webbs gave him just what he needed. His debt to them is plainly indicated by the language of his letter to *The Nation*. There he suggested establishing 'a Minimum Standard below which competition cannot be allowed but above which it may freely continue', to be achieved by a policy of remedying the patent inadequacy of existing social machinery. The evil to be removed was lack of organization in many areas of modern life, and those to which he specifically referred were casual labour and the misdirection of juveniles, what contemporaries were calling the problem of boy labour. Beyond this were vaguer references to a list of items drawn from the Webbs' proposals and topped off with old age pensions.[18]

Within a few days he was corresponding with Asquith about his political future as a possible president of the Local Government Board and sketching the same policy of the Minimum Standard: labour exchanges, boy labour, curative treatment of the unemployables, short-time working in seasonal and cyclical unemployment, and counter-cyclical public works programmes. 'Underneath, though not in substitution for the immense disjointed fabric of social safeguards and insurances which has grown up by itself in England, there must be spread—at a lower level—a sort of Germanised network of state intervention and regulation', was how he summed up his proposals.[19]

This is a remarkable passage and unlike the specific proposals just mentioned it owed little to the Webbs. It is interesting to note how, in his correspondence with Asquith, Churchill was combining the suggestions that he had taken from the Webbs with ideas that he had been turning over in his mind during his African tour, before he had come under their influence. He had set out on his voyage with his luggage well stocked with books on socialism, 'to see what the Socialist case really is', and he appears to have applied himself

---

[18] W. S. Churchill, 'The Untrodden Field in Politics', *The Nation*, 7 Mar. 1908, 812–13.

[19] W. S. Churchill to H. H. Asquith, 14 Mar. 1908, qd. in Churchill, *Winston S. Churchill*, ii. *Companion*, pt. 2, pp. 754–6. The letter has often been regarded as evidence of a reluctance to accept the Local Government Board. My reading of the letter is similar to that of Harris, *Unemployment and Politics*, p. 265, that Churchill was magnifying the arduousness of the office in whose work he was obviously very interested, in order to persuade Asquith to offer it to him with the rank of a Secretary of State. When Asquith decided after all to retain John Burns at the Local Government Board and offered Churchill the Board of Trade, he did in fact arrange for him to obtain the rank of a Secretary of State.

to his reading, for while in Africa he was holding forth on Liberal and Conservative views of socialism.[20]

Just what he said to his fellow passengers on the subject was not recorded, but two letters written at the time reveal an acquaintance with the German version of State socialism and an attempt to adapt what he may well have regarded as a Conservative response to the needs and priorities of a Liberal regime such as that of Britain. Security against the awful uncertainties of their lives he considered to be the main need of the working classes and the one thing that the democratic electorate would be certain to insist on. In England, he added, such security existed only for those able to subscribe to the voluntary organizations of mutual help. The flexibility, cheapness, and spontaneity of voluntary bodies was offset by their failure to meet the needs of all the population, and in this respect the very different system of State-provided security created in Germany had an enormous advantage. 'If we were able to underpin the whole existing social security apparatus with a foundation of comparatively low-grade state safeguards, we should . . . combine the greatest merits both of the English and of the German system.'[21] That was written in January, and in March his letter to Asquith showed him

[20] Henry Pelling, *Winston Churchill* (1974) p. 105, quoting A. G. Gardiner *Prophets, Priests and Kings* (new edn., 1924), p. 228, and F. A. Dickinson, *Lake Victoria to Khartoum* (1910), p. 82. Churchill's account with Hatchard's, his bookseller, records the purchase on 7 Aug. 1907 of seven books on socialism, including John Rae, *Contemporary Socialism* (1901), with its detailed account of the German academic socialists who had influenced Bismarck: Churchill Coll. Camb., Chartwell Papers, 1/85/8, 9. The books, which include Marx's *Capital* and the *Fabian Essays*, are somewhat theoretical in their approach; while it is not impossible that he may also have read a more direct description, such as Dawson's *Bismarck and State Socialism*, there is certainly no evidence to suggest it.

[21] W. S. Churchill to A. Wilson Fox, 4 Jan. 1908, qd. in Churchill, *Winston S. Churchill*, ii. *Companion*, pt. 2, p. 759. See also his letter to J. A. Spender, editor of the *Westminster Gazette*, qd. in Wilson Harris, *J. A. Spender* (1946), pp. 80–1. The suggestion in Pelling, *Winston Churchill*, p. 106, that he probably obtained the idea of a comparison with Germany from reading Beveridge's articles published in the *Morning Post* between 12 and 20 Sept. 1907 is not very likely. Churchill was at the time attending the French army manœuvres, and motoring to Venice and then to Vienna before embarking on his voyage. If despite such distractions he had read the articles, which were signed, and been impressed enough to have used them as the basis for ideas in Jan. 1908, it is unlikely that he would not have mentioned this to Beveridge, when he met him in Mar. 1908 at the Webbs, especially as the talk was very largely 'shop'. Beveridge wrote a detailed description of the meeting to his mother on the following day. It was only after he had met Beveridge in Mar. that Churchill placed an order for the *Morning Post* with his newsagent: Churchill Coll. Camb., Chartwell Papers, 1/85/87; LPES, Beveridge Papers II. b. 8.

still attracted by combining British voluntary initiative with State provision modelled on the German precedent.

When it is remembered how close the political relationship between Churchill and Lloyd George was soon to become, it is not surprising that it has commonly been assumed that the impetus for a British national insurance policy had originally come from Churchill, and that it was he who gave Lloyd George the idea of looking at German insurance.[22] Yet the evidence points the other way. As has already been demonstrated, Lloyd George had a more than adequate incentive of his own and had received a most explicit pointer from Harold Cox in the direction of German invalidity insurance. Churchill, on the other hand, was to show no interest in proposals for dealing with unemployment by means of insurance until after the Chancellor of the Exchequer had announced his conversion to an insurance policy.

What his appointment as President of the Board of Trade did was to give him an opportunity to pursue his interest in labour exchanges. When he had to seek re-election to his seat as MP for North-west Manchester on taking office, his manifesto signalled an intention to consider the question of unemployment in relation to the decasualization of labour.[23] He failed to be returned and it was some time before he found a seat at Dundee, but by the beginning of July he was firmly enough in office to contemplate putting his ideas into effect. Beveridge explained to his mother that the work for which he was being recruited to the Board of Trade would be 'Labour Exchanges and the rest of the unemployed problem from the side of the industrial organisation rather than relief'.[24] This in itself is an indication that insurance formed at that stage no part of the new policy, for in Beveridge's mind, as he had specifically stated in his *Morning Post* articles, unemployment insurance belonged to the sphere of relief.[25]

This interpretation is borne out by Churchill's response to the detailed memorandum on labour exchanges that Beveridge produced at his request. Beveridge had gone into the subject from every angle including their use as an adjunct to unemployment insurance. But when Churchill circulated the memorandum among the senior

---

[22] e.g. Gilbert, *Evolution of National Insurance*, p. 68.
[23] R. R. James (ed.), *Winston S. Churchill, Complete Speeches* (1974), i. 939–41.
[24] Beveridge, *Power and Influence*, p. 68.
[25] See above, pp. 157.

officials in the Board of Trade, he was strongly advised to omit all reference to unemployment insurance on the ground that the question of such insurance had not so far been raised, and that it was a mistake to suggest that 'the considerable sums asked for Labour Exchanges are to be followed by a demand for incomparably larger amounts for insurance against unemployment'. Churchill followed this advice and when he converted Beveridge's memorandum into one of his own for wider circulation he omitted all reference to insurance.[26] Then in October there was a sudden change of course. What had been considered out of the question in July had now become acceptable, and Llewellyn Smith, assisted by Beveridge, was told to draw up a scheme for insurance against unemployment. The following month Churchill produced a revised memorandum in which a proposal for unemployment insurance was linked to one for labour exchanges, just as Beveridge had originally suggested, and it was in that form that the project was submitted to the Cabinet in December.[27]

By the autumn of 1908 the two ministers were working closely together to prepare the ground for an insurance policy, but it is a significant pointer to the real origin of the new departure that, when in October Lloyd George invited the Webbs to breakfast to discuss his insurance scheme, the other non-official guest was Harold Cox. The Webbs did not at all approve of insurance against invalidity and they indicated this so firmly that Haldane, who was also present, had to step in as peacemaker between Lloyd George and them.[28] They were less fundamentally opposed to insurance against unemployment, and were of course firm advocates of labour exchanges. Churchill called upon them to explain the advantages of labour exchanges to a group of prominent Labour MPs at a breakfast at the Board of Trade. The presence of Lloyd George and Masterman, the two other ministers associated with the new policy, indicates that more was at stake than labour exchanges

[26] Confidential Memo on Labour Exchanges, by W. H. Beveridge, July 1908, Memo commenting on Beveridge's Memo, by D. F. Schloss, submitted to A. Wilson Fox, 13 July 1908, PRO, LAB 8/821. Memo by W. S. Churchill, qd. in Churchill, *Winston S. Churchill*, ii. *Companion*, pt. 2, pp. 827–31.

[27] José Harris, *William Beveridge: A Biography* (Oxford, 1977), pp. 169–70; Memo, *Unemployment Insurance: Labour Exchanges*, by W. S. Churchill, 30 Nov. 1908, circulated 11 Dec. 1908, PRO, CAB 37/96/159.

[28] Beatrice Webb's Diary, 16 Oct. 1908, in Webb, *Our Partnership*, p. 417. Churchill joined them after breakfast.

as such.[29] The meeting was part of the essential process of winning over the organized labour movement to the new policy, and was followed almost at once by the decision of the Parliamentary Committee of the TUC to send a delegation to Germany. It was to inquire into the feelings of German trade unionists towards the State system of insurance, and into the working of German labour exchanges.[30]

The TUC delegation found the German labour movement strongly in favour of State insurance as well as labour exchanges. The Board of Trade received a draft copy of its report, which became part of the evidence considered by the Cabinet in December 1908 when it decided in favour of a policy of compulsory insurance.[31]

In an article which Lloyd George's confidant, Harold Spender, wrote on unemployment insurance for the January number of the *Contemporary Review*, the new policy received a public airing.[32] By its condemnation of public relief works and its suggestion that the principles on which German State insurance had been built could be applied to the British unemployment problem, it expounded official thinking with considerable accuracy. The possibility that the Chancellor might under favourable circumstances deal at one stroke with insurance against infirmity, sickness, and unemployment was briefly touched upon, but the purpose of the article was to commend insurance as the answer to the problem of unemployment.

The most authoritative book on unemployment policy in England has come to the conclusion that the question of public

---

[29] Webb, *Our Partnership*, pp. 418–19.

[30] The Parliamentary Labour Party also decided to send two of its leading members to investigate the question of unemployment in Germany with special reference to insurance and labour exchanges. Unlike the trade union delegation they took no notice of any form of insurance apart from the few experiments in municipally sponsored unemployment insurance. They reported that these were 'only in an experimental stage', 'had obvious limitations', and 'could not be recommended for adoption in this country with any confidence'. As might be expected from advocates of the Right-to-Work Bill, they were on the look-out for municipal provision of work, but the bulk of their report dealt with the work of labour exchanges. They were frequently impressed by these and expressed no reservations about them. G. N. Barnes and A. Henderson, *Unemployment in Germany: A Report of an Inquiry into the Methods Adopted in Germany for Dealing with Unemployment, Presented to the Labour Party* (n.d. [1908]).

[31] *Workmen's Insurance Systems in Germany:Report of Delegation*, Dec. 1908, PRO, CAB 37/96/169; W. S. Churchill to H. H. Asquith, 29 Dec. 1908, in Churchill, *Winston S. Churchill*, ii. *Companion*, pt. 2, pp. 862–4.

[32] Harold Spender, 'Unemployment Insurance', *Contemporary Review*, 115 (1909), 24–36.

insurance against unemployment scarcely entered into the discussion of social problems before 1907.[33] Yet by the end of 1908 the government had embarked on the policy that was to produce Part 2 of the National Insurance Act of 1911.

Those who had most to do with the making of British unemployment insurance have emphasized that their model was drawn not from abroad, where no satisfactory precedent existed, but from the practice of British trade unions. As the Webbs put it, it was not 'made in Germany'.[34] This is certainly true. Yet the transition from 1907 to 1909 is too important to be ignored in any study of the German precedent in British social reform. For it was no accident that the transition from policies of public relief works to unemployment insurance should have coincided so closely with the similar transition from tax-provided old age pensions to insurance-based infirmity and sickness benefits. These were not two processes but one. Although foreign examples of unemployment insurance, none of which recommended themselves for adoption, had been frequently described, and although at least one senior official at the Board of Trade had considered the form that it might take, 'if it were done at all', it was the shift in the attitude of ministers and their immediate advisers towards the idea of compulsory State-supported insurance that set the subsequent process of policy-making in motion.[35] In that shift the contemplation of the German State insurance schemes and of their advantages played a crucial part.

Yet another connection between the government's unemployment policy and existing German institutions is to be found in the field of labour exchanges, for it was generally agreed that without a system of labour exchanges unemployment insurance was impossible to administer. In this sense the Labour Exchanges Act of 1909 formed an integral part of the policy of insurance. By establishing a

[33] Harris, *Unemployment and Politics*, p. 299.

[34] Beveridge, *Power and Influence*, p. 82; S. and B. Webb, *English Poor Law History* (1929), pt. 2, vol. ii, pp. 663–4.

[35] For the examination of these foreign examples, see *Report to the Board of Trade on Agencies and Methods for dealing with the Unemployed in certain Foreign Countries*, by D. F. Schloss, 1905 Cd. 2304 LXXIII. 471; Percy Alden, *The Unemployed: A National Question* (1905). RC on the Poor Laws, Mins. of Ev., Appx. XXI (K) Insurance against Unemployment in Foreign Countries, 1910 Cd. 5066 XLVIII; RC on the Poor Laws, Mins. of Ev., Evidence of A. Wilson Fox, esp. Q. 99115, 1910 Cd. 5068 XLIX. D. F. Schloss, *Insurance against Unemployment* (1909).

national network of labour exchanges, it went significantly beyond anything that had been achieved in Germany. But the exchanges that had already been set up in many German towns provided a model and one that was studied by everyone involved in formulating the British policy both before the Act was passed and when it came to be implemented.[36]

---

[36] In addition to references in nn. 16, 31, 35, see Dawson, *The German Workman; Economic Journal*, 18 (1908); *Economic Journal*, 20 (1910); PRO, LAB 2/210, 211; LAB 8/821. Also G. W. Askwith, *Industrial Problems and Disputes* (1920), pp. 272–81.

II

National Insurance—Old Attitudes and New

DURING the course of October 1908 the new policy of compulsory contributory insurance was launched by means of memoranda and consultation with interested bodies. It was a startling new departure when one remembers what had been said and done up to the summer of that year, and it implied a very different attitude to the German insurance schemes from that which had been dominant until then. The German experience was now relevant to the thinking of official policy-makers as it had not seemed relevant before. Not merely is this obvious now; it was an acknowledged fact at the time.

Lloyd George had announced his conversion when he returned from his German visit in August 1908.[1] The consultations that he and Churchill had with trade union leaders had led these in turn to dispatch a delegation to Germany in November.[2] Its consultation with German trade union leaders and visits to four German cities had provided the delegation with detailed information on the workings of the insurance system and of labour exchanges. It had also been convinced that the introduction of compulsory workers' insurance, far from injuring trade unions, had provided these with opportunities for propaganda and organization. The practical impact of this investigation on the reshaping of attitudes can be found in the subsequent internal debates within the labour movement and in its negotiations with the government.[3]

As for Churchill, he too was prepared to proclaim his conviction

[1] *Daily News*, 27 Aug. 1908.
[2] *Workmen's Insurance Systems in Germany: Report of Delegation*, Dec. 1908, PRO, CAB 37/96/169.
[3] e.g. Caxton Hall Conference on Labour Exchanges and Insurance, Mar. 1909, reported in National Union of Boot and Shoe Operatives, *Monthly Report*, Mar. 1909, pp. 158–9; Conferences on Labour Exchanges between Churchill and the TUC Parliamentary Committee, June 1909, PRO, LAB 2/211.

of the relevance of the German experience. As was his way he managed to draw what he had learnt into a single strategy. We find him urging Asquith in December towards what he called a policy of Social Organization in emulation of what had been achieved in Germany.

Germany with a harder climate and far less accumulated wealth has managed to establish tolerable basic conditions for her people. She is organised not only for war, but for peace. We are organised for nothing except party politics. The Minister who will apply to this country the successful experiences of Germany in social organisation may or may not be supported at the polls, but he will at least have left a memorial which time will not deface of his administration. It is not impossible to underpin the existing voluntary agencies by a comprehensive system—necessarily at a lower level—of state action.

He argued that the government had at least another two years, and sketched a six-point programme that would 'not only benefit the state but fortify the party'. 'Thrust a big slice of Bismarckianism over the whole underside of our industrial system, and await the consequences whatever they may be with a good conscience.'[4] We have no record of how Asquith took to this language. He must have been accustomed by that time to the rhetorical extravagance of his ambitious young colleague.

The government's commitment to the insurance policy was announced by Lloyd George in his budget speech of 29 April 1909. It is significant that the announcement was preceded by a discussion of the pledges given in the previous year to supplement the old age pensions proposals and followed immediately and logically from a statement refusing to lower the pensions age to 65. As already in June 1908, when he introduced the Old Age Pensions Bill, Lloyd George drew attention to the distress caused by premature breakdown in health, by the death of the breadwinner, and by unemployment, and declared that this had a greater claim on the government's immediate attention. But in contrast to the previous year he now launched into a panegyric of Bismarck's 'superb scheme' of insurance for the German workmen and their families. It had saved an incalculable amount of undeserved human misery and improved the efficiency of the German workman by protecting him

---

[4] W. S. Churchill to H. H. Asquith, 29 Dec. 1908; the complete text is printed in Churchill, *Winston S. Churchill*, ii. *Companion*, pt. 2, pp. 862–4.

from anxiety. Lloyd George reiterated several of the points that he had made on his return from Germany: that the scheme was accepted there by all classes of society, and that its cost to the government was relatively small. He then firmly grasped the nettle of compulsion. He committed the government to compulsory insurance for the sick, the disabled, widows, and orphans, financed by contributions from 'the classes more immediately concerned' and supplemented by a State contribution. He promised to do nothing to damage benefit and provident societies but rather to encourage them, and if practicable, to work through them. Together with existing old age pensions and accident insurance his plans would, he thought, put the country on a level with Germany, and he added, with reference to the recent agitation for increased naval construction, 'I hope our competition with Germany will not be in armaments alone'. The announcement of the government's proposals for unemployment insurance formed the next part of his speech.[5]

We find here the twin themes of imitation and rivalry that were to characterize Lloyd George's response to German forms of administration. Imitation, but of course not the kind of imitation then being advocated by proponents of universal military service or of tariff reform. With German methods being quoted over so wide a field, a free trade Liberal had to be careful when he joined in that chorus.

Why adopt the worst methods and ignore the best. The scientific training, the technical instruction of Germany are ignored on Tory platforms. All they want is the black bread of Germany, the conscription of Germany, the low wages of Germany. In addition to these there is another side of the great industrial life, the insurance of Germany against sickness and invalidity . . . it has given a sense of security to the workman . . . They have got the knowledge that this great gigantic State system is at their back . . . That is the sort of thing we ought to copy, and not tariffs.

And once again he coupled imitation with rivalry: 'We have provided for a State contribution which is twice as large as that of Germany, so that although the Germans have had the system for 20 years, Free Trade Britain in a single year is able to provide twice as much as Protectionist Germany after 20 years.'[6]

    [5] 5 *Hansard* 4 (29 April 1909) 482–7.
    [6] Speech at Reading in support of Rufus Isaac's re-election, by Lloyd George, 1 Jan. 1910, qd. in Herbert Du Parq, *Life of David Lloyd Geroge* (1912), iv. 748–51.

The crisis over the 1909 budget and two election campaigns intervened before the promises of April 1909 could be honoured. As this quotation shows, they gave the Liberal leaders an opportunity to present German workers' insurance in a new and more favourable light. This was just as well, for a very different set of attitudes was deeply entrenched.

'A system of regulation and a system of regimentation which . . . is utterly alien to the tradition of this country': Masterman's phrase during the Third Reading debate on the Old Age Pensions Bill reiterated what had become commonplace in relation to the German insurance scheme. 'The German system could not be transplanted here', Asquith had said, 'for one simple and sufficient reason—that it is founded on the two pillars of inquisition and compulsion'.[7]

Regimentation in this context usually referred to the compulsory nature of the scheme; *regulation* to its administrative provisions. Even Sidney Webb could use the current clichés when it suited him. In 1907 he had dismissed 'all contributory schemes of old age pensions as inherently and completely impossible, whether optional or compulsory. If compulsory they involve an impossible regimentation.' Charles Booth had regarded 'the complicated nature of the German old age pensions scheme and the practical impossibility of exercising any compulsion of this character on our people' as fatal objections. The proposals for unemployment insurance naturally also ran into the same objection that 'a compulsory scheme scarcely appeals to our English ideas'.[8]

For compulsion to be workable a record had to be kept of everyone within the scope of the scheme. The German old age and invalidity scheme provided each workman with a card which was filed by the employer. It was the latter who was responsible for purchasing insurance stamps and sticking the correct amount on to each card. 'The workingman in this country would not submit to the system of dossiers and registration to which the German workingman submitted', was the view of one Conservative MP. 'Sifted and regimented' was how G. N. Barnes, the Labour MP, put

[7] 4 *Hansard* 192 (9 July 1908) 142; ibid., 190 (16 June 1908) 828.

[8] *Suggestions as to Old Age Pensions*, by S. Webb, 29 Sept. 1907, Bodl., Asquith Papers 75, fo. 137; C. Booth, 'Enumeration and Classification of Paupers and State Pensions for the Aged', *Jour. Royal Statistical Soc.*, 54 (1891), 600–34, at 634; Harris, *Unemployment and Politics*, p. 309.

it when making the same point, and from the Liberal front bench Asquith had agreed. 'You cannot, even if you would, set up and work here the complicated and irritating machinery by which in Germany the necessary funds . . . are extracted from the pockets of both employers and employed'.[9]

Explanations for these impossibilities were usually given in terms of the wider political and social differences between the two countries. J. A. Spender had argued in 1892 that the idea of the State as disciplinarian and guide was in no way outlandish to those who were accustomed to the discipline of compulsory military service. *The Times* had said that sort of thing in 1889; there was no dearth of similar comments in 1908.[10]

These quotations are drawn almost entirely from Liberal or Labour sources, for it was the conversion of their own supporters that was to matter most to the ministers. In certain Conservative circles compulsory insurance schemes and the relevance of the German precedent had also become more acceptable during the course of 1908. Thus for instance Austen Chamberlain and his militant tariff reform circle, which included the editor of the *Morning Post*, published a manifesto in that paper in which they commended a sweeping social reform programme to the Conservative Party. 'Old age pensions', they argued,

should be treated as part of the bigger question of State insurance against the incapacity to work, from whatever cause the incapacity may arise. That question should be considered and dealt with in relation to other questions of national organisation and it is probable that its solution will be found in a contributory system. Such a system would carry with it the incidental advantage of effecting the registration of our industrial population which is a condition essential to the solution of unemployment and other pressing problems. This new pension which, as in Germany, might be called the infirmity pension, would, as in that country, gradually replace the existing incomplete, illogical and arbitrary distribution of State pensions'.[11]

These words could have been written by Beveridge, so closely did they echo the ideas of his *Morning Post* articles. In May 1911, with

[9] Leverton Harris, MP for Tower Hamlets, in 4 *Hansard* 190 (15 June 1908) 651–2; G. N. Barnes, ibid. 806–7; Asquith, ibid. 828. See also Alfred Mond, Liberal MP, putting a businessman's point of view, ibid., 640–2.

[10] J. A. Spender, *The State and Pensions in Old Age* (1892), pp. 73–6; 'State Socialism in Germany', *The Times*, 19 June 1889.

[11] *Morning Post*, 8 Oct. 1908, qd. in Sykes, *Tariff Reform*, pp. 196–7.

Austen Chamberlain as spokesman, the Opposition front bench was to give the National Insurance Bill a favourable reception, and only gradually, as it became obvious how much opportunity the details of the Bill presented for fishing in troubled waters, was their acquiescence to give way to hostility both in detail and in general.

The creation of a national scheme of insurance against sickness and invalidity, like the establishment of old age pensions in 1908, was the responsibility of the Chancellor of the Exchequer and his advisers at the Treasury. But just as the office of Chancellor was now occupied by Lloyd George instead of Asquith, so equally there appears to be little overlap in the civil servants connected with the two schemes. This was partly due to Lloyd George's unconventional choice of adviser; W. J. Braithwaite, the civil servant most closely involved in the making of what was soon to be called 'health insurance', was in fact a specialist from the Inland Revenue. As an expert on income tax, he had been sent to Germany a few months previously to investigate the German system of local income tax. English local government was badly in need of additional sources of revenue, but Braithwaite had convinced Lloyd Geroge that the German tax system had nothing to offer, and the Swiss, which he was subsequently sent to investigate, even less. Lloyd George was impressed by him and when, on taking up the insurance problems once more after the election of 10 December, he needed someone to investigate German insurance he asked for him again.[12]

Braithwaite was certainly no expert on Germany. He could read German only slowly and spoke it with difficulty, using another Treasury official as an interpreter. Nor had he any specialist knowledge of German institutions. For his investigation into insurance, as previously into taxation, he had to brief himself from scratch. On the first occasion he had read up the German literature on taxation. Far from being impressed with the German scientific approach he had found the assumption on which it was written, that there was such a thing as a generally applicable science of public finance, uncongenial to his mind. 'That there was a science was all fudge, an official pretence. But there was a very interesting history of taxation, totally different from England's, a wholly different set of problems and outlook, and much very useful and necessary information.'

[12] The other Treasury official closely involved in the legislation was J. S. Bradbury. He had played the principal role in 1909 and 1910.

He had felt uncomfortable in Germany during his first visit and had found a widespread hostility towards Englishmen, but he returned impressed with what he had seen of the efficiency of German municipal administration and the visible well-being of the population. This was so much at odds with the rhetoric of free trade politicians, who were constantly emphasizing the low living standard of the German people, that it left him uneasy. Hamburg, he felt, was beyond all comparison better than Liverpool. He noticed that German civil servants were paid low salaries, but was surprised by the lavish staffing, equipment, and accommodation, as well as by their thoroughness and competence. In contrast to 'strenuous, orderly, high-strung Germany', he found German-speaking Switzerland 'a land of happy noisy children, untidy streets and slovenly, incredibly slovenly, administrations'. 'If democracy really managed things like this, how can it survive?' he asked himself. His reaction to the French was even more unfavourable.[13]

All this was recent memory when he began to brief himself for his investigation into insurance. Among the papers he received was an article on 'The Insurance of the Working Classes in Germany', commissioned in 1905 by W. T. Stead for the *Review of Reviews*, an article that had made little impact at the time.[14] But more important was the outline of a scheme that had been negotiated with the leaders of the Friendly Society movement by Lloyd George between December 1908 and April 1909, submitted to the government actuaries, and returned with comments by them in March and August 1910.[15]

Braithwaite came to his task with a high regard for the Friendly Society movement and a faith, strengthened by his own social work in east London, in the institutions of mutual help as the basis of working-class self-respect. He strongly believed in the importance of working men managing their own institutions.

The basic political necessity, recognized by Lloyd George and all others, of associating the Friendly Societies in the construction of an insurance scheme found therefore in Braithwaite a response based on personal commitment. He wanted more than the political

[13] 'Memoirs 1910–1912', typescript, pp. 1–20, LPES, Braithwaite Papers I (d) vol. 1.

[14] The author was Percy Ashley, a Board of Trade official.

[15] LPES, Braithwaite Papers II. 1–6. For details of these negotiations see Gilbert, *Evolution of National Insurance*, pp. 295–303.

acquiescence of the Friendly Society movement; he wanted a scheme that would benefit the societies and lead to the extension of the principle of mutual association and self-government. He was not reassured to find that the provisional scheme sketched out in 1909 proposed to guarantee the special funds that the Friendly Societies were required to establish against any deficit arising from their failure to realize the expectations of the actuaries. He knew that in return for such a guarantee the government was bound to insist on detailed supervision, and indeed in their report the government actuaries made it quite clear that this was exactly how they saw the matter. He decided that this was a development that had to be resisted.[16] Thus he went to Germany with a set of attitudes not at all uncharacteristic of a Liberal Englishman—a belief in self-government, a distrust of bureaucracy, and a feeling of unease at the possible implications of State compulsion for voluntary initiative and the character traits associated with it.

He subsequently claimed that what had impressed him most during his first-hand investigation of German insurance, besides the usual German thoroughness, was the complexity and harshness of this 'social' legislation. 'It was amazing to find prosecutions for breaches of regulations running to many thousands in Berlin only', he wrote. He visited the offices of a sickness fund and commented: 'It all seemed very complicated to me . . . I noted that 126 officials were required to manage this Society of 120,000 members'. 'German methods of officialdom and compulsion . . . were awful warnings to me. Something simpler and more self-working must, I thought, be found for England.'

When he reported to Lloyd George he placed the emphasis accordingly. Dealing with invalidity insurance, he stressed that the insurance depended on a government guarantee and was administered by the government with truly Prussian thoroughness. He displayed a book of statistics, which was passed round amid exclamations of dismay, and which showed the reduction in the number of pensions which had followed the visits of government inspectors. There were reductions of up to 40 per cent. He rubbed it in that, though this was truly Prussian, it was demanded by efficient administration!

[16] *Provisional Scheme for Insurance against Sickness, Invalidity etc.*, in *First Report of the Actuaries*, p. 53, *Second Report of the Actuaries*, p. 9, LPES, Braithwaite Papers II. 4. See Bunbury, *Lloyd George's Ambulance Wagon*, pp. 73–81.

Turning to the sickness insurance scheme, he similarly emphasized the large number of prosecutions for non-payment of contributions, 'the Germans as usual relying upon force or compulsion'. 'I hoped that I had not been tendentious', was his comment on his report, which was, as so often with Lloyd George's advisers, given by word of mouth, 'but I had certainly tried to kill indirectly the notion of a Government guarantee.' He noticed that Lloyd George was discouraged by finding how much had already been done in Germany but attracted by some of the details of the scheme, especially by the idea of making employer or employed pay for extra sickness caused by either, as the Germans had done.[17]

Here we have the three attitudes which together made up the stance of the British policy-makers towards what they had found in Germany: *revulsion, imitation,* and *rivalry*. With Braithwaite the element of revulsion appears to have been dominant. This has already become apparent from the use that he made of the bureaucratic character of German invalidity insurance in order to argue in favour of giving the approved societies within the British scheme maximum responsibility for their own financial solvency. He was particularly pleased to find that these tactics had paid off and that the idea of a government guarantee had been dropped. The societies were thus given a financial incentive to attempt to control malingering among their members. The view that they were in a far better position to do so effectively than anybody else became a prominent justification for reliance on mutual associations in preference to bureaucratic structures.[18]

The other matter to which Braithwaite devoted much attention was his insistence that the scheme should be based on proper actuarial principles, i.e. should accumulate adequate funds with which to meet future liabilities. The alternative approach would have been to proceed on the assumption that contributions would always be forthcoming with which to meet liabilities, and that there would therefore be no need to accumulate large funds in advance. German old age and invalidity insurance had an accumulating fund; German sickness insurance did not. It was revealing that it

---

[17] Ibid., pp. 85–7.
[18] Ibid., pp. 93–5. The passage on this subject in the *Explanatory Memorandum* that accompanied the Bill was the work of Braithwaite, as indeed was the whole of the section devoted to contrasting British self-government advantageously with German bureaucracy. See ch. 12 below.

was this aspect of the German sickness scheme that Braithwaite emphasized, suggesting that it led to profligate use of available funds and inadequate thought for the future. There were numerous other occasions when he used the German scheme, or some aspect of the three German schemes, as an example of what to avoid.[19]

Lloyd George himself tended more frequently to regard the German schemes as a quarry for devices to be copied. To give just one example of many, he was delighted with his discovery that the Germans paid benefits only from the fourth day of sickness. Friendly Societies had always paid from the commencement of sickness; this device would help to spin out the money. Braithwaite would occasionally reject a suggestion of this kind by referring to its failure in Germany, but he found that it was sometimes prudent to accept these suggestions, even when he felt that German experience had not justified Lloyd George's hopes. Thus in their different ways both Lloyd George and Braithwaite found the mere existence of a working model of what they wished to create a great advantage. Braithwaite systematically combed the German material to find out what snags he was likely to encounter, so as to arm himself against them.[20]

As for Lloyd George, more important than the willingness to imitate the Germans was the determination to outdo them. This sense of rivalry was an important political factor in the overall situation and is well caught in Lloyd George's remark made while preparing the speech with which to introduce the measure to the Commons. When Braithwaite commented on the length of the speech, adding that he did not see what could be cut except a long passage of comparison with the German scheme, Lloyd George replied: 'I would rather get up and tell them what the rates are to the employer and employed in Germany, and that my scheme does not charge so much, and does more, and then sit down without having made a speech, than leave that out'.[21]

This sense of rivalry influenced more than just the style of presentation. It influenced the substance of the scheme by making it more ambitious than it would otherwise have been. On 5 April 1911 the Cabinet approved a draft Bill for national health insurance. It was to be financed by weekly contributions of 4*d.*

---

[19] Ibid., pp. 86–7, 88–9, 105, 110, 156.
[20] Ibid., p. 113.
[21] Ibid., pp. 152–3.

from male and 3*d.* from female workers, 2*d.* from employers, and from the State one-quarter of the cost of benefits, i.e. somewhat less than 2*d.* per head. There were still many details to be settled, but it was on this basis that the actuarial calculations had been presented to the Cabinet. About this time the Treasury team working on the Bill was augmented by W. H. Dawson, the Board of Trade official and expert on German social administration, who was commissioned to produce a paper setting out the German insurance contributions and benefits. On 21 April, when this had been completed, Braithwaite found Lloyd George greatly perturbed at the large amount paid by German employers and workers, and 'afraid that his own scheme looks small by the side of Germany'. Pacing his room in much agitation, he decided to increase the employer's contribution by 50 per cent, from 2*d.* a week to 3*d.* a week.

Earlier that month Lloyd George had discovered with a shock that his proposals did not provide women with any payment during a confinement. The Germans paid a minimum of six weeks' maternity benefit at normal sickness rates to female contributors, but child-bearing had never been regarded as sickness by British Friendly Societies and so had not been included in the British scheme. Now it was possible to remedy this and to pay a 30*s.* maternity grant on what was a more generous basis than that in force in Germany.[22] More important still, it became possible to increase the money available to all contributors for medical treatment. Here too the original figures had been based on Friendly Society practice, notoriously unsatisfactory though this was. The sum allocated had been 4*s.* per year per head; it could now be increased to 6*s.* As Braithwaite recorded in his diary: 'The new 1d makes everything possible—Maternity benefit and decent doctoring'. Asquith's consent was quickly obtained, the actuaries were told to revise all their calculations, and Dawson was commissioned to write a further memorandum on sickness and invalidity insurance in Germany. All this took place less than two weeks before the presentation of the Bill.[23]

In preparing the German section of his speech, Lloyd George worked with Dawson, and the figures that he quoted were drawn

---

[22] The Germans provided insured women workers with sickness pay during confinement; the British maternity grant could also be claimed by all insured male workers on the confinement of their wives.

[23] Bunbury, *Lloyd George's Ambulance Wagon*, pp. 139, 144, 149–50.

from Dawson's memorandum.[24] That speech, which introduced the measure to the House of Commons on 4 May, contained nine distinct references to Germany, and a further one in the subsequent section devoted to unemployment insurance. All the three attitudes that we have noticed are represented there. Four times the German scheme is cited as an example to be followed,[25] twice as a warning of what to avoid.[26] But three passages, including two of the most prominent, are clearly intended to demonstrate the superiority of the British product.

[24] *German Sickness and Invalidity Insurance: The Benefits Provided and their Cost*, 10 pp., printed 4 May 1911, LPES, Braithwaite Papers, II. 70. It was circulated as a Cabinet paper and can also be found in the PRO, CAB 37/106/56.

[25] Collection of contributions by the use of stamps; health education by lectures and pamphlets; disability allowance conditional on the patient obeying doctor's orders; also a long and important passage dealing with the principle of compulsory contributions from employers. This quoted the opinion of German employers to the effect that it increased the efficiency of their workers, and then showed that the employers' contribution in Germany was higher than the 3*d.* proposed in the Bill.

[26] Exclusion of casual labour; excessively generous treatment of those already over 50 at the expense of young contributors.

12

Comparison

LLOYD George's speech formed only one part of the elaborate comparisons with the German precedent that were so prominent an aspect of the presentation of the National Insurance Bill to Parliament. The Bill itself was supported by three further documents, which took up the same theme, a general explanatory memorandum, and two other memoranda dealing specifically with the existing German scheme. Of these, one presented a detailed comparison between the two schemes; the other provided testimonials by German workers, employers, and Poor Law authorities to the acceptability and success of what had been done in Germany.[1]

Comparison with the German precedent was therefore made deliberately into a prominent feature of the way in which the measure was presented to Parliament and to the public at large. The fact that compulsory contributory health insurance had originally been designed by Germans to suit their own conditions was treated no longer as a liability by those who were now proposing a British version of that same idea. By 1911 the parallels could be asserted and comparisons put forward, provided that these comparisons were favourable to the British proposal. Emulation and rivalry was the nature of the game, and in the process attention was repeatedly drawn to two aspects of the proposal: to its financial benefits and to its administrative structure and organization. This chapter will examine each of these in turn.

A prominent passage in Lloyd George's introductory speech dealt with the workers' own contribution to the scheme. In England that was to be 4d. per week for men. In Germany the payment varied in

---

[1] *National Insurance Bill, Memorandum Explanatory of the Bill*, 8 May 1911, 1911 (HC 147) LXXIII; *Memorandum on Sickness and Invalidity Insurance in Germany*, 14 pp., printed May 1911, 1911 Cd. 5678 LXXIII. 213; *Memorandum Containing the Opinions of Various Authorities in Germany*, 13 pp., printed May 1911, 1911, Cd. 5679. LXXIII. 227.

proportion to the rate of wages, but a worker earning 24s. a week, the average British wage, would be paying 9d. 'For that 9d.', said Lloyd George, 'the benefits he gets will not be equal to the benefits we shall be able to give under our Bill twenty years hence.'[2] He did not at that stage pause to comment on the actual rates of benefit written into the Bill. These were to be distinctly lower for as long as it was necessary to carry the higher risks presented by the older part of the insured population, who had built up no previous contributions and were in effect subsidized by the younger and healthier contributors. To compare existing German benefits with something set so far in the future was to strain comparison almost to breaking-point. It is remarkable that Lloyd George was prepared to make it as prominent as he did.

When he turned to comparing the contributions made by the State in Britain with those in Germany he included in his calculations the very considerable cost of tax-provided old age pensions under the Act of 1908. By adding these two legislative measures one to the other, he was able to make the British scheme appear incomparably more generous than the German, and so obtained political credit for the high cost of a system whose principles he had now rejected. The £13 million which old age pensions were costing by then he calculated as equivalent to a weekly contribution of 5d. 'We certainly could not have offered the benefits we are offering in this measure . . . had it not been that the whole burden of pensions over seventy years of age had been taken over by the State.'[3] This way of making the comparison was to prove useful at a subsequent stage when he wished to ward off requests for a more generous State contribution.[4]

In addition he pointed out that the minimum period of regular contributions that would entitle a British worker to a disability allowance was a mere two years compared with the five years that were required in Germany.[5]

That the British financial provisions gave better value than the German ones and were supported by a more generous State

[2] 5 *Hansard* 25 (4 May 1911) 615.   [3] Ibid. 619.

[4] See his appeal for restraint in his budget statement, and his reference to the comparative figures when refusing a request on behalf of women contributors, 5 *Hansard* 25 (16 May 1911) 1868–70; *National Insurance Bill, Report of Deputations*, p. 14., 1911 Cd. 5869 XXIX. 241.

[5] According to Cd. 5678, published a few days later, the qualifying period in Germany was four years not five.

contribution was also one of the principal emphases of the opening section of the explanatory memorandum, while the special memorandum on German insurance published at the same time was principally devoted to establishing point by point the financial superiority of the British Bill.

This document was based on information that Dawson had provided in late April and which had been made available to the Cabinet, but that original paper had been added to and extensively rewritten so as to make the comparison between the two schemes more explicit.[6] It did not, however, refer to the reform of the German insurance laws which was then being planned, and some of the favourable comparisons were to be outdated before the Bill had passed through Parliament. This applies for instance to the consideration of the proportion of the population covered by the compulsory provisions of the schemes. Because the German sickness insurance law had so far excluded agricultural labourers, domestic servants, home-workers, and certain other categories, it did not cover the 30 per cent or so that the British Bill was estimated to affect. These anomalies were removed by the revision of July 1911, and the difference between the two countries in this respect was to be insignificant.[7] Nor was the fact that the Germans were about to introduce widows' and orphans' pensions alluded to. Once Lloyd George had had to drop his own plans for this area of need under political pressure from the life-insurance industry prior to the elections of January 1910, it was naturally not a subject he chose to dwell on.[8]

It was a carefully constructed presentation. A table which showed that British workers would be paying less than Germans on a comparable wage had been used to good effect by Lloyd George in his introductory speech. Employers' contributions did not show up so favourably in a reworked table whose figures differed from

---

[6] See p. 178 above. The former document, *German Sickness and Invalidity Insurance: The Benefits Provided and their Cost*, was completed by 27 Apr. 1911 and printed on 4 May for consideration by the Cabinet, LPES, Braithwaite Papers II. 70, or PRO, CAB 37/106/56. For details, see Bunbury, *Lloyd George's Ambulance Wagon*, pp. 150–1.

[7] For the provisions of the German insurance law of July 1911, see Dawson, *Social Insurance in Germany 1883–1911*.

[8] Originally such provisions had strongly appealed to him and in 1908 he had made a point of announcing that the Germans were about to introduce them. *Daily News*, 27 Aug. 1908. For his reluctant change of position see Gilbert, *Evolution of National Insurance*.

the ones he had used in his speech. However, the memorandum quickly added on the cost of accident insurance lest anyone should doubt that British employers were getting off lightly compared with their German competitors. Since accident insurance had been brought into the picture exclusively for that purpose, it was not thought necessary to draw attention to the very much higher benefits available to German workers in cases of industrial injury.

Indeed the information on the benefits available in the two countries was equally carefully selected. The memorandum rightly drew attention to the maternity benefit of 30s. which would be given to the wives of all insured male contributors as well as to insured working women. In Germany the slightly higher benefit was available to insured working women only. But the section on medical benefit, which in Britain was not to include family dependants whereas in Germany optional arrangements for this purpose were not uncommon, was distinctly uninformative. It provided no figures for comparison. Dawson had originally come up with a figure of 8s. 10d. per head for Germany compared with the 6s. per head that at this stage was being proposed for Britain. Since that figure included expenditure on dependants, which was sometimes covered by an additional voluntary contribution and sometimes not, it was not strictly comparable and did not appear in the published document.[9]

On other matters rough and ready comparisons were more acceptable. Schemes that bore really so little resemblance to each other could be compared in terms of benefits provided only by overlooking many differences. Thus German invalidity pensions were not merely graded according to income classes, as explained below, but depended also on the number of contributions that the claimant had paid. British disablement benefit after two years' contributions had been paid was set at 5s. per week and did not vary. Fairly young men suffering from total disablement were

---

[9] Cf. *German Sickness and Invalidity Insurance: The Benefits Provided and their Cost*, PRO, CAB 37/106/56, p. 2, with *National Insurance Bill, Memo on Sickness and Invalidity Insurance in Germany*, pp. 8, 9. The explanation is provided briefly in Bunbury, *Lloyd George's Ambulance Wagon*, p. 139, and fully in *National Health Insurance, Medical Benefit under the German Sickness Insurance Legislation*, p. 3, 1912–13 Cd. 6581 LXXXVIII. Ultimately, as a result of the threat of the doctors to boycott the scheme, the amount for medical benefit in the UK was to be increased to 9s. per head.

therefore favoured by the British arrangements; fairly old men by the German. By comparing the 5s. of the British claimant with the entitlement of the German worker who had paid his contributions over twenty years, the document still just about managed to produce a favourable set of figures. Had it chosen thirty years and thirty-four years, i.e. workers in their late 40s and early 50s, as Dawson was to do in the book that he published in 1912, the comparison would have looked much less good.[10]

Nor was this the only respect in which comparisons of the cost of contributions and benefits between the two countries were bound to be arbitrary. The British scheme operated in principle by means of uniform contributions from all members, distinguishing only between men, who paid 4d. per week, and women, who paid 3d. For this it provided a uniform level of benefits. The German worker by contrast contributed on a graduated scale according to the size of his earnings, and similarly received graduated benefits in accordance with the level of his contributions. This applied both to sickness insurance and to invalidity and old age insurance, although, as always when it came to details, the two German schemes operated in different ways. That means of course not only that the burden of contributions fell on German workers proportionately to their ability to pay, but that benefits received by the well-paid were considerably greater than those received by the lower-paid.

This was the really fundamental difference between the schemes in the two countries. It is surprising how little comment it attracted at the time. The detailed memorandum on German insurance gave no explanation. The general explanatory memorandum mentioned it as a point of difference, but merely added that the British system of uniform contributions would reduce the inconvenience to employers. A short passage in Lloyd George's speech to the Commons on the First Reading of the Bill comes much nearer to the real explanation. He drew attention to the small sums received in benefit by the lower-paid in Germany, and added that he had decided in favour of a uniform flat-rate scale as being the simplest means of providing benefits large enough to keep the contributors' families from want. The passage is both short and obscure and was

[10] Cf. the table in *National Insurance Bill, Memorandum on Sickness and Invalidity Insurance in Germany*, p. 10, with those in Dawson, *Social Insurance in Germany*, pp. 145–6.

ignored in subsequent discussion of the measure.[11] But it contains the germs of a genuine explanation. British health insurance, like British unemployment insurance, was intended to supersede the Poor Law as the protection against want caused by those factors over which the individual had no personal control. It was an aspect of the politics of poverty, and was judged by what it did to protect the families of the poor from want. It derived its impetus from the conjunction of two political considerations. One was a concern to protect the human resources of the nation at a time of international competition, both economic and military. The other was the need to reassure the citizen-voter that he would not be allowed, for reasons over which he had no control, to fall into the non-citizen class of paupers. It was therefore not the maintenance of comfort but the prevention of want that was at stake.

The German scheme was intended to appeal primarily to the strong, not to the weak, among the German working class. It did less to rescue the very poor from dependence on poor relief—indeed this was often used to supplement inadequate insurance benefits. It did more to provide the better-paid element among the workers with benefits suited to their requirements and therefore worthy of their attention and co-operation. The reason for this contrast must presumably be sought in the different political situation out of which the German legislation had emerged. It is the total political situation not just Bismarck's personal intention that matter in this connection. Had Bismarck had his way, the German old age and invalidity scheme would indeed have been far closer to the British Act of 1911, for in 1887 the first draft of the German Bill had proposed low, flat-rate contributions and benefits, discriminating only between men and women and varying benefits merely according to the length of time that contributions had been paid. The intention was to provide all workers with the possibility of a modest existence, and to leave it to the higher-paid workers to improve on that by means of additional arrangements of their own. That was so similar to the subsequent British provision that it lent itself to a very similar interpretation, namely that the Poor Law was merely being replaced by a more honourable alternative. What is significant, however, is that this did not come about. The measure reached the statute book in 1889 only after a process of political

---

[11] 5 *Hansard* 25 (4 May 1911), 616. I have paraphrased what I take to be its meaning.

give-and-take which had enabled the National Liberals to insist on a graduated scheme designed to achieve quite different objectives.[12] When the Social Democratic Party subsequently condemned the inadequate pensions available to the lower-paid and demanded higher minimum levels to be financed from higher State subsidies, it made it clear that it had no intention of rejecting the proposals for differential benefits tied to differential contributions at the upper end of the wage scale.[13]

Of course the political problem in Britain was also how to obtain the co-operation of the comfortable working class, since it was its institutions that were to be used for the administration of the scheme. In consequence there were advantages held out to it, in particular the fact that the government scheme would make it unnecessary for Friendly Societies to draw on their accumulated funds for the purpose for which these had, after all, been accumulated, i.e. to pay basic sickness benefits to their existing members. They were left free to use this amount, estimated at the time at some £10–12 million, to provide their members both past and future with additional benefits.[14]

Even so, the difference remains, and it is significant. The success of the British scheme was judged by its ability to protect the weak from want. The enforced contributions from worker and employer, not to mention the State subsidy, were distributed on a flat-rate basis so as not to disadvantage the less well-paid. The aspirations of the better-paid for higher levels of comfort at times of sickness and disability were to be met by additional payments of a voluntary nature, not built into the structure of compulsion as was the case in Germany. Indeed, the only concession to the principle of graduated compulsory contributions to be found in the British scheme was designed to favour those with exceptionally low wages. They were to pay less than the standard rate of contribution while still being entitled to the standard benefits. It was the employer of low-wage labour who was obliged to make up the balance of the contribution, and in extreme cases the State added 1*d.* per week.[15] This was

[12] Ritter, *Social Welfare in Germany and Britain*, pp. 44–5, 70.

[13] G. V. Rimlinger, *Welfare Policy and Industrialization in Europe, America and Russia* (New York, 1971), pp. 127–8.

[14] Bunbury, *Lloyd George's Ambulance Wagon*, pp. 77–9. See the critical comments on this in 'The Insurance Bill: Compulsory Charity at the Expense of the Poor', *The Times*, 7 Aug. 1911.

[15] See 2nd Schedule of the Act.

graduation of a sort, but, by protecting the level of the benefit and not reducing it in line with the reduction in the worker's contribution, it was intended to achieve the opposite of what the Germans were doing. The success of the German scheme was not dependent on what it would do for the very poor, for these constituted no political menace on their own. It was dependent rather on the degree to which it appealed to the aspirations of the active and economically strongest section of the working class.

It is this contrast in the political context of the two pieces of legislation that accounts not only for the difference between graduated and uniform provision but also for the fact that this feature of the German scheme evoked so little interest or even comment in 1911. Earnings-related benefits, a matter of such interest to policy-makers in this country in recent years, belong to a political context very different from the preoccupation with minimum provision that characterized the Edwardians.

This contrast between the political contexts out of which the legislation in Britain and in Germany arose throws light not only on the financial provisions of the two schemes. It is also important for an understanding of the way in which the two schemes were organized.

German sickness insurance was organized on the basis of various kinds of sickness insurance funds (*Krankenkassen*) which with insignificant exceptions were controlled by their contributors. Since contributions were divided between workers and employers on a 2 : 1 basis this control was exercised by bodies on which workers' representatives outnumbered employers' representatives by two to one. In practice this enabled the workers through their chosen representatives to exercise the decisive control over the sickness funds. Old age and invalidity insurance was administered on a much more bureaucratic basis, but there were consultative committees composed in equal numbers of workers' and employers' representatives as well as appeals tribunals on which workers and employers served in equal numbers under the chairmanship of a civil servant.[16] This was unpaid service and associated workers' insurance with a long and respected tradition in which the obligation to give honorary service in local administration had been

16 Dawson, *Social Insurance in Germany*, chs. 2, 3, 5.

one of the marks of citizenship. Trade unions had naturally taken advantage of the scope that this reliance on workers' representatives offered and in particular through its Workers' Secretaries played an active part in the organization of this machinery of self-government.[17]

How was the comparison between the administration of British and German insurance actually presented to the British public? Once again our main sources are the memoranda that accompanied the Bill in May 1911. Although both of these devoted far more space to the details of comparative costs and benefits, they gave prominence to what they considered to be the greater merits of the British form of organization. The general explanatory memorandum made three points:

1. The administration would be handed over to the Friendly Societies already established or thereafter to be founded.
2. Since deficits due to malingering were not to be made good by the State, the members of the society would have every inducement to look after their own affairs.
3. In Germany the system was much more bureaucratic in its management, and did not nearly to the same extent adopt the principle of self-government.[18]

The more detailed memorandum on sickness and invalidity insurance opened with the statement that the most fundamental difference between the two schemes was that of organization. The British scheme combined sickness and invalidity insurance, whereas in Germany these were administered separately.[19] Apart from cheapness and simplicity, this meant that 'the workman will from first to last be able to continue in the provident society of his choice . . . and that at every stage of his membership his society will have a direct inducement to take an interest in his welfare'. Here, as already in the other document, the emphasis was on the way in which the Friendly Society movement 'will be further stimulated and strengthened by the Bill'.[20] This too is the stress in a subsequent

---

[17] August Müller, *Arbeitersekretariate und Arbeiterversicherung in Deutschland* (Munich, 1904); comments in Gerhard A. Ritter, *Staat, Arbeiterschaft und Arbeiterbewegung in Deutschland* (Berlin and Bonn, 1980), ch. 2.

[18] *National Insurance Bill, Memorandum Explanatory of the Bill*, p. 2.

[19] The fact that in Germany both invalidity pensions and old age pensions were administered together, whereas in Britain they were quite separate, was not alluded to.

[20] *National Insurance Bill, Memorandum on Sickness and Invalidity Insurance in Germany*, p. 2.

section, devoted to administration, whose opening paragraph declared:

There is no counterpart in German insurance legislation to the unconditional autonomy which the National Insurance Bill secures to the Approved Societies of insurers, to which the execution of the principal beneficiary provisions of the Bill will be entrusted. The Bill requires that the affairs of these Societies shall be subject to the absolute control of the members.[21]

The element of self-government in the German schemes was shortly described. By comparison with the absolute control proclaimed for the British approved societies it seemed small, and appeared to justify the unfavourable comparison made in this respect in both memoranda.

It is clear that what mattered in the presentation of the Bill was to emphasize that the scheme possessed the virtues of Friendly Societies. Comparison with German administration was basically made with this object in mind. This in turn points to the really fundamental fact. In so far as there was ever a model for the architects of British health insurance, it was not the German scheme but the practice of British Friendly Societies.

The formulation of a British scheme of health insurance had not been preceded by a detailed study of the German system. Lloyd George's hurried tour was hardly that, and it is a telling fact that the report that was subsequently produced by the Treasury in December 1908 was limited to the German invalidity and old age pensions scheme and still totally ignored the much more illuminating practices of German sickness insurance.[22] There is some evidence that Lloyd George asked Dawson at the Board of Trade for a copy of a paper on German sickness insurance that Dawson had written, but there is no sign that he ever received it.[23] It was not among the papers given to Braithwaite in December 1910 for his briefing, nor among the other working papers in connection with the Bill. Much more important were the early negotiations with the representatives of the Friendly Society movement in 1908–9.

This fundamental fact is reinforced by the role that Braithwaite played in the construction of the Bill from January 1911 onwards.

[21] Ibid., p. 13.
[22] *Memorandum Prepared in the Treasury on Invalidity and Old Age Insurance in Germany*, Dec. 1908, LPES, Braithwaite Papers II. 1. 11–14.
[23] W. H. Clark (Treasury) to W. H. Dawson, 23 Dec. 1908, Birm. Univ. Lib., W. H. Dawson Papers 173.

The man with the best opportunity to study the German scheme and consider how to adapt it to British conditions had not been interested in doing anything of the kind. More even than Lloyd George's earlier advisers, he was orientated towards Friendly Society practices and was not interested in discovering any fundamental alternatives in Germany. Had he wished to do so, he would soon have come up against obstacles, but the point is that no one ever seriously tried to consider the uses of German insurance for the shaping of a British scheme except at the most trivial level of borrowing individual devices. Just as unemployment insurance was undoubtedly constructed on the basis of trade union experience and practice, so health insurance took shape in relation to the experience and practice of Friendly Societies.

Friendly Societies were essentially voluntary associations, and no one in the Treasury team ever questioned the first of the two principles on which voluntary associations were necessarily constructed, i.e. that contributors should be free to choose their society. The other principle, equally basic to a voluntary association, was the freedom to refuse admission to undesirable applicants. In a sense this principle was incompatible with compulsory insurance. The combination of compulsion to join some society with freedom to be rejected by them all was liable to produce a residue of uninsured persons whom no society wanted. In this sense it was impossible to administer a compulsory scheme through voluntary associations. Yet this was exactly what Lloyd George and his advisers wished to do. It forced them into the position where they would have to make some other kind of arrangement for a residue of contributors whom no society wished to admit. No one knew how many of these there would be, but in March 1911 Lloyd George decided to make only minimal provision for such people and to rely on the societies to keep that residue small. This minimal provision was in fact neither insurance nor State subsidy; it was no more than a deposit account in the Post Office. It was politically acceptable only if the number of such 'deposit contributors' was in fact to be insignificant. In Braithwaite's words 'the bill was finally a gamble. Would the Societies compete for members?'[24] Lloyd George built the Bill on the belief that they would.

Comparison with the 1870 Education Act will illustrate the

[24] Bunbury, *Lloyd George's Ambulance Wagon*, pp. 119–20. See also ibid., p. 123.

significance of Lloyd George's decision. The School Boards created under that Act were comparable to the arrangements made for 'deposit contributors' in the sense that they too had been designed to fill the gaps that still remained in the provision made by approved and subsidized voluntary bodies. In the case of educational provision a new administrative structure was devised capable of filling gaps of a very considerable size.[25] In 1911 it was hoped that the voluntary bodies approved and subsidized for the provision of sickness benefit would leave very few gaps, and very inadequate provision was made to fill them.

The decision to rely on the Friendly Societies was among other things a decision to administer compulsory health insurance with a minimum of direct contact between the State and the citizen. It arose from a strong dislike of multiplying civil servants and an acute awareness of the limitations of bureaucracy. As the explanatory memorandum put it:

The greatest evil which has to be guarded against in all benefit schemes of this character comes from the danger of malingering . . . The only really effective check . . . is to be found in engaging the self-interest of the workmen themselves in opposition to it. That is why a purely State Scheme . . . would inevitably lead to unlimited shamming and deception. This Scheme is so worked that the burden of mismanagement and maladministration would fall on the workmen themselves . . . Once they realise that, then malingering will become an unpopular vice amongst them, and they will take the surest and shortest way to discourage it.[26]

It could be argued that under such circumstances Friendly Societies would do well to be cautious in their acceptance of new members, and leave the doubtful cases to find acceptance elsewhere. How reasonable was it to expect societies that had up to then been more noted for their caution to step out boldly into the unknown? And how likely was it that significant numbers of new approved societies would be forthcoming? In the Bill as submitted to Parliament in May such societies were intended to have all the constitutional characteristics of existing Friendly Societies, i.e. to be 'subject to the absolute control of the members, and with provision for the election of all committees, representatives and officers by the members'.[27]

[25] Donald K. Jones, *The Making of the Education System 1851–1881* (1977).
[26] *National Insurance Bill, Memorandum Explanatory of the Bill*, p. 15.
[27] *National Insurance Bill, Memorandum on Sickness and Invalidity Insurance in Germany*, p. 13; for fuller details see *Memorandum Explanatory of the Bill*, s. 5A.

In short the policy on which Lloyd George had embarked was certainly a gamble. By leaving societies free to reject members and yet creating no proper alternative organization, he had left his scheme of compulsory insurance extremely vulnerable.

In June 1911 the powerful industrial insurance companies and Collecting Friendly Societies, both engaged in the sale of life insurance and never before associated with sickness insurance, decided that they wished to participate in the government's scheme. They took this step in defence of their lucrative life-insurance business, which they feared would be absorbed by the Friendly Societies once these had established contact with households through the administration of health insurance. They decided that it would be better to administer health insurance through their own agents and to use the opportunity to sell profitable life insurance as well.[28]

This decision transformed the situation. Until then the Bill had envisaged that health insurance would be administered by approved societies modelled on the normal Friendly Society pattern. Yet industrial insurance companies were very different kinds of institutions. Friendly Societies consisted of self-governing local 'lodges' affiliated to national 'orders'. They ran the business of their lodge by means of honorary officers. Industrial insurance companies were centralized companies, conducting business with their customers through an army of local agents who sold policies on the doorstep and thereafter collected weekly subscriptions by calling at the house. The fact that they were paid by commission gave the agents a strong financial interest in the sale of policies. The system was strongly criticized both then and subsequently for the high proportion of the premiums that was absorbed by commissions and other administrative costs and for the tendency to sell to ignorant people policies that were more to the agent's financial advantage than to the customer's. In all these respects the so-called Collecting Friendly Societies were similar to the insurance companies. The latter were limited liability companies run by directors responsible to their shareholders. The former were non-profit-making societies run by officers formally responsible to their members. But since these members had no corporate identity and no connection with the society except through its collectors, it was the collectors who in

---

[28] For this and the next three paras., see the detailed exposition in Gilbert, *Evolution of National Insurance*, pp. 318–43, 358–83.

practice exercised the voting rights and controlled the society in their own interests.

There was at least one other respect in which these bodies differed from normal Friendly Societies. Since they had never administered sickness insurance, they provided no medical treatment and had no relations with medical practitioners.

The pressure that these bodies put on the government has been described in detail by Bentley Gilbert. Their army of agents, perfect door-to-door canvassers, gave them considerable political leverage. But the same active force, in contact with the very people whom the Friendly Societies had not been able to recruit, meant also that the companies had something to offer that the government badly needed, if the large numbers of the wage-earning population, previously untouched by the Friendly Society movement, for whom the compulsory insurance scheme was intended were to be enrolled in approved societies. In the first session of a new Parliament it was this fact, at least as much as the companies' capacity for exerting political pressure on Parliament, that explains their successful campaign to modify those clauses of the Bill that had laid down that approved societies should in essentials be like Friendly Societies. In its final version the Bill permitted them to participate without abandoning their own specific characteristics. It dropped the insistence on local branch organization, and separated the provision of medical treatment from the administration of insurance payments. Although the insistence on self-government remained formally written into the Bill, it had become capable of being nullified by the administrative discretion of the Insurance Commissioners, and this was what happened. The non-profit-making character of approved societies was retained, but, since they could now be associated with profit-making bodies under what was in effect the same management, this presented no obstacle to the insurance companies. In addition a very generously pitched margin for administrative costs was included in the actuarial calculations to cover the notoriously high administrative expenses of the collectors.

The result of this assertion of political power by commercial interests was that the British health insurance scheme was in effect less self-governing than the German one. The good intentions of May 1911 were overtaken by events. If the Friendly Societies properly so-called compared favourably with the German sickness funds, this was certainly not true of those approved societies connected with the commercial companies or with the so-called Collecting Friendly Societies, not even when the restrictions to be imposed on the local funds (*Ortskrankenkassen*) by the German law of 1911 are taken into account.[29]

The final version of the explanatory memorandum, printed in January 1912 to accompany the Bill as passed by the House of Commons, still proudly proclaimed that 'in Germany the system is much more bureaucratic in its management, and does not nearly to the same extent adopt the principles of self-government'.[30] Yet as far as self-government was concerned this was no more than a form of deception, and the administrative decisions taken in the course of the next few months served to make this clear.

The coupling of less bureaucracy with more self-government that came so easily to the British mind was in fact profoundly misleading. It had been the original determination to avoid the methods of bureaucracy and to rely on voluntary associations for the administration of the scheme that had led directly to the whittling away of the element of self-government. It had made the government vulnerable to pressure from those bodies capable of organizing what the government was unwilling to organize directly through its own bureaucratic structures. At first it had seemed that this would imply no more than a working relationship in which the State lent its support to Friendly Societies, whose mutuality and self-government made them deserving recipients of the resources of a State organized on the principles of Liberalism.

However, the decision to leave the field open to the initiative of voluntary associations also left it open to another set of voluntary associations with very different characteristics, i.e. commercial companies. In the ensuing competition the greater resources of the commercial bodies compared with the bodies of mutual help became only too obvious, first in the political competition for the compliance of politicians, secondly in the organizational competition for the recruitment of contributors. The pages of Braithwaite's

---

[29] This was intended to reduce the autonomy of bodies many of whom had come under the control of Social Democrats. The changes are itemized in Dawson, *Social Insurance in Germany*, pp. 34–8, 165–81. The matter is most fully discussed in Florian Tennstedt, *Geschichte der Selbstverwaltung in der Krankenversicherung* (Bonn, 1977), esp. pp. 60–3.

[30] *National Insurance Bill, Memorandum Explanatory of the Bill as Passed by the House of Commons*, p. 2, 1911 Cd. 5995 LXXIII. 69.

memoirs and Bentley Gilbert's book amply demonstrate the superior political skill of the representatives of the commercial world, or rather their greater ability and willingness to hire the professional skills required. The professional advisers of the insurance companies and their allies, particularly Kingsley Wood, emerge as the really able men in this struggle. As for the Friendly Society leaders involved, Braithwaite called them an extraordinarily thick-headed crowd and added:

They were intensely worthy . . . But oh they were so difficult—often so suspicious—and always so unintelligent and unadaptable. No doubt National Insurance and the complexities of legislation were too much for men often of humble circumstances and education. But why did they not get good advice? Why did they allow themselves to be outwitted every time?[31]

The subsequent history of national health insurance shows that in the competition for contributors the commercial companies were far and away the more successful. When health insurance was investigated in 1928, it had come to be generally recognized that insurance through approved societies had failed to create a system of self-government.[32]

The reasons for this ability of commercial undertakings to act more effectively in the politics of 1911, and subsequently in society as such, than voluntary mutual-help associations based on participation touch on some of the deepest changes in British society between the 1880s and 1920s.[33] But they acquire a peculiar importance in this connection because of the determination to minimize the role of the bureaucratic State. For there was in theory an alternative to the use of approved societies, namely bureaucratic structures in direct contact with the insurance contributors. They would certainly have been more expensive to the Treasury, and would thereby have increased the need for higher taxation, with political complications which the government was anxious to avoid. (Whether they would have been more expensive for the nation than the generous administrative costs allowed to the approved societies is quite another question.) Such considerations

[31] Bunbury, *Lloyd George's Ambulance Wagon*, p. 92.
[32] R. W. Harris, *National Health Insurance in Great Britain 1911–1946* (1946), chs. 4, 5. *RC on National Health Insurance, Majority Report*, ch. 8., *Minority Report*, paras. 38–40, 1926 Cmd. 2596 XIV. 311.
[33] See S. C. Yeo, *Religion and Voluntary Organisation in Crisis* (1976).

were undoubtedly important to the Chancellor of the Exchequer. But they were not the only considerations. The preference for voluntary associations was a positive preference, and it was only when it was too late to withdraw from the decision that its full implications became apparent.

The evidence presented in this chapter indicates that the comparisons which formed so prominent a part of the means by which the Bill was presented to the British public in 1911 were very different from those that a historical observer would wish to make. They were profoundly misleading for the simple reason that they were chiefly an expression of rivalry.

Indeed the financial comparison derived entirely from Lloyd George's judgement that an appeal to rivalry was an effective tactic in the contemporary situation. The comparison of organization and structure also owed something to the political need to reassure the Friendly Societies and the Liberal conscience. It was largely the work of Braithwaite and reflected his emphasis.

It would be unrealistic to expect comparisons presented so obviously for the sake of political persuasion to go far to satisfy a historian's rather different interests. From that point of view the documents in question are both evasive and misleading. Their value lies rather in what they tell us about the way in which political perceptions had been transformed. Here they point to two conclusions. On the one hand they indicate that the sense of rivalry could make acceptable what might have been expected to be a political liability. On the other hand they suggest the degree to which the territory that lay ahead was still uncharted.

The long-standing objection to the regimentation of the population had been transformed into a boast that in the United Kingdom one-third of the entire population would be liable to compulsory insurance compared with 24 per cent in Germany under invalidity and a mere 21 per cent under sickness insurance.[34] Little was now heard of the long-standing objection to the cost of administration of a compulsory contributory scheme. In 1908 the Treasury had produced a memorandum on German invalidity and old age insurance in which this item was described as 'extremely heavy',

[34] *National Insurance Bill, Memorandum on Sickness and Invalidity Insurance in Germany*, p. 3. The contrast was somewhat exaggerated and the extension of the German insurance under the law of July 1911, not mentioned in this context, was to make the figures in the two countries roughly the same.

accounting for 7.4 per cent of total income,[35] and in 1911 the figure
was stated to be 8.1 per cent and to be between 7.6 and 8 per cent
for Sickness Insurance.[36] No comparison with the British proposals
was attempted on that occasion, and in view of the high price that
was ultimately to be paid for the inclusion of the industrial
insurance companies and Collecting Friendly Societies that reticence
was well-judged. Ten years after the introduction of British health
insurance, roughly 13 per cent of total income was being spent on
its administration.[37]

This brings us back to the unexpected concessions that proved
necessary under the new circumstances. To appreciate these one
needs to bear in mind just how novel these circumstances were. In
1908 the government had still been reluctantly yielding to the
pressures to provide benefits out of general taxation to support
certain deserving categories of the needy and to rescue them from
dependence on the Poor Law. By deciding to provide benefits by
means of compulsory insurance it replaced an emphasis on taxation
by an alternative emphasis on regulating the conduct of workers
and employers. It had to find new methods of control that would
make it possible to enforce such conduct, and its distrust of
bureaucracy led it to rely heavily on negotiating arrangements with
bodies that were already in the field. Their willingness to co-operate
and the degree to which they would be able to insist on their own
terms was almost entirely unexplored. As Bentley Gilbert has pointed
out, it introduced an even bigger element of bargaining than usual
into the process of legislation.[38] Moreover, since so much of the
administration of the schemes depended on the initiatives taken by
such bodies, what could and what could not be achieved under the
Act was in practice subject to considerable uncertainty.

Meanwhile Braithwaite set about the winding up of his relationship with his German mentors on a suitably guarded note of
courtesy. As soon as they were in print he sent the German

[35] *Memorandum Prepared in the Treasury on Invalidity and Old Age Insurance
in Germany*, Dec. 1908, p. 7, Braithwaite Papers II. 1. 14. See also comments by
Alfred Mond, Liberal MP, E. A. Goulding, Conservative MP, and G. N. Barnes,
Labour MP, on this matter, in 4 *Hansard* 190 (15 June 1908) 640–2; ibid. (16 June
1908) 745–6, 806–7.
[36] *National Insurance Bill, Memorandum on Sickness and Invalidity Insurance in
Germany*, p. 13.
[37] Evidence of Sir Walter Kinnear, *Mins. of Ev.* to the RC *on National Health
Insurance*, para. 290 (Non-parliamentary Publication, 1925).
[38] Gilbert, *Evolution of National Insurance*, pp. 289–90.

insurance authorities copies of the Bill, of Lloyd George's speech of 4 May introducing it to the Commons, and of the two memoranda explaining the health insurance and the unemployment insurance provisions respectively. What he did not include was the memorandum on sickness and invalidity insurance in Germany, with its massaged figures and its dubious claims.[39] Not that such caution made any difference. The German authorities were following the British initiatives with the greatest interest and soon possessed copies of the relevant documents as well as much British and German newspaper comment. Even the Kaiser asked for a briefing, and in preparation for this the Ministry of the Interior produced a document which set out the circumstances and analysed the British Bill from the German official perspective.[40] It naturally dwelt on the debt that the legislators owed to the German model both in its details and its principles, and singled out eight matters in particular:

1. The compulsory nature of the insurance.
2. The reliance on contributions from both employers and employees with the addition of a State subsidy.
3. The responsibility of the employer for the payment of the joint contribution, and his right to deduct the worker's contribution from his wages.
4. The use of stamps and insurance cards.
5. The use of the Post Office.
6. Treatment in sanatoriums, and the organization of health education under the scheme.
7. The inclusion of voluntary insurance within the scheme.
8. The similarity in the categories of benefit provided: medical treatment, medicines, sickness benefit, and maternity benefit, and in the length of entitlement.

This last item was perhaps claiming too much, and there was no attempt to distinguish the practice of Friendly Societies from those matters, such as maternity benefit, which really were borrowed from abroad. One device that could have been added under the last heading and was overlooked was the four-day waiting period

---

[39] Letter, 12 May 1911, LPES, Braithwaite Papers II. 76.

[40] Zentral Staatsarchiv, Potsdam, Rmdj. No. 824, 272–81 Rs. See Florian Tennstedt, 'Anfänge sozial-politischer Intervention in Deutschland und England— einige Hinweise zu wechselseitigen Beziehungen', *Zeitschrift f. Sozialreform*, 29 (1983), 631–48.

before entitlement to benefit, which had had such an attraction for the Chancellor of the Exchequer.

Much emphasis was placed in the German document on the political concern of the Liberal government for working-class support and its dependence on the Labour Party votes for its majority in the current Parliament. This was adduced to help to explain the consideration shown to working-class institutions, as well as the willingness to provide what was by German standards a substantial State contribution. Rather more surprising is the document's claim to have identified the strong influence of 'socialist-communist ideas' in the Liberal government's policy. It instanced the provision of old age pensions in 1908 at the expense of the taxpayer, and saw the same principles still at work in those clauses of the 1911 Bill that relieved the lowest-paid of some of their contributions at the expense of their employer, and that gave the insured in receipt of sickness benefit some protection from ejection for non-payment of rent. Interestingly enough it saw the same ideas behind the 'extensive egalitarianism' of the flat-rate contributions and benefits, which took no account of income levels or of the diversity of needs due, for instance, to differences between conditions in town and country.

It is not to be expected that an official German comparison between the two schemes would meekly accept the judgements expressed in the British government's memorandum on the subject. For one thing the author was unimpressed by the superior virtues claimed for self-governing Friendly Societies compared with the German system and drew attention to the disadvantaged position of those excluded by the approved societies and relegated to the limited benefits of the Post Office deposit insurance. The German document made much of this point and reckoned that it would apply to practically half the insured population under the British Bill. Certainly at that time, before the industrial insurance companies had appeared on the scene, no one could have known the outcome of Lloyd George's gamble. But as it turned out the German assessment was very wide of the mark. By 1913 the number of Post Office deposit contributors was a mere 3 per cent of the total insured population in Britain.[41]

[41] Calculated from figures in *Annual Report for 1913–14 on the Administration of National Health Insurance*, 1914 Cd. 7496, LXXII. 3. By 1924 the percentage had fallen to 1.5%. *RC on National Health Insurance, Report*, p. 174, 1926 Cmd. 2596 XIV. 311.

For another thing the German document was quick to stress the contrast between the contributions required and the benefits obtainable under the two schemes, 'outwardly so similar in kind, yet inwardly completely different'. A flat-rate system, and one that in addition granted a standard disability pension irrespective of the length of time that contributions had been paid, did not lend itself to comparison with what was available in Germany, it pointed out with reference to the figures produced in the British memorandum. Even so it took the British set of figures more seriously than might have been expected. If the British worker obtained benefits for a lower contribution, it pointed out somewhat primly, the reason was that the British had made inadequate provision to cover future costs.

There is one further comparison to be made, although it is to be found neither in the British nor in the German document. No doubt there were many German precedents that were not followed when Britain turned its attention to constructing a system of national insurance. Among the most significant must be reckoned the establishment of a separate system of insurance for white-collar workers, which was being introduced at that very time in Germany. There was no interest at all in that idea. The British Act applied to 'artisans, mechanics, miners, clerks, shop assistants, servants, sailors', and many others, 'whether paid by the hour, day, week, month or year'. While excluding those earning more than £160 a year and those in pensionable jobs, it made no attempt to distinguish the manual worker from the low-paid white-collar worker. There was no basis for such a distinction in treatment in the politics of Edwardian Britain. In this respect, although Habsburg Austria led the way and Wilhelmine Germany soon followed, they provided no precedent for Britain then or later.[42]

[42] For the German *Angestelltenversicherung* of 1911, see Ritter, *Social Welfare in Germany and Britain*, pp. 91–8. For the Austrian law of 1906 see Herbert Hofmeister, 'Austria', in Peter A. Kohler and Hans F. Zacher (eds.), *The Evolution of Social Insurance 1881–1981: Studies of Germany, France, Great Britain, Austria and Switzerland* (1982).

13
Conclusion

THE relationship of British social reformers to the German insurance precedent as it has been presented here falls fairly clearly into five phases of unequal length. The 1880s were dominated in England by Canon Blackley's proposals that embraced compulsory insurance against both sickness and old age. In Germany they span the years between the launching of Bismarck's new social policy in 1881 and the introduction of the third and last of his new measures of compulsory workers' insurance, the Old Age and Invalidity Insurance Law of 1889. These were years of great fluidity for German social policy. They witnessed a bewildering series of draft proposals for legislation followed by revisions and amendments. This process must have been difficult for outsiders to understand and was certainly not followed closely by British social reformers. The second phase began in 1890 with the publication of Burt's Return on pauperism in old age and was dominated in Britain by the various proposals for old age pensions. This was followed by the period between August 1906 and May 1908 when old age pensions legislation was being drafted at the Treasury. The fourth phase consists of the six months from June to December 1908 during which the Liberal government was converted to the German approach, i.e. to compulsory contributory insurance. The fifth and final phase began in 1909 and saw the making of the National Insurance Act of 1911 and the utilization of the existing German arrangements for this purpose.

The six months from June to December 1908 provide the turning-point in that story, and its significance has already been expounded at length. Something more ought to be said, however, about the significance of the transition from the first to the second phase. The narrowing of the focus that occurred at that point had important effects on the way in which German workers' insurance was perceived in Britain.

The decisive rejection of the sickness-insurance component in

Blackley's proposals and the long drawn-out debate over old age pensions focused whatever interest British social reformers showed in German insurance schemes on that for old age and invalidity pensions, except in so far as the problem of employers' liability drew their attention to that for accident insurance. Even when the shortcomings of the 1908 old age pensions legislation encouraged some people to turn to German precedents for ways to reduce the pensions age for those for whom the age of 70 was unrealistically high, it was to the invalidity pensions, which formed part of the German old age and invalidity pensions provisions, that they turned their attention. As late as December 1908 the Treasury was confining its attention to the law of 1889 as amended in 1900 when briefing the Chancellor of the Exchequer on German precedents.[1]

Yet old age and invalidity insurance, with its bureaucratic structure of insurance institutions, stood in marked contrast to the other two schemes, in neither of which the State directly undertook the provision of insurance. It compelled its citizens instead to belong to approved associations of mutual insurance over which it exercised some degree of supervision. In the field of accident insurance, this involved the compulsory creation of associations of employers (*Berufsgenossenschaften*) and made the element of regimentation appear particularly prominent in the eyes of British commentators. But, in the case of the largely disregarded sickness insurance scheme, many of the sickness funds on which the scheme relied had already been in existence when the law was passed. Some of these, the factory funds, had been established compulsorily under earlier legislation, others were the creation of workers' mutual help or of other forms of initiative. The problem that had faced the legislators in 1883 and for the decade thereafter had been how to decide on the conditions under which existing bodies should be approved as suitable to participate in the scheme.[2] If only for that reason the sickness insurance scheme had far more of relevance to show to British social reformers than did the scheme for old age and invalidity insurance.

A few better-informed commentators did occasionally point out that the Germans had been prepared to accommodate existing

---

[1] See p. 189 above.
[2] This is dealt with only shortly in English: see Dawson, *Social Insurance in Germany*, pp. 4–10, 33. For a fuller treatment see Tennstedt, *Geschichte der Selbstverwaltung in der Krankenversicherung*.

institutions of mutual help in designing their insurance, and that the existence of such bodies as the British Friendly Societies was therefore no insuperable obstacle to a British variant of the German scheme.[3] Yet even Beveridge and Cox had done so merely to make a debating point in a climate in which it had been automatically assumed that German workers' insurance was inapplicable to the British scene with its flourishing Friendly Society sector. The point was never pursued far enough for anyone actually to inquire how the German State had treated these bodies and what lessons might be drawn from that experience. In other words, even when attention was drawn to those features of the German sickness insurance scheme that differed significantly from the better-known old age and invalidity pensions system, the references were superficial and the issues raised were never pursued.

For much of the period there was therefore little appreciation among British social reformers that the variety of different approaches which characterized the German experiment in compulsory social insurance could be of some use to them. It was not until Lloyd George and Braithwaite got down to the details of constructing a National Insurance Bill that this changed. Braithwaite was well aware that he had two models to draw upon, even if his references to the third model, the employer-dominated accident insurance model, are rare. It is true that by and large his approach to German precedents was negative, that is, he looked for aspects that did not work well. Yet even on that basis the value of studying the German precedent was greatly enhanced because there were in fact at least two proven experiences upon which to draw.[4] This flexibility, and Lloyd George's magpie eye for the useful idea wherever it was to be found, were far removed from the stolid description of the individual German schemes that was the best that Dawson's expertise seemed capable of providing. Certainly at this late stage, even if not before, it was appreciated that the German precedent was not one of uniformity but of variety, and that this enhanced its usefulness.

Such an interest in detail, it might be argued, only made sense once the fundamental rejection of the German insurance model had been replaced by a more sympathetic view. That is not altogether true. This book has, it may be hoped, provided sufficiently

---

[3] See pp. 166, 136, 144 above.
[4] See pp. 176–7 above.

adequate explanations for the course of events up to 1908 for it not to be supposed that we are dealing with a lack of appreciation based merely on ignorance. Yet by ignoring the most liberal of the variants of German social insurance, the one that Bismarck had himself criticized for being too conciliatory to the voluntary principle[5] and which therefore displayed most points of contact with British institutions, British observers saddled themselves with a view of German insurance that was far removed from reality. The bureaucratic nature of the 1889 scheme with its emphasis on regulation, and the forced and artificial creation of mutual associations of employers across the whole economy required by the accident insurance scheme, which seemed to exemplify the worst aspects of German regimentation, had undoubtedly strongly coloured British perceptions. Such matters were alien to the kind of social arrangements of which Englishmen approved. But the attempt by the German architects of sickness insurance to incorporate a multitude of existing bodies into a coherent system belonged to a world for which at least some British social reformers had much sympathy. Had they paid more attention to it, they would have recognized it as an attempt to impose greater completeness and some systematic organization on what was really rather an immature stage of social development.

In 1910 there were more than 23,000 separate German sickness funds, and they greatly varied in size.[6] In the world of insurance, where security is achieved by pooling risks, small is not beautiful. When Lloyd George's advisers were planning British health insurance they too were confronted by a multitude of small societies, but they were also able to deal with large national 'orders', such as the Foresters, Oddfellows, and Rechabites, and with large centralized societies, such as the Hearts of Oak, and it was these bodies that dominated the field. Alongside them were those trade unions that operated as benefit societies and were, like

[5] Vogel, *Bismarcks Arbeiterversicherung*, p. 151.

[6] 34% of the funds were factory funds with an average membership of 415, and 35% were parish funds with an average membership of 210. Between them they contained 35% of the total insured population. The local funds (*Ortskrankenkassen*), which accounted for just on half the insured population, had a more satisfactory average membership of 1,442, but since this category of funds varied enormously in size and contained some very large funds with a membership of over 100,000, the average, which is all that the official statistics provide, concealed the existence of quite small units even here. Figures from the insurance statistics for 1910, reproduced in Dawson, *Social Insurance in Germany*, p. 34.

British trade unions in general, organized on a national basis. The same was true to an even greater extent of the industrial insurance companies and the Collecting Friendly Societies which forced their way on to the scene in the summer of 1911. There were simply no German parallels to that degree of national organization among the sickness funds, although by the amalgamation of local trade-based funds some of the local sickness funds had become very large.

The German consolidating law of 1911 set out to reduce the multitude and diversity of the sickness funds, and increased the minimum size from 50 to 250 in the case of all but two categories, the factory-based and the guild-based funds.[7] At the same time Braithwaite was considering the same issue, that of a minimum permitted size for approved societies. Except for funds established by employers, for which a special guarantee was required, he came up with a minimum of 10,000 members; smaller societies would have to become part of an association. This drastic attempt to establish actuarialy viable units did not pass through Parliament unscathed. In the end small societies were not altogether excluded from the scheme, but they had to be grouped in units of at least 5,000 members for the purposes of pooling surpluses and deficits.[8] This preserved the best of both worlds, small units for close supervision but large units for the sharing of risks. The contrast between the minimum size of units in the two countries is striking.

It is not an isolated contrast. Despite the frequency with which the superior social organization of the German Empire was lauded by British reformers, it should be recognized that there were many respects in which it was Britain that was more coherently organized. It was after all a smaller territory and had a denser population. It was a unitary and not a federal State, and the dominance of London, not least its dominance within the railway network, made it easier to organize many aspects of British life on a national basis, although Ireland provides something of an exception to this. Because of this degree of national organization in British society, and the absence of entrenched federal structures in the constitution, the British State had in many respects a less difficult task when it came to establish a national insurance system.

---

[7] Ibid., pp. 35–7.
[8] *National Insurance Bill, Memorandum Explanatory of the Bill*, para. 5 (A); *Memorandum Explanatory of the Bill as Passed by the House of Commons*, para. 6 (3).

Thus the federal nature of the German Empire inevitably required a multiplication of top-level supervisory authorities. In 1910 there were thirty-one of these on a territorial basis and ten others for special categories of the insured. Even after the consolidation of the administration by the law of 1911 the individual states were still entitled to retain their own supreme insurance office alongside that of the Reich.[9] By comparison the four Insurance Commissions set up in 1911 for England, Scotland, Wales, and Ireland, made necessary by the exigencies of nationalist politics, appeared to be simplicity itself.

This point would not be worth making were it not so much at variance with the picture that was commonly drawn of Germany as a country whose national life was more coherently and completely organized. Reality was less simple and more diverse and it would have been possible to have come up with a more discriminating view. The way in which in Dawson's conscientious and detailed publications image and evidence occasionally failed to coincide has been mentioned already.[10] Most publicists and reformers turned abroad with a highly selective eye. It was the condition of England that interested them; their diagnosis of its needs did not derive from the study of other political systems. German precedents were grist to their mill and chosen for that purpose. The image of German national life as more coherently and completely organized, an image built up since at least the 1860s by those with a particular interest in education, helped social reformers to know what they were looking for. That the picture which they drew was far from being the whole picture is less significant than what they did see and how they used it.

This brings us back to the heart of the subject as it has been presented here, the decision to embark on a policy of national insurance and its consequences. This decision certainly involved a degree of compulsion and organization greater than had previously existed, just as the German initiative had done in the 1880s. Why did it happen? And what use was the earlier German experience?

In Britain the introduction of National Insurance was a response to the successful mobilization of demands for income in times of hardship over whose causes the individual had no control. That organized labour played an important role in this process is

[9] *Reichsversicherungsordnung*, 1911, para. 105.
[10] See p. 35 above.

significant, but more significant is the width of the appeal that such demands could make to the electorate and the consequent response that they evoked among MPs. 'However willing the working classes may be to remain in passive opposition merely to the existing social system', Churchill had written in 1907, 'they will not continue to bear . . . the awful uncertainties of their lives.'[11] It was a perceptive and influential assessment.

What was mobilized was a demand not for insurance but for income to be provided as of right at the expense of the community, i.e. out of general taxation. It was demanded in such a way as to leave the status and freedom of action of the mutual-help institutions of working-class life unaffected. There was to be no means test to discourage contributions to benefit societies, no payments to compete with those to benefit societies, and no subsidies to such societies to create a threat to their independence.

Even had the demands been met out of general taxation in the form in which they had originally been formulated, it is likely that they would have led not just to higher taxation but to greater State regulation. Benefits from public funds could not have been unconditional. Qualifications for entitlement would have had to be observed, conditions and records kept. From the point of view of the recipient this would have been far less onerous than dependence on the Poor Law, but from the perspective of society a new administration would have been required dealing with far more people than the Boards of Guardians ever dealt with. Moreover any departure from a purely universalist policy would have required still more regulations. Whatever might be conceivable in other political cultures, in Edwardian Britain State generosity would certainly have been accompanied by political accountability and therefore by greater regulation. Nor would the institutions of working-class life have been left as untouched by the process as was intended. In the Labour Party's Right-to-Work Bill lurked many a hidden question about the relation between the trade unions and the proposed unemployment committees. For these reasons it can be argued that, if the democratic impulse pointed to redistribution of income, it also pointed inevitably to greater State regulation.

The fact is, however, that the demands were not met in the form in which they had been presented. The policy on which the

---

[11] W. S. Churchill to J. A. Spender, qd. in Wilson Harris, *J. A. Spender* (1946), p. 81.

government embarked was deliberately intended to limit the call on general taxation and to rely instead to a much greater extent on the regulating powers of the State. It is in this way that national insurance differed from what was being asked for and from what had been reluctantly and partially provided in 1908. As has been suggested in the Introduction, this is what the interest in the German town-planning precedents had in common with that in workers' insurance. In each case the raised expectations of publicly provided benefits, whether income in time of need or improved dwèlling-space, led the government to increase the amount of regulation over the life of its citizens as a partial alternative to increasing taxation.

Had the response to the demands been indeed to offer higher benefits paid out of higher taxation, it is unlikely that British social reformers would have found much to interest them in Germany apart from a revenue tariff. Those who thought in such terms and looked to Germany as a protectionist State do not feature prominently in this book. We are mainly concerned with those at the free trade end of the political spectrum, who accepted the need to reform the system of direct taxation to increase its yield but at the same time wished to make this process politically manageable by moderating demands. It is true that they were at the same time looking to Germany for means to increase direct taxation, but they found little that was usable.[12] It was at the point at which they wished to divert further demands for direct taxation that German precedents had something to offer.

That is not surprising when it is remembered that compulsory insurance was pioneered by a political authority, the German Reich, which possessed no powers of direct taxation and for which, therefore, an ambitious policy of meeting working-class aspirations out of direct taxation was out of the question. A Chancellor who wished to enhance the political authority of the Reich by embarking on a policy of financial benefits for the workers was obliged to find the necessary resources in some other way, since it was the individual states that possessed the right of direct taxation.

[12] Braithwaite had been sent to Germany in 1910 to investigate local income taxes and had returned with an unfavourable report: 'Memoirs 1910–1912', typescript, LPES, Braithwaite Papers I (d) vol. 1. The taxation of site values was regarded as a more promising matter. For an interest in German precedents, see Offer, *Property and Politics 1870–1914*, pp. 193, 326–7.

Bismarck had intended to rely on two sources of revenue, indirect taxation on tobacco and contributions from employers, both of which, he assumed, could be passed on to the consumer. The Reichstag refused to grant him the former and he had ultimately to rely on contributions from both employers and workers. The contributory or insurance system had therefore arisen from the specific circumstances of Germany's federal constitution. But it was well suited to any government which wished to provide benefits for the mass of wage-earners without levying additional direct taxes or taxing articles of consumption. The real affinity between the politics of the German Reich in the early 1880s and those of the Asquith government was fiscal.

It is not to be found, as is occasionally suggested, in a common response to a 'socialist threat'. There the differences are more striking than the similarities. It seems generally agreed that for Bismarck workers' insurance was the carrot designed to accompany the stick of the anti-socialist laws. Electoral politics was to be made impossible for the Social Democrats, who had become established spokesmen of important sections of the organized working class and were growing in influence. Lloyd George's relationship to the established spokesmen of organized labour in Britain was totally different. Nothing brings out this fact better than the way in which the Liberal government was prepared to obtain the support of the Labour Party for the National Insurance Bill by agreeing to a trade union measure that would reverse the Osborne judgment of 1909, which had ruled that it was illegal for trade unions to spend their funds for political purposes. The legalization of the political levy that was brought about by the Trade Union Act of 1913 assured the expansion, indeed the continued existence, of a Parliamentary Labour Party. To Bismarck the 'socialist threat' had meant an attack on the Reich; its suppression was seen as the defence of the political structure established in 1871. To the Asquith government and its supporters the 'socialist threat' meant an attack on the purse, not revolution but profligacy.

The moral overtones of that word perhaps describe the stance of some Liberals more than others. For Lloyd George himself it was more a matter of political inexpediency. Insurance, as he explained to his private secretary, was for him necessarily a temporary expedient. He hoped that at no distant date the State would acknowledge full responsibility in the matter of making provision

for sickness breakdown and unemployment, not through the Poor
Law as it did already but in a way that was honourable and not
degrading. Insurance, he added, would then be unnecessary. There
is much retrospective irony to be extracted from those words in
view of the long and much lauded role that social insurance has
played in twentieth-century Britain. Nothing illustrates better the
truth of the dictum, attributed to the historian George Unwin, that
policy begins as expediency and ends up as principle.[13]

To answer the question 'Why did it happen?' exclusively in terms
of democratic pressure is, however, to present that process in
misleading isolation. The policy could be and was supported also
on grounds of maximizing the human resources of the nation and
protecting them from deterioration. It was to some degree a
response to anxieties caused by international rivalry. One objection
to the concentration of resources on the needs of the elderly,
expressed by Lloyd George himself, was that it ignored the needs of
the more active sections of the population at a time when these
ought to loom large in the consideration of social reformers.[14]
Whether, in the absence of democratic pressure for increased
income benefits, these considerations alone would have sufficed is
quite another question. It was the powerful conjunction of both
considerations that produced the support for a hazardous task of
political reorientation.

Nevertheless it should be borne in mind that reliance on
compulsory insurance was not particularly well suited to maximizing
the nation's human resources and protecting those most at risk
from deterioration. Dependent as it was on the regular contributions
of the wage-earner and his employer, it was suited only to those in
regular wage-earning employment. It was therefore difficult to
apply to the casually employed or to the self-employed, while the
inclusion of the needs of dependants was liable to put an excessive
burden on the contributors. Yet the casually employed had been

[13] Lloyd George to G. R. Hawtrey, 7 Mar. 1911, in Bunbury, *Lloyd George's
Ambulance Wagon*, pp. 121–2. The dictum by Unwin in its original version runs:
'Policy, as actually found in history, is a set of devices into which a government drifts
under the pressure of practical problems, and which gradually acquire the conscious
uniformity of a type, and begin, at last, to defend themselves as such', George
Unwin, *Studies in Economic History* (1927), p. 184.
[14] See his budget speech announcing the new policy, in 5 *Hansard* 4 (29 Apr.
1909), 484.

repeatedly identified as the heart of the problem of poverty,[15] and as central to the unemployment problem.[16] This fact should serve to remind us that on any comprehensive view of national efficiency there were other groups at risk. Yet their needs counted for little compared with those in regular employment, who were more likely to have qualified for the vote and to belong to organizations by whom the political demands were being voiced. The policy of insurance did not address itself *first and foremost* to need, whether formulated in terms of the individual or of the nation. It was a bold extension of the circle of the more privileged, intended to give certain deserving categories protection from dependence on the Poor Law. It addressed itself first and foremost to demands.

That is to put the matter starkly, but the object of politics is usually to blur alternatives not to stress them. We are dealing with a conjunction of two considerations, and every effort was made to minimize the differences between them, i.e. to stretch the insurance concept to cover those groups that did not fall into the category of regular wage-earners.

In the case of the temporarily unemployed Lloyd George had intended to permit them to suspend their contributions without penalty, and stressed that this made the proposed British insurance more generous and more adequate than its German counterpart.[17] That clause did not survive the parliamentary process, and the problem of the unemployed, piling up arrears of contributions and being penalized for it, became one of the problems of operating a

[15] Charles Booth, *Life and Labour of the People in London*, i (1889; 3rd edn. 1902). It could have been argued since the publication of B. S. Rowntree's *Poverty: A Study of Town Life* (1901), that, if York was typical of English towns, other causes of poverty, such as low wages earned by the regularly employed, were more important. But even from Rowntree's figures such a conclusion does not necessarily follow. It would have to ignore those whom Rowntree counted as being in secondary poverty. In 1909 the older view was still being expressed in the most respected quarters: see *The Relations of Industrial and Sanitary Conditions to Pauperism*, by A. D. Steel-Maitland and Rose E. Squire, p. 178, *RC on the Poor Laws*, app. vol. XVI 1909 Cd. 4653 XLIII.

[16] W. H. Beveridge, *Unemployment: A Problem of Industry* (1909), esp. chs. 5, 9, 10, 11. Beveridge regarded unemployment insurance as subordinate to the organization of the labour market on a national basis by means of labour exchanges and the decasualization of the labour force. It made sense only in conjunction with it. See also nn. 20, 23 below.

[17] *National Insurance Bill, Memorandum on Sickness and Invalidity Insurance in Germany*, p. 2.

contributory scheme in the age of high long-term unemployment after the war.[18]

In 1911 the proponents of compulsory insurance were more preoccupied with stretching the provisions to cover the casually employed. Braithwaite had noticed how the Germans, by excluding casual labourers from their sickness-insurance contributions, had actually encouraged their employment.[19] German invalidity insurance was different. There casual labourers were generally included, but so many grounds for exception were provided that the question of who was compelled to contribute and who was not had become a labyrinth. He was determined that the British scheme should be wide enough to include most forms of casual labour. In that case there was bound to be a problem over the employer's contribution. Some employers would be penalized by having to pay the whole week's contribution for less than a week's work; others would get off free. What might be regarded as an awkward administrative problem was closely connected with fundamentals, since the existence of casual labour on a large scale was widely considered as a major cause of poverty and as encouraging an improvident and unreliable way of life among the work-force. The fact that casual employment failed to meet the conditions on which the success of compulsory insurance normally depended was therefore not necessarily a disadvantage. Those who hoped to use the power of the State to diminish the extent of casual employment saw an opportunity here, and the Act offered employers the chance of reduced contribution if they co-operated in arrangements which would lead to more regular forms of employment. Yet that co-operation was only very rarely obtained. The hope entertained by such civil servants as Beveridge that contributory insurance could be used to hasten the decasualization of the labour market, precisely because such insurance schemes depended for their effective operation on a labour force regularly employed by the week, was to be disappointed.[20]

[18] For the long list of measures dealing with the problem, partly at the expense of the unemployed, whose entitlement was reduced although never allowed to disappear, partly at the expense of the insurance funds, and finally at the expense of the taxpayer, see B. B. Gilbert, *British Social Policy 1914–1939* (1970), pp. 294–300.

[19] Bunbury, *Lloyd George's Ambulance Wagon*, pp. 110, 255–7.

[20] For details, see Gordon Phillips and Noel Whiteside, *Casual Labour: The Unemployment Question in the Port Transport Industry 1880–1970* (Oxford, 1985), ch. 3.

The third group to present the architects of National Insurance with a special problem were the self-employed. They were to be allowed to join sickness insurance on a voluntary basis, but paying a higher contribution to compensate for the non-existence of the employer's share. This option was taken up to such an insignificant extent that the privilege was withdrawn in 1918.[21]

Finally it must be borne in mind that the Act of 1911 imposed no obligation on approved societies to pay for medical treatment for anyone but the contributor himself. Apart from the maternity grant, wives qualified only if they too were wage-earners. Children did not qualify at all. Approved societies were permitted to pay for the medical treatment of dependants at their own discretion out of surplus funds. It fell into the category of matters that were desirable but not essential. Nothing demonstrates more clearly than this limitation of compulsory provision to the breadwinner how little the legislation was designed to improve the physical condition of the nation. The provision was against poverty, and against illness only in so far as it led to an interruption of earnings.

From all this it may be seen that, although compulsory insurance significantly increased the numbers who enjoyed some protection against the consequences of illness and of unemployment, the limitations inherent in this way of financing and organizing the benefit inevitably set bounds to the degree of comprehensiveness obtainable. Truly national insurance in the sense of nationwide insurance, even for those below a certain income, was unobtainable in this way.

This is a matter that should not surprise us in view of the origins of the device. That was not the purpose for which compulsory insurance had been designed when introduced in Germany. It had been aimed at a limited section of the working class, picked on account of its ability to express political preferences. Sickness insurance was introduced in a piecemeal manner, and domestic servants, and agricultural and forestry workers, were not included until the law of 1911. Much the same was true of accident

[21] Voluntary insurance continued to be available for another class that did not fit the assumptions on which compulsory insurance was based, i.e. those who had once been employed and built up an entitlement but then become self-employed. The number of those who chose to become voluntary insurers was very small, *RC on National Health Insurance, Mins. of Ev.*, QQ. 42, 23, 398 (Non-parliamentary Publication, 1925).

insurance.[22] There was no pressing reason why Bismarck and his subordinates should have wished to include the whole working-class population. On the contrary there was a distinct advantage in excluding occupations that existed in different social and political contexts from that of industrial workers. Chamberlain had done the same in 1897 for a similar mixture of political and administrative calculations. The conclusion is clear. Compulsory insurance, whether in Britain or in Germany, was not about provision for the whole working-class population. That was ruled out by the methods on which it relied.

The weakness of a form of provision which relied so heavily on the contributions of the wage-earner in regular employment and of his employer might have become apparent more rapidly than it did but for the onset of the war. Wartime demands for manpower and for production reduced unemployment and the under-employment of the casual worker to previously unknown levels.[23] The pent-up demand for consumption created almost equally exceptional conditions in the immediate post-war period. This situation led to a misplaced optimism about the applicability of the insurance system, which showed itself most clearly in the extension of unemployment insurance to all wage-earners by 1920. The conflict between the assumptions inherent in the insurance model and the strong political pressures in the post-war world for maintenance for all the unemployed rapidly exposed the limitations of the former.[24] Under the pressures of long-term unemployment the distinction between

---

[22] *Persons Insured as a Percentage of Total Population*

	Sickness Insurance	Accident Insurance
1885	10.0	7.0
1895	15.4	32.5
1904	19.2	30.9
1914	23.0	36.7

Figures for 1885, 1895, and 1904 from Reichsversicherungsamt, *Statistik der Arbeiterversicherung des deutschen Reichs 1885–1904*, bearbeitet von G. A. Klein (Berlin, 1906), p. 8; figures for 1914 are calculated from Kaiserliches Statistisches Amt, *Statistisches Jahrbuch für das deutsche Reich* (Berlin), 1916, 1917. The figures for sickness differ slightly from those given in Ritter, *Social Welfare in Germany and Britain*, p. 187, table 1.

[23] For unemployment, see figures in B. R. Mitchell and Phyllis Deane, *Abstract of British Historical Statistics* (Cambridge, 1962), ch. 2. For casual labour at the docks, see Phillips and Whiteside, *Casual Labour*, chs. 4, 5.

[24] Gilbert, *British Social Policy*, chs. 2, 4.

insurance and provision of benefits out of general taxation was rapidly subverted.

The achievements of Part 1 of the National Insurance Act proved less evanescent, but it would be unrealistic to expect health insurance to have remained unaffected by the increase in unemployment between the wars. It carried the consequent loss in contributions largely from its accumulated funding. It was also affected by the cut-back in unemployment relief in the 1930s which drove more claimants on to health insurance. Many sanguine hopes for the expansion of provisions from accumulated funds that had blossomed between 1911 and the early 1920s withered in the harsher years that followed.[25] Indeed it is remarkable that social insurance was not more discredited. Even now, when on its revenue side it has become merely a device for additional taxation to be adjusted by the Chancellor of the Exchequer for any purpose of his choosing, and when on its expenditure side it is heavily dependent on the Exchequer, i.e. when all that characterizes insurance has evaporated, it remains firmly entrenched as an institution of the modern State.

[25] Noelle Whiteside, 'Private Agencies for Public Purposes: Some New Perspectives on Policy Making in Health Insurance between the Wars', *Journal of Social Policy* 12. 2 (1983), 165–93.

BIBLIOGRAPHY

Place of publication is London unless stated otherwise.

I MANUSCRIPT SOURCES

BIRMINGHAM UNIVERSITY LIBRARY:
JOSEPH CHAMBERLAIN PAPERS
W. H. DAWSON PAPERS

BODLEIAN LIBRARY, OXFORD: ASQUITH PAPERS

BRITISH LIBRARY:
JOHN BURNS PAPERS
CAMPBELL-BANNERMAN PAPERS
DILKE PAPERS
HERBERT GLADSTONE PAPERS

CHURCHILL COLLEGE, CAMBRIDGE: CHARTWELL PAPERS

LIBRARY OF POLITICAL AND
ECONOMIC SCIENCE, LONDON
SCHOOL OF ECONOMICS:
BEVERIDGE PAPERS
BRAITHWAITE PAPERS

PUBLIC RECORD OFFICE:
BOARD OF TRADE PAPERS
BRADBURY PAPERS
CABINET PAPERS
HOME OFFICE PAPERS
TREASURY PAPERS

ZENTRAL STAATSARCHIV, POTSDAM: REICHSAMT DES INNEREN

II NEWSPAPERS AND PERIODICALS

The *Athenaeum*
Blackwood's Magazine
The *Daily Chronicle*
The *Daily News*
Economic Journal
The *Examiner*
The *London Graphic*

The *Morning Post*
The *Nation*
The *Nineteenth Century*
Post Magazine and Insurance Monitor
The *Review of Reviews*
The *Spectator*
The *Times*

III PARLIAMENTARY PAPERS

RC on Popular Education (Newcastle Commission), Report on the State of Elementary Education in Germany, by Mark Pattison, 1861 [2794–IV] XXI.

Schools Inquiry RC, Report Relative to Technical Education, 1867 [3898] XXVI.

SC on Technical Education, Report, 1867–8 (432) XV.

SC on Employers' Liability, Reports, 1876 (372) IX; 1877 (285) X.

RC on Railway Accidents, Report, 1877 C. 1637 XLVIII.

Reports on the Laws in Force in France and Germany with Regard to the Insurance of Persons Employed in Mines and the Legal Liability of their Employers, 1880 C. 2607 LIX. 233; 1880 C. 2631 LIX. 249.

SC on National Provident Insurance, Mins. of Ev., 1884–5 (270) X; 1886 Sess. 1 (208) XI; *Report,* 1887 (257) XI.

RC on Technical Instruction (Samuelson), 2nd Report, 1884 C. 3981 XXIX; *Mins. of Ev.,* 1884 C. 3982–II XXXI.

SC on Employers' Liability Act (1880) Amendment Bill, Report and Mins. of Ev., 1886 (192) VIII.

Report on Accident Insurance Law of Germany, 1886 C. 4784 LXVII. 571.

Papers Respecting the German Law of Insurance against Old Age and Infirmity, Passed by the Reichstag on 23rd May 1889, 1889 C. 5827 LXXVII. 353.

Correspondence Respecting the Proposed Labour Conference at Berlin, 1890 C. 5914 CXXXI. 529.

Return . . . of the Number of Persons . . . in Receipt of In-door relief and of Out-door Relief Aged over 60 Returned in Quinquenniel Groups on 1st August 1890 (Burt's Return), 1890–1 (36) LXVIII. 563.

Reports from HM Representatives in Europe Respecting Assistance Afforded or Facilities Given by Foreign Governments to the Provision of the Industrial Population for Old Age, 1890–1 C. 6429 LXXXIII. 429.

Return . . . of the Number of Persons . . . over 65 Years and Upwards . . . in Receipt of In-door Relief and Out-door Relief on 1st Jan. 1892 and at Any Time during the 12 Months Ended Lady Day 1892 (Ritchie's Return), 1892 Sess. 1 (265) LXVIII. 619.

Memorandum on the Liability of Employers for Injuries to their Servants, by Sir Godfrey Lushington, *RC on Labour, App. CLIX to Mins. of Ev. Taken before the RC Sitting as a Whole,* pp. 348–59, 1893–4 C. 7063 III–A XXXIX, pt. i. 805.

Memo on Employer's Liability for Accidents in France, Germany and Austria, by Sir Godfrey Lushington, *RC on Labour, App. CLIX to Mins. of Ev. Taken before the RC Sitting as a Whole,* pp. 359–63, 1893–4 C. 7063 III–A XXXIX, pt. i. 805.

RC on Labour, Foreign Reports, vol. v, *Germany,* 1893–4 C. 7063–VII XXXIX, pt. ii.

Report on Agencies and Methods for Dealing with the Unemployed, 1893–4 C. 7182 LXXXII. 377.

Memo on the Evidence re Employers' Liability, Secretary's Summaries of the Evidence, App. V, 5th and Final Report, RC on Labour, Pt. II, pp. 556–62, 1894 C. 7421–I XXXV.

RC on the Aged Poor, Report, 1895 C. 7684 XIV; *Mins. of Ev.,* 1895 C. 7684–I XIV; 1895 C. 7684–II XV.

Report on the Operation of the Insurance Laws in Germany for 1895, Foreign Office Reports, General and Commercial, Miscell. Series, 418, 1897, C. 8278 LXXXVIII. 677.

Report on a Visit to Germany with a View to Ascertaining the Recent Progress of Technical Education in that Country: A Letter to the Duke of Devonshire, by Philip Magnus *et al.,* 1897 C. 8301 LXXXVIII. 403.

Departmental Committee on Old Age Pensions, Report etc., 1898 C. 8911 XLV.

SC on the Aged Deserving Poor, Report, 1899 (296) VIII.

Memos on Provision for Old Age by Government Action in Certain European Countries, 1899 C. 9414 XCII.

Report on Chemical Instruction in Germany and the Growth and Present Condition of the German Chemical Industries, by Frederick Rose, 1901 Cd. 430–16; *Supplementary Report,* 1902 Cd. 787–9.

Board of Trade, Seventh Abstract of Labour Statistics, 1901 Cd. 495 LXXIII.

British Foreign Trade and Industrial Conditions, 1903 Cd. 1761 LXVII; 1905 Cd. 2337 LXXXIX.

Interdepartmental Committee on Physical Deterioration, Report, 1904 Cd. 2175 XXXII.

Departmental Committee on Compensation for Injuries to Workmen, vol. i, *Report and Apps.,* 1904 Cd. 2208 LXXXVIII. 487; vol. ii, *Mins. of Ev. and Index,* 1905 Cd. 2334 LXXV. 487; vol. iii, *Memo on Foreign and Colonial Laws,* 1905 Cd. 2458 LXXXV. 897.

Report to the Board of Trade on Agencies and Methods for dealing with the Unemployed in Certain Foreign Countries, by D. F. Schloss, 1905 Cd. 2304 LXXIII. 471.

Departmental Committee on Life Insurance through the Post Office, Reports and Mins. of Ev., 1907 Cd. 3568 LXVIII. 163: 1907 Cd. 3569 LXVIII. 175.

Report on Sanatoria for Consumption and Certain Other Aspects of the Tuberculosis Question, by H. Timbrell Bulstrode, MD, *Supplement to Local Government Board, Annual Report of the Medical Officer for 1905–6,* 1907 Cd. 3657 XXVII. 1.

Return of Workmen's Insurance in Germany against Sickness, Invalidity and Old Age 1908 (102) XCVI. 1189.

Memo on the Old Age Pensions Scheme in Force in New Zealand and the Scheme of Insurance against Invalidity and Old Age in Force in the German Empire, 1908 (159) LXXXVIII. 391.

Cost of Living of the Working Classes: British Towns, 1908 Cd. 3864 CVII. 319; *German Towns,* 1908 Cd. 4032 CVIII. 1.

Workmen's Compensation Statistics, Annual Series, 1908–38.

RC on the Poor Laws, Reports, 1909 Cd. 4499 XXXVII; Mins. of Ev., 1910 Cd. 5066 XLVIII; Cd. 5068 XLIX.

The Relations of Industrial and Sanitary Conditions to Pauperism, by A. D. Steel-Maitland and Rose E. Squire, p. 178, RC on the Poor Laws, app. vol. XVI 1909 Cd. 4653 XLIII.

National Insurance Bill, Report of Deputations, 1911 Cd. 5869 XXIX. 241.

National Insurance Bill, Memorandum Explanatory of the Bill, 1911 (HC 147) LXXIII.

National Insurance Bill, Memorandum on Sickness and Invalidity Insurance in Germany, 1911 Cd. 5678 LXXIII. 213.

National Insurance Bill, Memorandum Containing the Opinions of Various Authorities in Germany, 1911 Cd. 5679 LXXIII. 227.

National Insurance Bill, Report of the Actuaries, 1911 Cd. 5681 LXXIII. 99.

National Insurance Bill, Report of the Actuaries on Pt. I of the National Insurance Bill as Amended in Committee, 1911 Cd. 5983 LXXIII. 143.

National Insurance Bill, Memorandum Explanatory of the Bill as Passed by the House of Commons, 1911 Cd. 5995 LXXIII. 69.

National Health Insurance, Medical Benefit under the German Sickness Legislation, 1912–13 Cd. 6581 LXXXVIII.

Annual Report for 1913–14 on the Administration of National Health Insurance, 1914 Cd. 7496 LXXII. 3.

Board of Trade, Seventeenth Abstract of Labour Statistics, 1914–16 Cd. 7733 LXI.

Departmental Committee on Workmen's Compensation (Holman Gregory), Report, 1920 Cmd. 816 XXVI. 87; Mins. of Ev., vol. i 1920 Cmd. 908 XXVI. 87; vol. ii 1920 Cmd. 909 XXVI. 605.

RC on National Health Insurance, Reports, 1926 Cmd. 2596 XIV. 311; Mins. of Ev. (Non-parliamentary publication 1925, 1926).

IV OTHER OFFICIAL PUBLICATIONS

Brooks, Compulsory Insurance in Germany: Fourth Special Report of the US Commission of Labour (including app. on Compulsory Insurance in Other Countries in Europe; Washington, 1893; rev. edn. 1895).

Congrès International des Accidents du Travail et des Assurances Sociales, Rapports et procès-verbaux (1894–1911).

German Imperial Insurance Office, The Workmen's Insurance of the German Empire: Guide Expressly Published for the World's Exhibition in Chicago (Berlin and London, 1893).

—— Guide to the Workmen's Insurance of the German Empire: Newly Composed for the World's Exhibition in Brussels (Berlin, 1897).

—— Guide to the Workmen's Insurance of the German Empire: Revised

Edition Brought up to date for the International Exhibition at Paris (Berlin, 1900).

—— *Guide to Workmen's Insurance of the German Empire: Revised Edition Brought up to date for the Universal Exposition at St. Louis* (Berlin and London, 1904).

Hansard, *Parliamentary Debates*.

Kaiserliches Statistisches Amt, *Die bestehenden Einrichtungen zur Versicherung gegen die Folgen der Arbeitslosigkeit im Ausland und im deutschen Reich* (3 vols.; Berlin, 1906).

—— *Statistisches Jahrbuch für das deutsche Reich* (Berlin, annual publication).

Labour Party, *Life and Labour in Germany* (1910).

NCOL, *Annual Reports and Balance Sheet 1900–1909* (1909).

—— *Ten Years' Work for Old Age Pensions 1899–1909* (1909).

Office de Travail, *Études sur les derniers résultats des assurances sociales en Allemagne et Autriche* (Paris, 1895).

Reichsversicherungsamt, *Statistik der Arbeiterversicherung des deutschen Reichs 1885–1904*, bearbeitet von G. A. Klein (Berlin, 1906).

TUC, *Proceedings* (1872–1914).

V   CONTEMPORARY BOOKS AND ARTICLES

Alden, Percy, *The Unemployed: A National Question* (1905).

Anon., 'National Insurance in Germany', *Chamber's Journal*, 8 Feb. 1890, 87–9.

Arnold, Matthew, *The Popular Education of France* (1861).

—— *A French Eton* (1864).

—— *Schools and Universities on the Continent* (1868).

—— *Friendship's Garland* (1871; 2nd edn. 1897; pop. edn. 1903).

Aschrott, P. F., *Das englische Armenwesen in seiner historischen Entwicklung und seiner heutigen Gestalt* (Leipzig, 1886), trans. H. Preston-Thomas (1888; 2nd edn. 1902).

Ashley, Anne, *The Social Policy of Bismarck* (Birmingham Studies in Social Economics; Birmingham, 1912).

Ashley, Percy, 'The Insurance of the Working Classes in Germany, with an Introductory Letter by Sir John Gorst', in W. T. Stead (ed.), *Coming Men on Coming Questions* (1905).

Ashley, W. J., *The Progress of the German Working Classes in the Last Quarter of a Century* (1904).

Barker, J. Ellis, *Economic Problems and Board of Trade Methods: An Exposure* (1908).

Barnes, G. N., and Henderson, A., *Unemployment in Germany: A Report of an Inquiry into the Methods Adopted in Germany for Dealing with Unemployment, Presented to the Labour Party* (n.d. [1908]).

Beveridge, W. H., 'Public Labour Exchanges in Germany' *Economic Journal*, 18. 69 (1908), 1–18.
—— *Unemployment: A Problem of Industry* (1909).
Blackley, W. L., 'National Insurance: A Cheap, Practical and Popular Means of Abolishing Poor Rates', *Nineteenth Century*, 4 (1878), 834–57.
—— *Collected Essays on the Prevention of Pauperism* (1880).
—— 'Prince Bismarck's Scheme of Compulsory Insurance', *Contemporary Review* 39 (1881), 610–28.
—— 'Mr. Goschen on National Insurance', *National Review*, 5 (1885), 490–503.
—— 'Mr. Chamberlain's Pension Scheme', *Contemporary Review*, 61 (1892), 382–96.
—— *Thrift and National Insurance as a Security against Pauperism: With a Memoir of the Late Rev. Canon Blackley and Reprint of his Essays by M. J. J. Blackley* (1906).
Bode, W., 'Old Age Pensions: Failure in Germany', *National Review*, 19 (1892), 26–31.
Bödiker, T., *Die Arbeiterversicherung in den Europäischen Staaten* (Leipzig, 1895).
Booth, Charles, *Life and Labour of the People in London*, vol. 1 (1889; 3rd edn. 1902).
—— 'Enumeration and Classification of Paupers and State Pensions for the Aged', *Jour. Royal Statistical Soc.*, 54 (1891), 600–43.
—— *Old Age Pensions and the Aged Poor* (1899).
—— *Pauperism, a Picture and Endowment of Old Age, an Argument* (1892).
Bowley, A. L., Review of *Economic Problems and Board of Trade Methods: An Exposure*, by J. Ellis Barker, *Economic Journal*, 18 (1908), 657–62.
Brooks, J. G., 'A Weakness in the German "Imperial socialism" ', *Economic Journal*, 2 (1892), 302–15.
—— 'Workmen's Insurance and the Chicago Exhibition', *Economic Journal*, 3 (1893), 138–45.
Bunbury, H. N. (ed.), *Lloyd George's Ambulance Wagon: The Memoirs of W. J. Braithwaite C.B. 1911–1912* (1957).
Chamberlain, Joseph, 'Old Age Pensions', *National Review*, 18 (1892), pp. 722–3.
—— 'The Labour Question', *Nineteenth Century*, 32 (1892), 677–710.
Churchill, R. S., *Winston S. Churchill*, ii. *The Young Statesman 1901–1914* (1967).
—— *Winston S. Churchill*, ii. *Companion* pt. 2 (1967).
Churchill, W. S., 'The Untrodden Field in Politics', *The Nation*, 7 Mar. 1908, 812–13.

Churchill, W. S., *The Complete Speeches*, ed. R. R. James (1974).

Dawson, W. H., *German Socialism and Ferdinand Lassalle: A Biographical History of the German Socialistic Movements during this Century* (1888; 2nd edn. 1891; 3rd rev. and enlarged edn. 1899).

—— *Bismarck and State Socialism* (1890; 2nd edn. 1891).

—— *The Unearned Increment: or Reaping without Sowing* (1890; 2nd edn. 1891; 3rd edn. 1910).

—— *Germany and the Germans* (2 vols.; 1894).

—— *Social Switzerland: Studies of Present-day Social Movements and Legislation in the Swiss Republic* (1897).

—— *German Life in Town and Country* (1901).

—— *Matthew Arnold and his Relation to the Thought of our Time: An Appreciation and a Criticism* (1904).

—— *Protection in Germany: A History of the German Fiscal Policy during the Nineteenth Century* (1904).

—— 'The German Workmen's Secretaries', *Economic Journal* 15 (1905), 443–7.

—— *The German Workman: A Study in National Efficiency* (1906).

—— *The Evolution of Modern Germany* (1908).

—— *Germany at Home* (1908; 2nd edn. of *German Life in Town and Country*, 1901).

—— *School Doctors in Germany* (Board of Education pamphlet, 1908).

—— *The Vagrancy Problem: The Case for Measures of Restraint for Tramps, Loafers etc.* (1910).

—— 'Insurance Legislation, the Larger View', *Fortnightly Review*, 95 (Mar. 1911), 534–47.

—— *Social Insurance in Germany 1883–1911: Its History, Operation, and Results, and a Comparison with the National Insurance Act 1911* (1912).

—— 'Social Insurance in England and Germany—A Comparison', *Fortnightly Review*, 98 (1912), 304–20.

—— *Industrial Germany* (1913).

—— *Municipal Life and Government in Germany* (1914).

—— 'The Campaign against German Trade', *Fortnightly Review*, 102 (Nov. 1914), 755–65.

—— *What is Wrong with Germany* (1915).

—— *The German Danger and the Working Man* (1915).

—— *Problems of Peace* (1917).

—— (ed.), *After-war Problems* (1917).

Dickinson, F. A., *Lake Victoria to Khartoum with Rifle and Camera* (1910).

Du Parq, Herbert, *Life of David Lloyd George* (4 vols.; 1912).

Felkin, H. M. 'The New National Insurance Laws of Germany', *Contemporary Review*, 54 (1888), 279–98.

Gainsborough Commission, *Life and Labour in Germany*, ed. J. L. Bashford (1907).

Gardiner, A. G., *Prophets, Priests and Kings* (new edn., 1924).

Gibbon, I. G., 'Insurance against Sickness and Invalidity and Old Age in Germany', *Economic Journal* 21 (1911), 185–201.

—— *Medical Benefits: A Study of the Experience of Germany and Denmark* (1912).

Gorst, Sir John, 'A Social Programme for Unionists', *Review of Reviews*, 3 (1891), 252, 272.

Haldane, R. B., *Education and Empire* (1902).

—— 'The Executive Brain of the British Empire', in W. T. Stead (ed.), *Coming Men on Coming Questions* (1905), pp. 133–4.

Hobhouse, L. T., *Democracy and Reaction* (1904).

—— *Liberalsim* (1911).

Hobson, J. A., *The Social Problem: Life and Work* (1901).

—— *The Crisis of Liberalism* (1909).

Hogarth, Janet E., 'The German Insurance Laws', *Economic Journal*, 6 (1896), 161–266.

Hooper, E. Grant, *The German State Insurance System for Providing Invalid and Old Age Pensions* (1908).

Horsfall, T. C., *The Government of Manchester: Paper Read to the Manchester Statistical Society* (Manchester, 1895).

—— *The Housing of the Labouring Classes* (Manchester, 1900).

—— *The Housing Question: An Address to the Jubilee Conference of the Manchester and Salford Sanitary Association, 24 April 1902* (Manchester, 1902).

—— *The Improvement of the Dwellings and Surroundings of the People: The Example of Germany: Supplement to the Report of the Manchester and Salford Citizens' Association for the Improvement of the Unwholesome Dwellings and Surroundings of the People* (Manchester, 1904).

—— *The Relation of Town Planning to National Life* (1908).

—— 'On the Interaction between Dwellings and the Occupant in Germany and England', *Town Planning Review*, 2 (1911), 99–112.

—— *The Housing Question in Manchester: Report Presented to the Liège Congress* (n.d.).

James, R. R. (ed.), Winston S. Churchill, *Complete Speeches* (1974).

Jastrow, Henriette, 'Workers' Insurance Legislation in Germany', *Fortnightly Review*, 61 (1897), 374–86.

Marr, T. R., *Housing Conditions in Manchester and Salford* (Manchester, 1904).

Maurice, Sir F. ('Miles'), 'Where to Get Men', *Contemporary Review*, 81 (1902), 78–86.

Müller, August, *Arbeitersekretariate und Arbeiterversicherung in Deutschland* (Munich, 1904).

NAPSS, *Sessional Proceedings* (1877–8).

Nettlefold, J. S., 'Speech made to Birmingham City Council on the Presentation of the Housing Committee's Report', in City of Birmingham, *Report of the Housing Committee, 3 July 1906* (Birmingham, 1906).

—— *Practical Housing* (Birmingham, 1908).

Pattison, Mark, *Suggestions on Academical Organization* (1868).

Preston-Thomas, H., *The English Poor-Law System, Past and Present* (1888; 2nd edn. 1902), trans. from Aschrott, P. F., *Das englische Armenwesen in seiner historischen Entwicklung und seiner heutigen Gestalt* (Leipzig, 1886).

Provand, A. D., 'Employer's Liability', *Nineteenth Century*, 34 (1893), 698–720.

—— 'Employer's Liability', *Contemporary Review*, 66 (1894), 137–52.

Rae, John, *Contemporary Socialism* (1901).

Riddell, George Allardice (Baron), *More Pages from My Diary 1908–1914* (1934).

Rogers, Frederick, *The Care of the Aged in Other Countries and in England* (1905).

—— *Labour, Life and Literature* (1913).

Rowntree, B. S., *Poverty: A Study of Town Life* (1901).

Ruegg, A. H., *The Laws Relating to the Relation of Employer and Workmen in England* (1905).

Schloss, D. F., *Insurance against Unemployment* (1909).

Schwedtman, F. C., and Emery, J. A., *Accident Prevention and Relief: An Investigation of the Subject in Europe with Special Attention to England and Germany* (New York, 1911).

Shadwell, Arthur, *Industrial Efficiency: A Comparative Study of Industrial Life in England, Germany and America* 2 vols.; 1905; (2nd edn. 1909).

Sheffield Daily Telegraph, *Life Under Tariffs: What We Saw in Germany* (Sheffield, 1910).

Spencer, Herbert, *The Study of Sociology* (1874).

Spender, Harold, 'Unemployment Insurance', *Contemporary Review*, 115 (1909), 24–36.

Spender, J. A., *The State and Pensions in Old Age* (1892).

Stead, F. H., *How Old Age Pensions Began to Be* (n.d. [1909]).

Stead, W. T. (ed.), *Coming Men on Coming Questions* (1905).

Tariff Reform League, *Reports on Labour and Social Conditions in Germany* (2 vols.; 1910).

Webb, B., *Our Partnership*, ed. Barbara Drake and Margaret Cole (1948).

Webb, S. and B., *Industrial Democracy* (1898).

—— *The Prevention of Destitution* (1911).

White, Arnold, *Efficiency and Empire* (1901).

Wilkinson, H. Spenser, *The Brain of an Army* (1890).

Williams, E. E., *The German Menace and its English Apologists* (1894).

—— *Made in Germany* (1896, reissued Brighton, 1973).
—— 'The Economic Revolution in Germany', *National Review*, 35 (1900), 922.
—— 'Made in Germany—Five Years Later', *National Review*, 38 (1901), 130–44.
Wolff, Henry, W., 'Accident Insurance', *Contemporary Review*, 67 (1895), 68–80.
Young, Thomas Emley, *The German Law of Insurance 1889 against Invalidity and Old Age: A Paper Read before the Institute of Actuaries 27 April 1891* (1891).
Zacher, Georg, *Die Arbeiterversicherung im Auslande, v. England (Grossbritannien)* (Berlin, 1899).

VI   LATER BOOKS AND ARTICLES

Alderman, Geoffrey, *The Railway Interest* (Leicester, 1973).
Alter, Peter, *Wissenschaft, Staat, Mäzene: Anfänge moderner Wissenschaftspolitik in Grossbritannien 1850–1920* (Stuttgart, 1982).
Argles, Michael, 'The Royal Commission on Technical Instruction 1881–1884: Its Inception and Composition', *Vocational Aspects*, 11.23 (1959), 98.
—— *South Kensington to Robbins: An Account of English Technical and Scientific Education since 1851* (1964).
Armytage, W. H. G., *The German Influence on English Education* (1969).
Ashby, Eric, and Anderson, Mary, *Portrait of Haldane at Work on Education* (1974).
Askwith, G. W., *Industrial Problems and Disputes* (1920).
Bartrip, P. W. J., 'The Rise and Decline of Workmen's Compensation', in Paul Weindling (ed.), *The Social History of Occupational Health* (1985).
Bartrip, P. W. J., and Burman, S. B., *The Wounded Soldiers of Industry: Industrial Compensation Policy 1833–1897* (Oxford, 1983).
Beveridge, W. H., *Report on Social Insurance and Allied Services* (1942).
—— *Power and Influence* (1953).
Brown, K. D., *Labour and Unemployment 1900–1914* (Newton Abbot, 1971).
Cardwell, D. S. L., *The Organisation of Science in England: A Retrospect* (1957).
—— (ed.), *Artisan to Graduate: Essays to Commemorate the Foundation of the Manchester Mechanics Institute* (Manchester, 1974).
Challinor, R. C., *The Lancashire and Cheshire Miners* (Newcastle, 1972).
Chamberlain, Austen, *Politics from Inside* (1936).
Cherry, Gordon E., *Factors in the Origins of Town Planning in Britain: The Example of Birmingham 1905–1915* (Working Paper No. 36,

Centre for Urban and Regional Studies; University of Birmingham, 1975).

Clarke, P. F., *Liberals and Social Democrats* (1978).

Collins, Doreen, 'The Introduction of Old Age Pensions in Great Britain', *Historical Journal*, 8 (1965), 246–59.

Davidson, R., 'Llewellyn Smith, the Labour Department and Government Growth 1886–1909', in Sutherland, G. (ed.), *Studies in the Growth of Nineteenth Century Government* (1972).

—— and Lowe, R., 'Bureaucracy and Innovation in British Welfare Policy 1870–1945', in W. J. Mommsen and W. Mock (eds.), *The Emergence of the Welfare State in Britain and Germany 1850–1950* (1981).

Dinsdale, W. A., *History of Accident Insurance in Great Britain* (1954).

Emy, H. V., *Liberals, Radicals and Social Politics 1892–1914* (Cambridge, 1973).

Flora, Peter, and Heidesheimer, Arnold J., *The Development of Welfare States in Europe and America* (New Brunswick, NJ, 1981).

Foden, Frank, *Philip Magnus, Victorian Educational Pioneer* (1970).

Freeden, Michael, *The New Liberalism* (1978).

Garvin, J. L., *Life of Joseph Chamberlain* (3 vols.; 1932–4).

Gilbert, B. B., *The Evolution of National Insurance in Great Britain: The Origins of the Welfare State* (1966).

—— *British Social Policy, 1914–1939* (1970).

Gooch, John, *The Plans of War: The General Staff and British Military Strategy c. 1900–1916* (1974).

Gwynn, Stephen, and Tuckwell, Gertrude, *Life of the Rt. Hon. Sir Charles W. Dilke* (2 vols.; 1917).

Haines, George IV, 'German Influence upon Scientific Instruction in England 1867–1887', *Victorian Studies*, 1. 3 (1958), 215–44.

—— *Essays on German Influence upon English Education and Science 1850–1919* (Hamden, Conn., 1969).

Hanes, D. G., *The First British Workmen's Compensation Act 1897* (New Haven, Conn., 1968).

Harris, José, *Unemployment and Politics* (Oxford, 1972).

—— *William Beveridge: A Biography* (Oxford, 1977).

Harris, R. W., *National Health Insurance in Great Britain 1911–1946* (1946).

Harris, Wilson, *J. A. Spender* (1946).

Harrison, Michael, 'Housing and Town Planning in Manchester before 1914', in A. Sutcliffe (ed.), *British Town Planning: The Formative Years* (Leicester, 1981).

Havighurst, A. F., *Radical Journalist: A Life of W. H. Massingham* (1974).

Hay, J. R., *The Origins of the Liberal Welfare Reforms 1906–1914* (1975).

—— 'Employers and Social Policy in Britain: The Evolution of Welfare Legislation 1905–14', *Social History*, 4 (1977), 448–50.

—— 'Employers' Attitudes to Social Policy and the Concept of Social Control 1900–1920', in Pat Thane (ed.), *The Origins of British Social Policy* (1978).

—— 'The British Business Community, Social Insurance and the German Example', in W. J. Mommsen and W. Mock (eds.), *The Emergence of the Welfare State in Britain and Germany 1850–1950* (1981).

Heclo, Hugh, *Modern Social Politics in Britain and Sweden* (1974).

Hennock, E. P., 'The Origins of British National Insurance and the German Precedent 1880–1914', in W. J. Mommsen and W. Mock (eds.), *The Emergence of the Welfare State in Britain and Germany 1850–1950* (1981).

—— 'Arbeiterunfallentschädigung und Arbeiterunfallversicherung: Die britische Sozialreform und das Beispiel Bismarcks', *Geschichte u. Gesellschaft*, 11 (1985), 19–36.

Hoffman, R. J. S., *Great Britain and the German Trade Rivalry 1875–1914* (New York, 1933).

Hollenberg, Günther, *Englisches Interesse am Kaiserreich* (Wiesbaden, 1974).

Jenkins, Roy, *Sir Charles Dilke: A Victorian Tragedy* (rev. edn., 1965).

Jones, Donald K., *The Making of the Education System 1851–1881* (1977).

Kennedy, Paul, M., *The Rise of the Anglo-German Antagonism 1860–1914* (1980).

Kohler, Peter, A., and Zacher, Hans F. (eds.), *The Evolution of Social Insurance 1881–1981: Studies of Germany, France, Great Britain, Austria and Switzerland* (1982).

Lowe, Roy, 'The Early 20th C. Open Air Movement: Origins and Implications', in N. Parry and D. McNair (eds.), *The Fitness of the Nation: Physical and Health Education in the 19th and 20th Centuries* (History of Education Society, 1983).

Machtan, Lothar, 'Risikoversicherung statt Gesundheitsschutz für Arbeiter: Zur Entstehung der Unfallversicherungsgesetzgebung im Bismarck-Reich', *Leviathan*, 13. 3 (1985), 420–41.

Mallalieu, W. C., 'Joseph Chamberlain and Workmen's Compensation', *Jour. of Econ. Hist.*, 10 (1959), 45–57.

Marsh, P. T., *The Discipline of Popular Government* (Brighton, 1978).

Masterman, Lucy, *C. F. G. Masterman* (1939).

Messerschmidt, M., *Deutschland in englischer Sicht: Die Wandlung des Deutschlandbildes in der englischen Geschichtsschreibung* (Düsseldorf, 1955).

Mitchell, B. R., and Deane, Phyllis, *Abstract of British Historical Statistics* (Cambridge, 1962).

Mosely, Russell, 'The Origins and Early Years of the National Physical Laboratory: A Chapter in the Pre-history of British Science Policy', *Minerva*, 16 (1978), 222–50.

Offer, A., *Property and Politics 1870–1914* (Cambridge, 1981).

Oppenheimer, Sir Francis, *Stranger Within* (1960).

Pelling, Henry, *Winston Churchill* (1974).

Philips, Gordon, and Whiteside, Noel, *Casual Labour: The Unemployment Question in the Port Transport Industry 1880–1970* (Oxford, 1985).

Reynolds, Josephine P., 'T. C. Horsfall and the Town Planning Movement in England', *Town Planning Review*, 23. 1 (1962) 52–60.

Rimlinger, G. V., *Welfare Policy and Industrialization in Europe, America and Russia* (New York, 1971).

Ritter, Gerhard A., *Staat, Arbeiterschaft und Arbeiterbewegung in Deutschland* (Berlin and Bonn, 1980).

—— *Sozialversicherung in Deutschland und England: Entstehung und Grundzüge im Vergleich* (Munich, 1983).

—— *Social Welfare in Germany and Britain* (Leamington Spa, 1986).

Robinson, H. P., *The Employers' Liability Assurance Corporation Ltd. 1880–1930* (1930).

Russell, A. K., *Liberal Landslide: The General Election of 1906* (Newton Abbot, 1973).

Sanderson, Michael, *The Universities and British Industry 1850–1970* (1972).

Saul, S. B., *Industrialisation and De-industrialisation? The Interaction of the German and British Economies before the First World War* (1980).

Searle, G. R., *The Quest for National Efficiency 1899–1914* (Oxford, 1971).

Seip, Anne-Lise, 'Motive Forces behind the New Social Policy after 1870: Norway on the European Scene', *Scandinavian Jour. of Hist.*, 9 (1984), 329–41.

Semmell, Bernard, *Imperialism and Social Reform: English Social–Imperial Thought 1895–1914* (Cambridge, Mass., 1960).

Sires, R. V., 'British Legislation for Old Age Pensions', *Jour. of Econ. Hist.*, 14 (1954), 229–53.

Spender, Harold, *The Prime Minister* (1920).

Spiers, Edward M., *Haldane: An Army Reformer* (Edinburgh, 1980).

Sutcliffe, Anthony, *Towards the Planned City: Germany, Britain, the United States and France 1780–1914* (Oxford, 1981).

—— (ed.), *British Town Planning: The Formative Years* (Leicester, 1981).

Sykes, Alan, *Tariff Reform in British Politics 1903–1913*, (Oxford, 1979).

Tennstedt, Florian, *Geschichte der Selbstverwaltung in der Krankenversicherung* (Bonn, 1977).

—— 'Anfänge sozial-politischer Intervention in Deutschland und England

—einige Hinweise zu wechselseitigen Beziehungen', *Zeitschrift f. Sozial-reform*, 29 (1983), 631–48.

Thane, Pat, 'Non-Contributory versus Insurance Pensions 1878–1908', in Pat Thane (ed.), *The Origins of British Social Policy* (1978).

Unwin, George, *Studies in Economic History* (1927).

Vogel, Walter, *Bismarcks Arbeiterversicherung: Ihre Entstehung im Kräftespiel der Zeit* (Brunswick, 1951).

Webb, S. and B., *English Poor Law History* (3 vols.; 1927–9).

Whiteside, Noelle, 'Private Agencies for Public Purposes: Some New Perspectives on Policy Making in Health Insurance between the Wars', *Journal of Social Policy*, 12. 2 (1983), 165–93.

Wickenhagen, Ernst, *Geschichte der gewerblichen Unfallversicherung* (2 vols.; Munich, 1980).

Wilson, Sir Arnold, and Levy, Hermann, *Workmen's Compensation* (2 vols.; 1939, 1941).

—— and Mackay, G. S., *Old Age Pensions: A Critical History* (1942).

Yeo, S. C., *Religion and Voluntary Organisation in Crisis* (1976).

VII   UNPUBLISHED THESES

Brown, John, 'Ideas Concerning Social Policy and their Influence on Legislation in Britain 1902–11', Ph.D. thesis (London, 1964).

Gupta, P. S., 'The History of the Amalgamated Society of Railway Servants 1871–1913', D.Phil thesis (Oxford, 1960).

McGlashan, J. J., 'German Influence on Aspects of English Educational and Social Reform 1867–1908', Ph.D. thesis (Hull, 1973).

Wilkins, C. T., 'The English Reputation of Matthew Arnold 1840–1877', Ph.D. thesis (Illinois, 1959).

Williams, P. M. (Pat Thane), 'The Development of Old Age Pensions in Great Britain 1878–1925', Ph.D. thesis (London, 1970).

INDEX

accident insurance, British compulsory 42–4, 45–6; *see also* workmen's compensation

accident insurance, German 1, 4, 20, 53, 54, 55, 56, 60–2, 64–6, 67, 68, 70–1, 83, 86, 87, 100, 102, 105, 109, 112, 113, 114, 183, 202, 203, 204, 213–14

and accident prevention 7, 65, 70, 71–2, 73–4, 75, 76–7, 83, 98

administration by *Berufsgenossen-schaften* 7, 66, 70–1, 71, 74, 76–7, 96, 202, 204

appeals 66, 67, 70, 73, 77, 80

collective trade responsibility 70–1, 74, 74–5, 76–7, 87, 91, 98–9

cost of administration 73

industrial diseases 99–100

levy 7, 70, 74

medical rehabilitation 43, 83, 98

for miners 43, 46

qualifying period 70

relation to sickness insurance 3, 61, 70–1

statistics 4, 54, 55, 57, 63, 64–5, 73, 214 n.

works covered 81, 88

accident insurance, other countries 60–1, 64, 67, 86, 87

Accident Offices Association 89, 104

accident prevention 7, 40, 42, 48, 63, 64, 66, 71–5, 83

German 7, 65, 66, 70, 71–2, 74, 75, 76–7, 83

Acts of Parliament:

Assurance Companies (1909) 90 n., 104

Criminal Law Amendment (1871) 40

Education (1902) 127

Education (1918) 28

Elementary Education (1870) 14, 190–1

Employers' Liability (1880) 47–8, 49, 50, 57, 60, 72 n., 80

Employers' Liability Insurance Companies (1907) 90 and n., 104

Housing (1890) 24

Housing and Town Planning (1909) 27

Labour Exchanges (1909) 166–7

Local Taxation (Customs and Excise) (1890) 14

National Insurance (1911) 4, 35, 166, 201, 215

National Insurance (Industrial Injuries) (1946) 94

Old Age Pensions (1908) 2, 27, 111, 153, 181, 201, 202

Technical Education (1889) 14

Trade Disputes (1906) 85

Unemployed Workmen's (1905) 153–4, 154, 157

Widows', Orphans' and Old Age Contributory Pensions (1925) 2

Workmen's Compensation (1897) 4, 39, 66–79, 72, 80, 82–3, 85, 91

extension of 81–5

Workmen's Compensation (1900) 81, 85

Workmen's Compensation (1906) 3, 82, 88, 91, 95, 100, 102

Workmen's Compensation (Silicosis) (1918) 100

Workmen's Compensation (1923) 93

Workmen's Compensation (1925) 93

Workmen's Compensation (Coal Mines) (1934) 93, 98

see also Bills

actuaries 174, 178

Africa 160, 161–2

agriculture 67, 96, 113, 182, 213

Amalgamated Society of Railway Servants 41, 45

Employers' Liability Bills (1874–80) 41, 45

Employers' Liability Bill (1881) 49

Employers' Liability Bill (1882) 49

Anglo–German Friendship Committee 32

anthrax 99

arbitration 66, 69

by employers and workers jointly 66,